Non-Western Perspectives on Human Communication

To those who welcome differences

Non-Western Perspectives on Human Communication

Implications for Theory and Practice

Ipac **Library**

MIN-SUN KIM

University of Hawaii at Manoa

SAGE Publications
International Educational and Professional Publisher
Thousand Oaks ▪ London ▪ New Delhi

For information:

Sage Publications, Inc.
2455 Teller Road
Thousand Oaks, California 91320
E-mail: order@sagepub.com

Sage Publications Ltd.
6 Bonhill Street
London EC2A 4PU
United Kingdom

Sage Publications India Pvt. Ltd.
M-32 Market
Greater Kailash I
New Delhi 110 048 India

Printed in the United States of America

Library of Congress Cataloging-in-Publication Data

Kim, Min-Sun.
Non-western perspectives on human communication:
    implications for theory and practice / by Min-Sun Kim.
        p. cm.
Includes bibliographical references and index.
    ISBN 0-7619-2350-0 -- ISBN 0-7619-2351-9 (pbk.)
1. Intercultural communication. 2. Communication and culture. I. Title.
    P94.6 .K56 2002
    302.2--dc21
                                2002005209

05 10 9 8 7 6 5 4 3 2

Acquiring Editor:	Margaret H. Seawell
Editorial Assistant:	Alicia Carter
Production Editor:	Claudia A. Hoffman
Copy Editor:	Meredith L. Brittain
Indexer:	Molly Hall
Cover Designer:	Sandy Ng

Contents

Preface

The battle over who we are" (Achenbach, 1993) shapes the field of human communication.

Something ugly is lurking inside the National Museum of Natural History. It lives among the bones of the dead. In a word: racism. It can be sensed, for example, in a corner of the Ice Age Mammals hall, in an antiquated exhibit called "The Emergence of Man [*sic*]," that might better be labeled "The Emergence of White Man [*sic*]." *Homo erectus*, an ancestor of modern humans, is represented by a painting of light-skinned brutes throwing spears at a mammoth in what is now northern Spain. Next in line comes the Neanderthal man, the most famous of protohumans, and not coincidentally a European too. Then comes the anatomically modern human. An illustration on the wall shows what he looks like. Caucasoid, naturally. Perhaps—judging from the features—Swede.

The irony is, this white guy on the wall was supposed to represent a liberal, progressive view of the work when painted back in 1966. The caption underneath makes the point that, over time, biological differences among humans have diminished but cultural diversity has increased. The white guy represents this cultural diversity simply because he's got long stringy hair and raggedy jeans, and is barefoot. He's a hippie! (The real tip-off is that he's playing a flute, the ultimate hippie musical instrument.)

"The implication is that there's this ascending progress that ends up with white hippies," says Bob Sullivan, the museum's associate director of public programming. "Issue number one we're facing is how to get the Eurocentrism out and how to replace it with a balanced view." ... It's no wonder that the museum is putting up a warning at the entrance to "The Emergence of Man [*sic*]." The warning says that the exhibit is defective. The museum calls this a "dilemma label." (Achenbach, 1993, pp. 127-129)

Museums are established to preserve and tell the history of a society but, often, a select few decide what items should be presented, and how. Although there is a deliberate effort to be open and unbiased, those making the selections unconsciously shape ideas of who we are: "Decisions about how cultures are presented reflect deeper judgments of power and authority and can, indeed, resolve themselves into claims of what a nation is or ought to be as well as how citizens should relate to one another" (Lavine & Karp, 1991, p. 2). As the dynamics of race change in the United States, so do the dynamics of museums that are responsible for educating and telling the story of the nation. This book proposes a "dilemma label" in the "museum" of human communication.

It is no secret that theories of human communication, as studied in Western academia, have been based in large part on individualistic assumptions and empirical research involving subjects from the mainstream U.S. culture (see Kim, 2001). All too often, claims regarding the universality of human communication phenomena are made on the basis of data obtained from—and by—persons from one ethnic group (i.e., Anglo) in one country (i.e., the United States). Although the development of a communication theory that is applicable to only the U.S. mainstream culture is of value, there is an ethnocentric tendency to assume that what is true of the mainstream United States is true of other parts of the world.

The vast majority of theory and research in social science, including human communication—at least the studies performed by Western scholars and published in Western outlets—assumes that people have individualistic notions of self (i.e., independent self-construals). The model that underlies virtually all current social sciences (including human communication) views the self as an entity that (a) comprises a unique, bounded configuration of internal attributes (e.g., preferences, traits, abilities, motives, values, and rights) and (b) behaves primarily as a consequence of these internal attributes. The individual's major normative task is to maintain her independence as a self-contained entity or, more specifically, to be true to her own internal structures of preferences, rights, convictions, and personal goals. According to this independent view of the self, there is an enduring concern with expressing one's internal attributes both in public and in private (see Markus & Kitayama, 1991, 1994). This single overarching model of human functioning prevails throughout the field of mainstream communication. This view stands as a major obstacle to a fuller understanding of communication phenomena.

In this book, I draw upon the results of numerous research projects on cultural differences and discuss their implications for modifying current conceptualizations of communication constructs and current theories of communication phenomena. Specifically, my intention is (a) to investigate the extent to which traditional studies on human communication have centered on Western independent self-orientations, (b) to investigate the extent to which those constructs and theories are inapplicable interculturally, and (c) to bring multicultural perspectives to scholarly analyses as well as to everyday understandings of human communication.

Individualistic values are characteristic of U.S. society and, therefore, tend to be reflected ethnocentrically in human communication theories. However, to progress toward a more universal and less culture-bound understanding of human communication, we must first examine the metaphors and values generating our research. Looking at the world from an interdependent perspective, both as communication scholars and in our everyday interpersonal interactions, requires a substantially different approach. In particular, I explore competent human communication behavior as defined in terms of an interdependent self-orientation. I illustrate my theoretical analysis by focusing on various important verbal communication phenomena—e.g., communication apprehension, assertiveness, argumentativeness, conflict management, deception strategies, silence, re-requesting, bragging, and so forth.

To summarize, an understanding of human communication from a multicultural perspective is of great pragmatic importance for both the individual and society. The extent to which individualists and collectivists differ in their conceptions of themselves and of others in relation to communication styles is just beginning to be studied empirically. I hope that this book will help to alert mainstream communication researchers to the need for examining communication phenomena across a diverse array of ethnicities within as well as outside the United States. If communication theories are to transcend culture, they must first address culture.

❖ ORGANIZATION OF THE BOOK

This book has four parts. Part I, "Introduction," on cultural conceptions of self, contrasts the concepts of the interdependent, relational self and the independent, separated self. I consider the different cultural values that shape individualistic and collectivistic orientations, with special emphasis on the distinctive constructions of personhood that they produce. This part ends with a discussion of some advantages in the individual-level approach to the study of cross-cultural communication behavior.

Part II, "U.S.-Centrism: Cultural Relativity of Communication Constructs and Theories," deals with the individualistic notions of self and questions some well-accepted Western theories of human communication. I examine how these individualistic assumptions have shaped theory and research on communication phenomena. I discuss the ideas of personhood that contemporary Western researchers almost inevitably bring to their understanding of human communication. I selectively review the burgeoning recent literature on cultural variations in ways of being and the implications for human communication phenomena. The literature I have reviewed spans many different communication phenomena, such as communication apprehension, assertiveness, conflict styles, attitude-behavior consistency, group conformity, locus of control, self-presentation, acculturative communication competence, deception, and silence. Throughout the chapters in Part II, I review pertinent research to bring out several unfortunate effects of the individualistic influence and to discuss approaches to the unbiased understanding of human communication. Specifically, I explore how the commonly accepted communication theories in the Western model can be modified from an interdependent perspective.

In Part III, "Toward a Bidimensional Model of Cultural Identity," two models of cultural identity are presented: the unidimensional model and the bidimensional model. One of the issues in conceptualization of self-construals has to do with the following question: Are independence and interdependence polar opposites of a single dimension, or are they separate dimensions? In previous comparisons of the self in different cultures and contexts, the focus has been on the contrast between those patterns of cultural participation that construct the person as an independent, autonomous entity and those that construct the person as an interdependent part of a larger social order. However, I argue that elements of both worldviews may exist at the cultural as well as the individual level. There is growing evidence that these concepts do not necessarily form opposite poles and may coexist in individuals or groups in different situations. The common tendency to pit independence against interdependence is not warranted. The unidimensional model of cultural identity is significantly limited in its vision of human potential. Awareness of these limitations is a crucial preparation for genuine understanding of cultural identity and human communication.

Part IV, "Conclusion," looks at research and theoretical developments that explore new combinations (coexistence, synthesis) of individualistic and collectivistic orientations. This research, as it matures, should lead to better conceptualizations in the field of human communication.

All these sections deal with different, yet related, topics. In addition, the chapters reflect the chronology of my own research work: an initial foray into culture-level comparisons of communication styles and then a stepping back to consider how this material sits in the wider framework of cultural identity. Parts III and IV bring the discussion back to the bidimensional model of cultural identity and, correspondingly, bicultural communication competence. At issue throughout the book are the questions of what it means to be a self and, especially, what it means to be a self who communicates in a particular culture. The first step is to consider the most basic term: the *self*. This is the explicit subject of the next chapter and is at the heart of my concern throughout.

❖ SEXIST LANGUAGE

Sexist language in direct quotations has necessarily been retained unchanged. Likewise, I have left in their original, gendered forms the quotations that open each chapter. To balance the historical use of sexist language in English, I chose to use "she" and "her" (rather than "he," "him," and "his") throughout the book. Where I could not avoid the male counterparts, I placed the masculine language second (e.g., "she and he").

Acknowledgments

To my two children, Tara and Arjun, who, even while being half-clones of myself, constantly pose to me the challenges and joys of understanding and loving "the Other."

To my beloved husband, Dr. Narayan S. Raja, who, with his wizard editing, like the fairy godmother, transformed my manuscript from a ragged Cinderella into a refined and presentable Cinderella.

To my brothers and sisters, who parented me in my young age, and who sent their dreams abroad with their youngest sister to follow the star.

Also to my mentors, especially the late Dr. Gerald Miller at Michigan State University, who, probably without knowing it himself, has influenced my scholarship to this day.

To the editors at Sage, Margaret Seawell and Claudia Hoffman, who accepted the proposal for this book, which gave me the courage to eventually finish the book. Also, to the copy editor at Sage, Meredith Brittain, who tirelessly combed through the whole manuscript and provided valuable editorial suggestions and finishing touches for the book.

And to my colleagues and students past and present, I thank you all!

I

Introduction

In recent years, social scientists have become increasingly sensitive to the ways in which their pursuit of knowledge is influenced by their cultural baggage. Researchers can be vitally influenced by the values and normative assumptions of the culture in which they participate (Gergen, 1979). Because they participate in the presumptive base on which the meaning of scientific conduct is premised, it is difficult to forge a body of knowledge independent of this base. The linkage between scientific conduct and cultural context raises questions of profound importance. In what specific ways and to what extent does cultural baggage hinder the quest for objective understanding? And what particular influences have shaped what passes for knowledge in present-day communication research?

There is a growing awareness on the part of communication scholars as to the social basis of their activities. Littlejohn (1996), who also authored the well-known textbook *Theories of Human Communication*, acknowledges that communication theory in the United States is a Eurocentric enterprise. That is, communication theory has a strong Western bias, and Eastern ideas that could contribute to the study of communication have not been adequately integrated into communication theory as understood in the West. Monge (1998), a former president of the International Communication Association, concurs: "There can be little doubt that the preponderance of contemporary communication theory has been developed from the singular perspective of the United States" (p. 4). And he rightly suggests that Eastern perspectives need to be drawn upon to broaden existing human communication theory (for further discussion on this issue, see Miike, 2000).

Furthermore, Gordon (1998/1999) remarks that the body of communication that is developed in the United States should not simply become the communication theory for the world. He adds that multicultural communication perspectives need to be generated and widely shared internationally so that our vision of humans communicating might be broadened beyond unicultural bias and ethnocentrism. Further, he writes,

> Into the decade of the eighties we Caucasian males still directed the American communication discipline's scholarship and theorizing; we were the editors of the journals, the authors of the scholarly papers and books, the major gatekeepers of the discipline. . . . The views that we have of "communication" have, as a result, been skewed. They have not represented a sample of all possible conceptual positions and vantage-points from which knowledge of communication can be constructed. (p. 3)

Similarly, Yum (1988) observes,

> The field of communication has reached a critical period, with an ever-increasing number of people studying communication, a proliferation of academic and practical journals, and Ph.D. programs in many universities. Much of this growth, however, has been within North America, and most research and theory is based upon Western philosophical foundations. As more scholars from Asia have entered the field of communication, there has been increasing dissatisfaction with the use of North American models of communication to explain communication processes in Asia, and even some aspects of communication processes in North America. (p. 374)

Ishii (1998) has commented on Japanese scholarship. He specifically discusses the issue of the body of communication theory that has been developed in the United States becoming the communication theory for the world:

For decades, Japanese communication scholars have been willing to import and apply Euro-America-centered research paradigms not only in the natural sciences but also in the social sciences and humanities. They have been doing so without trying to develop their own non-Western frames of research. Today Japanese researchers are expected to develop new research paradigms and perspectives based on their own Japanese cultural background and to contribute these to the international academic arena. (p. 109)

Recently, similar questions have been raised about the generalizability of communication theories based on Western models to other countries and to ethnic minorities in the United States (Gordon, 1998/1999; Kim, 1999; Kim & Leung, 2000; Kincaid, 1987). It becomes abundantly clear that there is a call across the field for significant change in American communication studies—a strong and urgent call for increasing diversity across racial, ethnic, and gender lines. The traditional field of communication, as exemplified by the North American tradition, is in dire need of reformulation. The field of communication, which has been built on top of the individualistic model of self-identity, precludes an adequate appreciation of the social basis of communication—an ironic state of affairs that should cause alarm to those in the field.

Most of what is known about the nature and effects of self-related variables—at least in Western cultures—is based on the unspoken assumption that people have more or less independent self-construals. But the so-called laws or rules of human communication may not apply (or may take a different form) in cultures in which people construe themselves as more interdependent. Even within the United States, this is a vital issue considering the prediction that by the year 2020, racial and ethnic minorities will together constitute the majority population of the United States (Sue, Arredondo, & McDavis, 1992).

Clearly, there needs to be a shift from an Anglo-centered field to a multipolar field. With the advent of multiculturalism as the "fourth force" within the United States (Pedersen, 1991), there has been an increased emphasis on alternative conceptual systems. Communication theories must be freed from the confines of the pervasive Euro-American belief in the autonomous individual. The study of human communication from alternative cultural perspectives will reveal how cultural frameworks powerfully structure both everyday and scientific understandings.

In attempting to come to grips with the cultural basis of communication research, it is valuable to consider the trends in various sister disciplines that show some progress along these lines. For instance, Buss (1975) outlines how psychologists may become more self-conscious of their discipline—that is, how they can achieve a broader perspective of the discipline qua discipline. Gergen (1973) has shaken the very foundations of traditional experimental social psychology. Arguing that social psychology is a historical inquiry, Gergen believes that current theories in social psychology reflect current cultural values, norms, and ideologies, and that as social conditions change, theories must also change in fundamental ways. Gergen's article has opened up debate on the culturally and historically bounded nature of social theories of behavior.

Although diverse European, American, and Asian theorists (e.g., Bond, 1998; Buss, 1979; Geertz, 1973; Ishii, 1998) have found fault with the individualistic model of self and its ability to reflect and account for social behavior, this critique, for the most part, has gone unheeded in theoretical and empirical analyses of communication behavior. Similar to Berry's (1978) recommendations on social psychology, the following three recommendations are important steps we need to take in the field of human communication: (a) cultural decentering away from Euro-American theory, (b) recentering the discipline within the cultures of interest, and (c) integrating the different cultural perspectives to move toward a truly universal theory of human communication.

In this book, I will show that within our field there is an emerging awareness of what may be called the cultural underpinnings of communication theories. I will attempt to apply this perspective to various theories and approaches within the field. Clearly, a systematic theoretical framework needs to be developed for progress to be made in this area. Although it is presently unclear how this step will be accomplished, any communication scholars interested in pursuing this goal will profit by closely scrutinizing the current theories from a cultural point of view.

There is little doubt that the individualistic notion of self has been embraced by mainstream human communication research. One does not question a fact that appears to be self-evident or natural. The acceptance of this normative base for a broad range of social science has made possible the claim of a value-free science. The study of human communication has developed within a European-American cultural framework and, not surprisingly, it incorporates a web of tacit understandings and implicit assumptions that are shared by researchers. The shared notions include a blend of normative beliefs and moral prescriptions about human nature and preferred modes of communication that are, for the most part, so obvious and taken for granted they are almost never spelled out (see Markus & Kitayama, 1998).

The social and cultural backgrounds of most of the theoreticians in our area would probably lead them to assume that the desire to be an autonomous individual is a human universal. They might, for instance, readily conclude that the desirability of high communication motivation (e.g., assertiveness) is a nonquestion. The evidence, however, suggests that this is far from the case. Being an independent and efficacious individual has been the goal of only a small portion of humankind (Inkeles & Smith, 1974). In fact, societies with such individualistic values are so rare that Meyer (1988) has formulated a theoretical approach aimed at specifying the nature of the institutional support that Western societies provide for such an individualistic view of the self.

One of the powerful ways in which cultural systems mold individuals' communication behavior is through their influence on an individual's ways of being a person in the world. Varied cultural, social-structural processes lead to differences in the emphasis placed on the importance of self-direction and other-direction, and corresponding communication patterns for the individual. Furthermore, such differences in emphasis may exist not only between cultures, but also within societies, especially those that are not homogeneous socially or culturally (Schooler, 1990).

In certain cultures, such as that of the United States, the core of the self-concept tends to be based on the person's "unique configuration of internal attributes (e.g., traits, abilities, motives, and values)" (Markus & Kitayama, 1991, p. 224). We now know that the independent or individualistic self is not universal but, rather, is a culture-specific belief system. There is an important alternative belief system that is held by about 70% of the world's population (Triandis, 1989); it is called *interdependence* or *collectivism*. Viewpoints on human communication from interdependence-oriented societies can help to balance the present ethnocentric skewing of human communication studies. There is a need to derive some intellectual nourishment from the Asian tradition (Gordon, 1998/1999; Ishii, 1998; Kim, 1999).

To what extent does a culture idealize personhood in terms of individual achievement and autonomy? To what extent does a culture idealize personhood in terms of relationships with others? Focusing on these questions and their implications for communication patterns may provide a unifying conceptual framework for considering the relationship between cultural values and human communication.

In examining the field of human communication, one must explain why some problems have taken precedence, some epistemological strategies have been promoted over others, and some conjectures have been vigorously pursued while others remain unnoticed. Preconceived notions of personhood that cannot address the challenges posed by cultural diversities should no longer be acceptable. Although culture has often been overlooked, it is to the person as water is to the fish. Culture is the medium through which one experiences the world. Cultures tell their members how to behave and tell their scholars how to think about the causes of behavior—or even whether to think about the causes of behavior (Caprara & Cervone, 2000).

I hope this book marks the coming of age of an endeavor to internationalize what was once a narrow Euro-American discipline. Unless the international dimension is introduced, American communication research may remain blind to its culture-bound assumptions and limitations. A similar point regarding social psychology was made by Berry (1983), who warned that "the discipline is so culture-bound and culture-blind that, as it stands now, it should not be employed as is in cultures outside the United States" (p. 449).

In the next three chapters, I will selectively review some of the recent literature on cultural variation in self-concept and the sociocultural ground for the self. Specifically, I will compare European-American models of independence with East Asian models of interdependence, thus contrasting two very different conceptions of the self and social behavior. Although many other cultural comparisons are possible and interesting, I focus on East Asia because so much of the recent research has been conducted there. Sufficient empirical work now exists to form a basis for this particular comparison.

1

"Who Am I?"

Cultural Variations in Self-Systems

The individual is the end of the Universe.

— Miguel De Unamuno,
The Tragic Sense of Life, p. 312

The discovery that many findings in social science are culturally specific led researchers to argue that culture should be incorporated as a parameter in social science theories (Smith & Bond, 1998). Explaining differences in communication behavior across cultures requires a search for the relevant independent variables "culture unpackaged," so to speak (Segall, 1986). At the very heart of the concept of culture is the expectation that different people will possess different values, beliefs, and motives, which are reflected in various behaviors. Travelers to foreign lands detect different behaviors quickly, sensing that they are viewing not only different lifestyles but also different attitudes toward life itself (Segall, 1986). A key attribute that distinguishes cultures is the meaning they assign to being a person. Anthropologists, and more recently psychologists (Geertz, 1973; Markus & Kitayama, 1991, 1998), have argued that cultural groups diverge in their understandings of selfhood and personhood.

According to Smith (1991), *selfhood* is a label for the criterial features of the human condition. Over the millennia, since people became *self-consciously* aware of their special place in the world, selfhood has been the primary puzzle (along with the cosmological puzzle) that myth, religion, and philosophy have addressed. Smith (1991) refers to this as the "universal features of being a person" (p. 20). The ways of being a person are shaped according to the means and practices of a given cultural community, and communities are maintained by these ways of being in the world. Each person is embedded within a variety of sociocultural contexts or cultures (e.g., country, ethnicity, religion, gender, family, etc.). Each of these cultural contexts makes some claim on the person and is associated with a set of ideas and practices (i.e., a cultural framework) about how to be a good person (Markus & Kitayama, 1998). The *self*, then, is an organized locus of the various, sometimes competing, understandings of how to be a person, and it functions as an individualized orienting, mediating, interpretive framework, giving shape to what a person notices and thinks about, what she is motivated to do, and (the focus of this book) how she communicates with others.

My approach is consistent with that of cultural psychologists who maintain that the person and the environment co-constitute one another and cannot be separated from one another. In describing the culture-specific nature of self, Markus, Mullally, and Kitayama (1997) suggest that cultural and social groups in every historical period are associated with characteristic patterns of sociocultural participation or, more specifically, with characteristic ways of being a person in the world. They call these characteristic patterns of sociocultural participation "selfways."

According to Markus et al. (1997), people do not live generally or in the abstract; rather, they live according to specific and substantive sets of cultural understandings. *Selfways* are defined as communities' ideas about being a person and the social practices, situations, and institutions of everyday life that represent and foster these ideas (Markus et al., 1997, p. 16). Thus, selfways include definitions and ideas of what it means to be a self and how to be a good or acceptable self, but they are not just a matter of such beliefs. They also include practices, habits, and customs that appear as subjectively natural ways of acting and interacting with others. Selfways are not just different ways of construing the self; they are, more generally, different ways of being, and different ways of knowing, feeling, and acting (see Heine, Lehman, Markus, & Kitayama, 1999).

Cultural meaning systems can exert formative influences on human psychological systems in such a way that these psychological systems become integral parts of the cultural systems themselves. For instance, when individuals' thoughts, feelings, and behaviors are consistent with the dominant selfways, they are likely to be repeated, sustained, and eventually habitualized to form a relatively independent (or interdependent) psychological structure. The emerging psychological system, in turn, is likely to generate responses that resonate with, and thus reconstitute, aspects of the cultural system itself. In this way, each person's psychological processes and structures are gradually integrated into the larger cultural context. In contrast, behaviors that do not fit well with the selfway will remain cognitively unelaborated. There have been some discussions of the implications of selfways on emotion, cognition, and social episodes in patterns of caretaking, schooling, religion, work, in the media, and so on (Markus et al., 1997). What has not been systematically investigated is how selfways are manifested in everyday communication theories. That will be the focus of this book.

In sum, *self-concepts* (i.e., selfhood, selfways) are the mental representations of those personal qualities used by individuals for the purpose of defining themselves and regulating their behavior (Niedenthal & Beike, 1997). The entire set of concepts used to describe the self is also referred to as the *self-system* (Markus & Wurf, 1987). Self-concepts are thought to contain information about the characteristic features of the self in specific situations, temporal contexts, and moods, as well as the relations between the features (Niedenthal & Beike, 1997). Views of the acquisition and structure of self-concepts are based on two philosophical positions that have different interpretations of the link between concepts of self and social relationships. Some theorists have argued that identity develops from social relationships and that relationships with others actually constitute identity, whereas other theorists suggest that identity develops as the individual separates from primary relationships and that features and experiences unique to that individual constitute identity (Markus & Kitayama, 1991). In the following sections, I review how the models of self as independent or as interdependent are reflected in philosophical and ontological ideas and ideologies constructed and preserved in the respective cultural contexts.

❖   EVOLUTION OF WESTERN SELF-CONSTRUCTION:
     "AMERICA'S CIVIL RELIGION"

The worldview and value system that lie at the basis of Western culture, which need to be carefully reexamined, were formulated in their essential outlines in the 16th and 17th centuries. The prevailing notion of *human being* in ancient Greece differed somewhat from the contemporary Western concept (Gill, 1996). The Greek concept was less centered on the individual than the Western concept that developed by the time of Descartes and Kant. The Greeks emphasized participation in interpersonal and communal relationships. To be a human being was to act on the basis of reason and to honor the obligations of membership in a community. Between 1500 and 1700, there was a dramatic shift in the way people pictured the world and in their way of thinking. The new mentality and the new perception of the cosmos gave Western civilization the features that are characteristic of the modern era. They became the basis of the paradigm that has dominated Western culture for the past 300 years (Capra, 1982).

Before 1500, the dominant worldview in Europe, as well as in most other civilizations, was organic. People lived in small, cohesive communities and experienced nature in terms of organic relationships, characterized by the interdependence of spiritual and material phenomena (Capra, 1982). The nature of medieval science in Europe was very different from that of contemporary science. It was based on both reason and faith, and its main goal was to understand the meaning and significance of things rather than to predict and control them. Medieval scientists considered questions relating to God, the human soul, and ethics to be of the highest significance. The medieval outlook changed radically in the 16th and 17th centuries. The notion of an organic, living, and spiritual universe was replaced by that of the world as a machine, and the world machine became the dominant metaphor of the modern era (Capra, 1982).

Newtonian physics, the crowning achievement of 17th-century science, provided a consistent mathematical theory of the world that remained the solid foundation of scientific thought well into the 20th century. The stage of the Newtonian universe, on which all physical phenomena took place, was the three-dimensional space of classical Euclidean geometry. In Newton's own words, "Absolute space, in its own nature, without regard to anything external, remains always similar and immovable. . . . Absolute, true, and mathematical time of itself and by its own nature, flows uniformly, without regard to anything external" (Capra, 1982, p. 65).

The elements of the Newtonian world that moved in this absolute space and absolute time were material particles. The Newtonian model of matter was mechanistic. This mechanistic view of matter was extended to living organisms and has had a profound effect on Western thought. It has taught people to be aware of themselves as isolated egos existing inside their bodies. The thinkers of the 17th and 18th centuries applied the principles of Newtonian mechanics to the sciences of human nature and human society. Following Newtonian physics, Locke developed an atomistic view of society, describing it in terms of its basic building block: the human being. When Locke applied his theory of human nature to social phenomena, he was guided by the belief that there were laws of nature governing human society, similar to those governing the physical universe. As the atoms in a gas would establish a balanced state, so would human individuals settle down in a society in a "state of nature." Thus, the function of government was not to impose its laws on the people but, rather, to discover and enforce the natural laws that existed before any government was formed. The ideals of individualism, property rights, and the free market, all of which can be traced back to Locke, contributed significantly to the thinking of Thomas Jefferson and are reflected in the Declaration of Independence (Capra, 1982). These ideas include social contracts, rational profit making, and the actions of a free market made up of individual players.

As the Western construction of the person as unique and special gained prominence, persons were no longer equated with their social roles, and these roles were no longer considered part of a person's essence. Thus, a person came to be understood as an individual entity with a separate existence independent of place in society (Klein, 1995). European-American notions of personality are afforded and maintained by a great many cultural meanings, including the idea that difference among people is obvious and good; the belief that a person can be separated from society or the social situation; and the assumption that social behavior is rooted in, and largely determined by, one's underlying traits. This developing sense of individual uniqueness and personal choice is reflected in changes in the meaning of the English words *individual* and *self"* over the past five centuries. In the 15th century, "individual" meant "indivisible." It could be used to describe the Trinity or a married couple, who were individual, not to be parted as man and wife. In the late Middle Ages in Europe, self was a noun representing something to be denied in favor of God and all "he" represented. The Protestant reformation and rise of capitalism combined to place personas in an individuated rather than mediated relation to God. By the 18th century, an emphasis on a person's unique qualities was amplified by the idea that each individual has a unique "potential." Thus, in Europe and North America, there has been the growing sense of individuation over the past few centuries (see Klein, 1995).

In the dominant mentality of contemporary Western culture, self is equated with the autonomous or self-sufficient individual. Gates (1993) called this individualistic view "America's civil religion." Therefore, in Western cultures, relationality is often constructed as undermining the "right" or most powerful kind of selfhood (Klein, 1995). To the extent that personal creativity and individuality are more valued than the relationship and to the extent that autonomy is characterized as the pinnacle of psychological and ethical development, there is the implicit suggestion that caring and a relational style of identity makes one less than one might be. Smith (1991) believes that "the individualistic version of selfhood that has characterized our Western tradition since the Renaissance, which we Americans have managed even to exaggerate, seems an increasingly poor fit to our requirements for survival in unavoidable interdependency" (p. 33).

Within the framework of individualistic ontological assumptions, the person is assumed to be a separate and somewhat nonsocial individual who exists independently. The individual has a right and responsibility, in fact a moral obligation, to become separate, autonomous, efficacious, and in control. The concern with individuality is also embodied in alienated individualism, the idea that social institutions are transitory and essentially invalid, and that to the extent that the individual identifies with social roles, she or he is fundamentally inauthentic (Niedenthal & Beike, 1997). It is within the independent view of the self, with all such variants encompassed in it, that theories of human communication have historically been constructed.

❖ INTERDEPENDENT SELF-CONSTRUALS: AN ALTERNATIVE FRAMEWORK

The pervasive influence of the individualistic ideal in many aspects of Western communication has recently been pointed out by several communication researchers (Kim, 1999; Kim & Leung, 2000; Kincaid, 1987). But the European-American view of the self and its relation to the collective is only one view. There are other equally powerful but strikingly different cultural notions about the self and its relation to the collective.

In some other cultures, there developed a philosophy of an inherent relatedness among individuals and the necessity of social relationships for the establishment of identity. Guisinger and Blatt (1994) noted that although the individualistic view is the dominant Western view of human nature, it is not consistent with the view of identity in, for instance, Eastern cultures. The worldviews expressed in Buddhist teachings, Taoist writings, and Confucian ideologies, among others, have exerted considerable influence on daily practices, discourses, and social institutions in East Asian cultures (Ames, Dissanayake, & Kasulis, 1994).

In East Asian cultures, the self is defined predominantly in terms of relationships and group memberships. In this alternative view, the self is inherently social—an integral part of the collective. The key feature of interdependence is not distinctiveness or uniqueness, but a heightened awareness of the other and of the nature of one's relation to the other. Interdependence is the first goal to be taken care of; it is crafted and nurtured in social episodes so that it becomes spontaneous, automatic, and taken for granted (Kitayama & Markus, 1999).

Far more than in the modern West, in many East Asian cultures one lives within a well-articulated social matrix intricately connected with one's own endeavors and sense of identity. Japanese are said to see babies as overly individualistic and in need of training to become connected; in the United States, babies are seen as too connected and in need of training to become individuals (Klein, 1995).

How do we deal with the powerful pulls between the experiences of relatedness and autonomy, connection and separateness? What it means to be a person is, of course, construed very differently in contemporary Western and East Asian cultures. By understanding the different ways in which different cultures construct personas as connected or separate, we can better understand the limitations of various theories.

2

Independent and Interdependent Models of the Self as Cultural Frame

Every man for himself, his own ends, the Devil for all.*

— Burton, *The Anatomy of Melancholy*
(quoted in Bartlett, 2000)

If you congregate, you live. If you scatter, you die.

— Korean proverb

Triandis (1989) proposed an explanation of culture's influence on behavior. He employed the concept of "self" as a mediating variable between culture and individual behavior. The self can be construed, framed, or conceptualized in different ways. Markus and Kitayama (1991) delineated two general cultural self-schemata: interdependence and independence. These two images of self were originally conceptualized as reflecting the emphasis on connectedness and relations often found in non-Western cultures (interdependent self) and the separatedness and uniqueness of the individual (independent self) stressed in the West. For instance, the more individualistic the culture, the more frequent the sampling of the independent self. In contrast, the more collectivistic the culture, the more likely it is that people will sample the interdependent self. Triandis (1989) introduced the term *sampling*. The probability of sampling refers to whether the element that will be used is more likely to be an element of the independent or interdependent self. Thus, if the independent self is complex, or well-developed, there are more "independent-self units" that can be sampled (see Triandis, 1989, for a similar argument on the sampling of the private, public, or collective self).

Independent and interdependent construals of self are the most important self-schemata for distinguishing culture. Markus and Kitayama (1991) proposed that whereas the self-system is the complete configuration of self-schemata (including, for example, self-schemata of gender, race, religion, social class, and one's developmental history; Markus & Wurf, 1987), the independent and interdependent construals of self are among the most general and overarching self-schemata in an individual's self-system. Based on an extensive review of cross-cultural literature, Markus and Kitayama (1991, 1998) argued that these two construals of self influence cognition, emotion, and motivation more powerfully than previously thought. The main difference between the two self-construals is the belief one holds regarding how the self is related to others. Those with highly developed independent construals see themselves as separate from others, whereas those with highly developed interdependent construals see themselves as connected with others.

❖ INDEPENDENT SELF-CONSTRUAL:
   INDIVIDUALISTIC ASPECTS OF SELF

In the independent construal, most representations of the self (i.e., the ways in which an individual thinks of herself) have as their referent an individual's ability, characteristic, attribute, or goal ("I am friendly" or "I am ambitious"). These inner characteristics or traits are the primary regulators of behavior. This view of the self derives from a belief in the wholeness and uniqueness of each person's configuration of internal attributes (Johnson, 1985). The normative imperative of individuals in such cultures is to become independent of others and to discover and express one's own unique attributes (Marsella, DeVoss, & Hsu, 1985). Thus, the goals of persons in such cultures are to stand out and to express their own unique internal characteristics or traits. This orientation has led to an emphasis on the need to pursue personal self-actualization or self-development. Individual weakness, in this cultural perspective, is to be overly dependent on others or to be unassertive (Bellah, Madsen, Sullivan, Swidler, & Tipton, 1985). This perspective is rooted in Western philosophical tradition and is linked to a Cartesian view in which the goal of existence is to objectify the self. According to Lebra (1992), the ontological goal of this perspective is to highlight the division between the experiencer and what is experienced—in other words, to separate the individual from the context.

❖ INTERDEPENDENT SELF-CONSTRUAL: GROUP-DERIVED IDENTITY

By contrast, in the interdependent construal, the self is connected to others; the principal components of the self are one's relationships to others (Markus & Kitayama, 1991). This is not to say that the person with an interdependent view of the self has no conception of internal traits, characteristics, or preferences that are unique to that person but, rather, that these internal, private aspects of the self are not primary forces in directing or guiding behavior. Instead, behavior is more significantly regulated by a desire to maintain harmony and appropriateness in relationships. Within such a construal, the self becomes most meaningful and complete when it is cast in the appropriate social relationship. Therefore, one's behavior in a given situation may be a function more of the needs, wishes, and preferences of others than of one's own needs, wishes, or preferences. As a result of this interdependent construal of the self, one may attempt to meet the needs of others and to promote the goals of others. Weakness in this perspective is to be headstrong, unwilling to accommodate the needs of others, or self-centered (Cross & Markus, 1991). According to Lebra (1992), this interdependent view of self can be traced to Buddhist philosophical traditions within which the very goal of existence is different from that assumed in the West. From this view, the core notion is not to objectify the self but to submerge the self and gain freedom from the self. The emphasis is on downplaying the division between the experiencer and the object of experience, and what is highlighted is connection with, rather than separation from, others and the surrounding context.

A focus on the sociocultural grounding of the self does not deny the individuality, idiosyncrasy, or uniqueness that can be observed in even the most tight-knit and coherent collectives. At least some of the remarkable variation among people results because they are unlikely to participate in the identical configuration of group memberships. Furthermore, the ways in which individuals participate in culture reflect their position and status in society (i.e., gender, socioeconomic status, age, ethnicity, etc.), so the effects of cultural participation will seldom be totalizing or uniform (Markus, Mullally, & Kitayama, 1997).

According to Markus and Kitayama (1991), on average, a larger percentage of individuals in Western cultures hold independent self-construals than individuals in non-Western cultures do. Within a given culture, however, individuals will vary in the extent to which they are typical and construe the self in the typical way. Thus, not all people who are part of an individualistic culture possess primarily independent self-construals, nor do all those who are part of a collectivistic culture possess primarily interdependent self-construals.

Thus, the distinctions between independent and interdependent construals must be regarded as general tendencies that may emerge when the members of the culture are considered as a whole. For instance, even in North America, a theme of interdependence is reflected in the values and activities of many of its cultures. Religious groups, such as the Quakers, explicitly value and promote interdependence, as do many small towns and rural communities (see, e.g., Bellah et al., 1985).

Nevertheless, any particularized sense of the self will be grounded in some consensual meanings and customary practices, and it will necessarily bear some important resemblances to similarly grounded selves (Markus et al., 1997). Although any two American selves will differ from one another in countless ways, as will any two Japanese selves, the fact of cultural participation in either the current system of American or Japanese practices and institutions will produce some important uniformities. Although Markus and Kitayama do not directly link their conceptualization of the self-construals to any culture-level dimensions, they discuss the cultural differences at the individual level under a framework similar to individualism-collectivism (Gudykunst et al., 1996). Cultural differences in self-construal have been well established by recent studies (Gudykunst et al., 1996; Kashima et al., 1995; Kim et al., 1996). Singelis (1994; Singelis & Brown, 1995), who developed a measure that taps the independent and interdependent dimensions of the self, found in Hawaii that participants from an Asian background were both more interdependent and less independent than those with a European background. Similarly, Bochner (1994) found that Malaysian self-construals were more interdependent and less independent than Australian and British self-construals. In fact, cross-cultural studies have reported a direct link between collectivism

Table 2.1   Characteristics of Independent and Interdependent
Self-Construals That Have Implications for Communication
Behaviors

Focus	Independent Self-Construals	Interdependent Self-Construals
Rationality vs. Relationality	A person is an autonomous entity defined by a somewhat distinctive set of attributes, qualities, or processes.	A person is an interdependent entity who is part of the encompassing social relationships.
Personality vs. Status	The configuration of internal attributes or processes determines or causes behavior (i.e., the origins of behavior are in the individual, and people are knowable through their actions).	Behavior is a consequence of being responsive to others with whom one is interdependent. The origins of behavior are in relationships, and people are knowable through their actions within a given social relationship.
Context-independent vs. Context-dependent	Individual behavior will vary because people vary in their configurations of internal attributes and processes, and this distinctiveness is good.	The precise nature of a given social context often varies, so individual behavior will vary from one situation to another and from one time to another. This sensitivity to social context and consequent variability is good.
Attitude-Behavior Consistency	People should express their attributes and processes in communication behavior, so there should be consistency and stability in communication behavior across situations and over time, and this consistency and stability is good.	Consistency is not a moral obligation, given the relatively tight organization of social life.
Control of others vs. Receptivity toward others	The study of attitude and personality is significant because it will lead to an understanding of how to predict and control communication behavior.	Predicting behavior is not a major concern. Being receptive to others or influenced by them is not a sign of inconsistency. Rather, it reflects self-control, flexibility, and maturity.

SOURCE: Adapted from Markus and Kitayama (1998).

and an interdependent self-construal and between individualism and an independent self-construal. Singelis and Brown (1995) suggest that cultural collectivism is positively related to the interdependent self and negatively related to the independent self. Kim and her colleagues (1996) report that culture-level individualism is systematically related to independent self-construals.

In this preliminary discussion of self in cultural context, I have tried to address a number of questions that I believe are basic to a culture-based research on human communication. First, I asked, "What is a person?" and suggested that there are at least two equally viable ways to answer this question. The independent view of the person, in which a person is seen as an autonomous entity comprising a set of internal attributes, is the view that is incorporated into most communication theorizing and into almost all theories of human communication.

Much more could be said about these apparently startling differences in ontological emphasis of different selves. But my purpose is to underscore that these divergent views of what the self should be are critical underpinnings of communicative processes. These ways of being are significant elements of the cultural frame (Markus & Kitayama, 1994) and form the framework for individual experience of communication behavior.

In summary, being a person requires incorporating and becoming attuned to a set of cultural understandings and patterns, including—notably, for the purposes of this discussion—culture-specific understandings of human nature and communication behavior. The tendency for the independent self is to see itself as distinct, autonomous, individualistic, and possessing unique internal attributes. On the other hand, the tendency for the interdependent self is to view itself as woven inextricably within the social tapestry of significant relationships and situationally specific behaviors and opinions, which develops into a sense of what borders on collective consciousness. Table 2.1 summarizes some distinctive characteristics of independent and interdependent self-construals that seem to have consequences for various communication behaviors.

3

Why Self-Construals Are Useful

Science is a great game. It is inspiring and refreshing. The playing field is the universe itself.

— Isidor I. Rabi, *New York Times*, 28 Oct. 1964, p. 38

In the last chapter, I examined the interface between culture and self. I dealt with how the concept of self varies with culture. This chapter examines some of the advantages in an individual-level approach to the study of cross-cultural communication behavior. The notion of self-construals is of great interest to a wide range of researchers. Increasing numbers of intercultural-communication researchers are recognizing the importance of conceptualizing culture along meaningful dimensions of sociopsychological variability and developing ways to measure these dimensions on the individual level. Theoretical analyses rooted in the distinction between these two models of the self have proven to be quite powerful in integrating cross-cultural differences in human communication as well as in cognition, emotion, and motivation (for extensive reviews on this issue, see Gudykunst et al., 1996; Kim et al., 1996; Markus, Mullally, & Kitayama, 1997). Specifically, the interest can be traced to the following two main factors:

- Parsimony of explanation: impact of culture
- Cultural relativity of communication constructs

❖ PARSIMONY OF EXPLANATION: IMPACT OF CULTURE

The theoretical analysis rooted in the distinction between these two models of the self has proven to be quite powerful in integrating cross-cultural differences in communication behavior. From this observation, it may seem quite sensible to assume that people in different cultural contexts tend to internalize and thus to believe the cultures' respective models of the self.

Individualism-collectivism (IC) has been considered "the single most important dimension of cultural difference in social behavior" (Triandis, 1988). Its popularity with those researching cross-cultural communication derives from its use as a culture-level explanation for observed cultural differences in behavior. Two widely held world-views or cultural dimensions have become evident in the cross-cultural literature as variables on which most cultures vary: individualism and collectivism. These dimensions tap the cultural assumptions of the fundamental nature of personhood. Individualism characterizes cultures in which the self is emphasized. Collectivism characterizes cultures in which the group is emphasized.

Individualism and collectivism have been proposed as typical East Asian and U.S. value orientations that influence communication styles. A main reason for the criticism of individualism-collectivism is that it is misused as a stand-in for a variety of social and cultural independent variables in the explanation and prediction of behavior (Kagitcibasi, 1996). The typical method of comparing findings in different cultures is frequently used to examine the impact of culture on communication behaviors. Although this method is useful in evaluating whether cross-cultural differences exist, it is far less helpful in explaining why culture has an effect. Therefore, a better way to evaluate the effect of culture on communication behavior is to examine the mediating role of self-construals.

There have been several notable attempts to measure self-construals at the individual level (Gudykunst et al., 1996; Leung & Kim, 1997; Singelis, 1994) and to relate the individual differences in self-construal to differences in communication behaviors (e.g., Gudykunst et al., 1996; Kim, Aune, Hunter, Kim, & Kim, 2001; Kim et al., 1996). Recent cross-cultural research on the self has suggested that the self-concept is an important mediator of cultural behavioral patterns (Ting-Toomey, 1989; Triandis, 1989). The concept of self has been linked to many of the communication styles previously associated with cultural dimensions, such as individualism and collectivism. The notion of self-concept as a mediating variable permits us to better specify the precise role of the self in regulating preferences for conversational styles. That is, locating variables that are affected by culture and that subsequently affect communication styles may further our understanding of the complexities of culture's influence on communication (see Singelis, 1994).

Many theoretical approaches in intercultural communication at some point invoke individual-level processes (e.g., self-concept, identity) as an explanation of cultural differences (see Collier & Thomas, 1988; Cronen, Pearce, & Tomm, 1985). However, there is a conspicuous lack of empirical evidence about the specifics of the self-systems of people from different cultural backgrounds. A major determinant of preferred conversational style seems to be the kind of self that operates in a particular culture. It is widely recognized that culture is a fuzzy concept that is difficult to define and impossible to operationalize. Several major cultural dimensions (e.g., individualism vs. collectivism, high-context vs. low-context) emerge from the literature as high-order psychological concepts that can help explain cross-cultural differences in behavior over a wide range of situations. In many cases, a broad concept is invoked to explain major aspects of the behavior of an entire cultural population. However, high-level concepts such as individualism and collectivism tend to be loosely defined. It is also difficult to determine their validity, because the delimitations of these broad concepts (i.e., the boundaries between aspects of behavior that are covered by the concept and those that are not) remain unclear.

Self-construals appear to be a strong intervening variable that can help explain how culture affects communication behavior. Elements of the self-system (e.g., independent and interdependent selves) help us to more precisely understand the processes by which culture influences communication behavior. Because self-concept provides a link between the norms and values of culture and the everyday behavior of individuals, it may be a promising means of explaining intercultural conversational style. At the individual level, the problematic categorization of people as either individualistic or collectivistic is ameliorated (Singelis, 1994).

Furthermore, the measures of individualism and collectivism on the individual level are advantageous because they allow us to characterize the IC nature of different groups and to examine the relative importance of individualism and collectivism in those groups. Using such measures, researchers would no longer have to assume that the groups in their studies are individualistic or collectivistic; they could demonstrate the nature of the groups empirically (Matsumoto, Weissman, Preston, Brown, & Kupperbusch, 1997). For theorists to better understand the impact of culture, it is essential to explain how psychological differences between people from varying cultural backgrounds shape their beliefs and behaviors (Brockner & Chen, 1996).

Recent between-culture analyses that include self-construals provide converging evidence of the critical role played by self-construals (Gudykunst et al., 1996; Kim et al., 1996; Singelis & Brown, 1995). Self-construals provide a parsimonious explanation of differences between cultures in the impact of self-related variables and communication behavior. Recent studies (Kim et al., 1996; Kim et al., 2000; Kim & Sharkey, 1995; Kim, Sharkey, & Singelis, 1994) also show that the degree of independent and interdependent construal of self systematically affects the perceived importance of "conversational constraints" (Kim, 1993, 1995) within a culture as well as across different cultural groups. Furthermore, Kim et al. (2001) found that culture influences mediating processes (self-construals) that affect the motivations for verbal communication. Stated differently, cultural variability does not have a direct impact on verbal communication motivations per se but, rather, its influences are indirect through other processes.

The notion of self-construals (as individual-level correlates of individualism and collectivism) potentially clarify and elaborate the fuzzy construct of culture, not only providing more "concise, coherent, integrated, and empirically testable dimensions of cultural variations but also linking psychological phenomena to a cultural dimension" (Rhee, Uleman, & Lee, 1996, p. 1037). Coherent theoretical efforts can be made only through the logical connection between culture-level analysis on one hand and individual-level analysis on the other. To summarize, self-construals appear well-suited to account for both the between- and within-culture variation in the expression of communication behavior (Singelis, 1994).

❖ CULTURAL RELATIVITY
   OF COMMUNICATION CONSTRUCTS

The increased attention on individual-level cultural dimensions was a further healthy step. Some began asking whether new or complementary theories, constructs, and methodologies could be teased from the collective worldview (Kim, 1999; Kim, 2001; Kim & Leung, 2000). Instead of merely applying Western theories or translating Western instruments, could non-Western communication researchers originate such scientific creations from their own cultural legacy? By doing so, they could rebalance the scientific center of gravity. According to Brockner and Chen (1996), the consequences of self-related variables in cultures in which people usually have independent self-construals may be very different from the consequences observed in cultures in which people have more interdependent self-construals.

The main focus of Part II of this book will be the cultural relativity of the constructs and theories used in human communication. The field of human communication was largely developed in the United States, using the theme of research and the contents of the theories serving its own society. The ultimate goal of science is the production of general statements about all relevant phenomena, using appropriate theoretical and methodological tools (Berry, 1978). Communication theories have been imported from the United States to other societies, and they are used to study topics that are central to the established literature, with little regard to what is actually happening in that other society or to how it may best be studied. Of course, applying theories developed in the mainstream United States to the mainstream United States is entirely appropriate. But clearly, the two problems with such theories are their importation and use in other cultures and subgroups of a culture, and their masquerading as the universal human communication (see Berry, 1978, for a similar argument in social psychology).

Many of the findings currently regarded as basic to human communication may be a function of particular cultural frameworks that may be unseen and unexamined because they are shared by investigators and subjects alike. Conversely, the seemingly anomalous failure in replicating these standard phenomena in other cultures makes sense when we understand the cultural models with which people are thinking, feeling, judging, and acting—including the models of persons (Fiske, Kitayama, Markus, & Nisbett, 1998).

The scientific theories, concepts, categories, and models are based on studies that are designed, conducted, and interpreted with reference to a very particular framework. Communication researchers often disregard the cultural frameworks that are limiting conditions for their results— sometimes tacitly assuming that the social forms and communicative practices of the modern West are representative of the human species. Consequently, most human communication theories reflect and incorporate a vast set of cultural meanings and practices that are nearly invisible from within their own subcultures.

The individualistic model of the self is implicitly or explicitly also used by most of the field of human communication. Rooted in Western philosophical presuppositions about human nature and in layers upon layers of practices and institutions, this model seems a characterization of objective reality. It has been a useful framework for organizing empirical work on the human communication of European and American subjects who operate with reference to these individualistic axioms. However, this model of persons and socialities is not based on objective empirical evidence about most other cultures.

In this book, I use the notion of independent and interdependent self-construals to illustrate the problems in a monocultural perspective of the field. Within the last two decades, social scientists' view of the self-concept has undergone a dramatic transformation (e.g., Kagitcibasi, 1996; Markus & Kitayama, 1991). The notions of self-construals have emerged primarily in the field of cultural psychology and pertain to how people define themselves and their relationships with other people. After a brief review of the major individualistic tenets, I will isolate several underlying assumptions concerning the nature of cultural identity. I shall then examine how the same assumptions have shaped theory and research on interpersonal and intercultural communication as well as other areas of human communication research.

II

U.S.-Centrism

*Cultural Relativity
of Communication Constructs and Theories*

The individualistic model of the self that provides the infrastructure for traditional Western theories and models of communication, as well as for most of the social sciences, may seem an obvious and natural one. However, it is not the only model of how to be a person or the only answer to "What is a person?" Another model of the self that is significantly different from individualism in many of its assumptions, yet very widely held, suggests that persons are not independent entities but are instead fundamentally interdependent with one another (see Markus & Kitayama, 1998). Mainstream communication theories, for the most part, have largely ignored this model by assuming an autonomous, bounded, temporally stable and consistent person who can first be identified by means of an assortment of personality inventories and, only subsequently and secondarily, put back into the social milieu.

In the chapters that follow, I underscore how most current theories of human communication are rooted in Western philosophical presumptions about persons and in layers of practices and institutions that reflect and promote these presumptions. Most other ontologies and ideologies of personhood have yet to be reflected in the literature on human communication, and analyzing human communication in a cultural context will bring some of these alternative ways to light (see Markus & Kitayama, 1998, for a similar argument on personality research).

Given its original orientation to social context, the field of human communication could have come to recognize that culture is the most basic and far-reaching context in which communicative processes are engaged and thus formed. Yet communication research in the last half century has largely failed to develop these insights of its founders so as to include the cultural perspective in its modern conceptual frameworks. Recently, similar arguments have been made in social psychology, child development, and counseling, as well as in other social sciences (for discussion of this issue, see Berry, 1983; Fiske, Kitayama, Markus, & Nisbett, 1998; Kagitcibasi, 1996; Markus & Kitayama, 1998). For instance, the value implications of psychological concepts, particularly those in the areas of personality, social, and developmental psychology, have been traced back to the sociohistorical context of emerging individualism (Buss, 1975; Hogan & Emler, 1975; Riegel, 1972). Gergen (1973) suggests that the current terminology reflects an arbitrary labeling based on Western value preferences: "For example, high self-esteem could be termed egotism; need for social approval could be translated as need for social integration; creativity as deviance; and internal control as egocentricity" (p. 312).

Similarly, LeVine (1973) introduced "The Japanese problem," referring to challenges Japan poses to Western psychoanalytic theories. He argues that psychoanalytic theorists must revise their conceptions of what is normal, necessary, and adaptive in the psychic development structure and functioning of humans. In other words, Japan can function for Americans as a powerful tool to destabilize the taken-for-granted assumptions about psychoanalytic theories. According to Tobin (2000), "The Japanese problem" does not have to be about Japan. In theory, any culture could play this role of calling into question the ethnocentricity of our commonsense understandings and our social scientific theories. It presents a challenge not only to psychoanalytic theories, but more generally to our basic assumptions about interpersonal relations and communication patterns. In short, Japan (the useful other) for

Americans presents a fundamental challenge to both our scholarly and conventional understandings of the nature of person.

Although current descriptions of the largely independent and autonomous self could be argued to be reasonably adequate for European-American selves, a growing body of evidence suggests that they are simply not valid for many other cultural groups. Furthermore, at least in the United States, the analysis of the selves of those groups in society that are marginalized—women, members of nondominant ethnic groups, the poor, the unschooled—reveals a more obvious interdependence between the self and the collective when compared with other societal groups. For example, many women describe themselves in relational terms, and they do not reveal the typical preference for being positively unique or different from others (Gilligan, 1982; Lykes, 1985). Gilligan (1982) voiced her criticism that the separate self is predominantly a male perspective, whereas women's conception is one of self-in-relationships. The individualistic view of the self may be more descriptive of men in U.S. society than of women in U.S. society. Many theorists have echoed this view (e.g., Belenski, Clinchy, Goldberger, & Tarule, 1986; Chodorow, 1989). For instance, Jordan (1991) argued that the "Lone Ranger" model of the self simply does not fit many women's experience because women's sense of self seems to involve connection and engagement with relationships and collective. Findings also suggest that those with power and privilege are those most likely to internalize the prevailing European-American cultural frame to naturally experience themselves as autonomous individuals (Markus & Kitayama, 1994).

Heine, Lehman, Markus, and Kitayama (1999) also point out that it is perhaps most accurate to view the vast amount of self research amassed over the past few decades largely as a reflection of contemporary North American culture. Unfortunately, because the cultural specificity of social psychological theories is rarely highlighted, often the implicit assumption is that these theories reflect pancultural psychological processes. Hogan (1975) also suggested that "much American psychology can plausibly be described as theoretically egocentric" (p. 534).

Similarly, human communication theories of the self focused on the individuated self-concept—that is, the person's sense of unique identity differentiated from others. Cross-cultural perspectives, however, have brought a renewed interest in the social aspects of the self and the extent to which individuals define themselves in terms of their relationships to others and to social groups. Central to this new perspective is the idea that connectedness and belonging are not merely affiliations or alliances between the self and others but entail fundamental differences in the way the self is construed. Increasingly throughout social sciences, including the field of human communication, there are indications that the individualistic model of the self is too narrow and fails to take into account some important aspects of communication phenomena. I will illustrate the process whereby cultural views of self are transformed into psychological tendencies and then into communication styles.

The aim of Part II, which consists of 11 chapters, is to emphasize the relationship between fact and value within the field of communication and thereby help to make communication scholars more self-conscious of the implications their research has with respect to creating a specific image of humans and society. Values and social sciences are intimately interlocked, and this interdependent relationship must be made explicit and understood (Buss, 1975). Both cultural perspectives on human communication are powerful and viably animate their respective worlds. The point, however, is not to argue for one or the other. Instead, my goal is to underscore how cultural frameworks structure both everyday and scientific understandings of human communication.

4

Communication Apprehension

Deficiency or Politeness?

Those who talk do not know. Those who do not know talk.

— Lao Tzu

He who converses not knows nothing.

— John Ray, *English Proverbs*, 1670, p. 5

Few things are more basic to an individual's communication style than the amount that she or he talks. Simply describing an unknown person as either quiet or talkative will evoke very different images in people's minds. Research that employs such descriptions has found dramatically different perceptions of the persons described.

A substantial body of cross-cultural research exists in the area of verbal communication predisposition. Studies indicate that significant differences exist both cross-culturally and intraculturally in regard to communication approach and avoidance. However, the role that communication motivation plays in intercultural communication is virtually unknown.

Although talk is probably a vital component in interpersonal communication and the development of interpersonal relationships in all cultures, people differ dramatically from one another in the degree to which they actually value talk. This variability in talking behavior among people is alleged to be rooted in "willingness to communicate" (McCroskey and Richmond, 1987). Studies on verbal communication skills have focused on the perceptual impact of reticence or apprehension without specific regard to the cultural factors associated with the communication receiver or object of her perception. Yet cross-cultural communication research clearly demonstrates the norms for verbal behavior, as well as the consequent perceptions associated with these norms, which vary to an extraordinary degree from one culture to the next.

Research on communication motivation, like many other branches of communication, was born and nourished by the philosophical foundations of individualism. We now discover that individualism is not a universal, but rather a culture-specific, belief system (Greenfield, 1994). The view of communication motivation from interdependence-oriented societies can help to balance the ethnocentric picture of the individualistic value placed on communication approach. In the individualistic culture, talk is considered positive and is generally rewarded. Many other cultures do not place as high a premium on the amount or frequency of talk as does the U.S. culture. This analysis of verbal communication motivation implies the necessity of reformulating theories in this and related areas.

The work in this area has been biased by the individualistic assumption that confrontation is more desirable than avoidance, which limits a full understanding of the dispositional communication motivation. Given the general assumption of the desirability of direct confrontation of matters, it is not surprising that researchers have conceptualized the avoidance styles as generally destructive and reflective of low concern for self as well as for the other. This assumption is taken so much for granted in individualistic cultures that it has rarely been stated explicitly. Similarly, some researchers consider argument (direct confrontation of matters) to be a beneficial and prosocial mode of conflict resolution and view avoidance as less socially acceptable (e.g., Infante, Trebing, Shepherd, & Seeds, 1984; Rancer, Baukus, & Infante, 1985). According to Miike (2000), people from Asian cultures are, in general, one-sidedly labeled by Western communication researchers as "passive communicators." And in most cases, the connotation associated with this label is that Asians are less communicatively competent than Westerners and need to be trained to communicate better.

Notably, most cross-cultural research on communication disposition has explored how it applies and operates in the U.S. culture in comparison to other cultures. Because culture shapes human communication behavior, the amount of talking in which a person engages is dependent, at least in part, on that person's cultural orientation (Barraclough, Christophel, & McCroskey, 1988). For instance, it is likely that different cultures perceive, manifest, and respond (reward and sanction) differently to communication approach and avoidance (Olaniran & Roach, 1994). This chapter reviews and critically synthesizes, from a cultural standpoint, research on people's predispositions toward avoiding social interaction.

❖ MOTIVATION TO AVOID VERBAL COMMUNICATION

Lustig and Andersen (1991) argue that "No communication variable has been examined more during the past two decades than has communication apprehension" (p. 299). *Communication apprehension (CA)* is "an individual's level of fear or anxiety associated with either real or anticipated communication with another person or persons" (McCroskey, 1977, p. 78). Previous cross-cultural studies on communication apprehension have focused on comparisons of other cultures as either higher or lower in communication motivation (e.g., CA and argumentativeness) than the U.S. culture (McIntyre, Mauger, Margalit, & Figueiredo, 1989; Prunty, Klopf, Ishii, 1990; Watson, Monroe, & Atterstrom, 1989).

Recently, Kim (1999) reviewed cross-cultural variations in general levels of communication apprehension. The cross-cultural research reviewed clearly demonstrates that the norms for verbal behavior, as well as the consequent perceptions associated with these norms, vary to an extraordinary degree from one culture to the next. The overall results of past research indicate that samples from collectivistic cultures, such as China and Japan, display higher levels of verbal communication apprehension than comparable samples in individualistic cultures, such as Australia and the mainland United States. Gudykunst and Ting-Toomey (1988) contend that the finding that members of collectivistic cultures have higher levels of communication apprehension than members of individualistic cultures should not be taken to imply that communication apprehension is a problem in collectivistic cultures; in fact, the opposite is probably true.

This line of argument is consistent with the view that high-context communication predominates in collectivistic cultures and, therefore, high scores on communication apprehension are to be expected in collectivistic cultures (Gudykunst & Ting-Toomey, 1988). Hence, without information about a culture's general predisposition toward verbal communication, research on communication apprehension in a given culture may not be very useful. The amount of talk and the degree of quietness endorsed by a culture may have an overpowering impact on the communication motivation of most people in that culture. Given findings reporting significant cross-cultural differences, it is critical to be careful when generalizing about the nature of communication apprehension and other related communication orientations. The present review suggests that such relationships may be extremely culture-bound and nongeneralizable from one culture to another.

McCroskey (1977) outlined three general propositions regarding the effects of high apprehension about communication: (a) People who experience high apprehension about communication will withdraw from and seek to avoid communication when possible; (b) As a result of withdrawal from and avoidance of communication, people who experience high apprehension about communication will be perceived less positively than people who experience lower apprehension about communication by others in their environment; and (c) As a result of their withdrawal and avoidance behaviors, and in conjunction with the negative perceptions fostered by these behaviors, people who experience high apprehension about communication will be negatively affected in their economic, academic, political, and social lives. Indeed, individuals with high levels of CA were found to withdraw from and avoid communication whenever possible, to be perceived less positively than individuals with low levels of CA, and to experience negative consequences in various aspects of their daily lives (McCroskey, 1982). Results from numerous studies conducted in the United States indicate that communication apprehension plays a negative role in the process of interaction.

Specifically, those with high CA, reticence, unwillingness to communicate, and so on, have been found to talk less (Burgoon, 1976), disclose less (McCroskey & Richmond, 1987), and engage in less information seeking (Burgoon, 1976) than those with low CA. Numerous researchers have reported that people described as uncommunicative are perceived to be less attractive than their verbal counterparts on a host of dimensions, including social and task attraction (e.g., Daly, McCroskey, & Richmond, 1977) and perceived sexuality (e.g., McCroskey, Daly, Richmond, & Cox, 1975).

Early research in communication apprehension suggested that individuals with high public speaking apprehension would experience high levels of negative thinking in anticipation of presenting a speech as well as during the delivery (Meichenbaum, 1977). Recent studies support the assumption that individuals high in public speaking anxiety report more negative thoughts prior to speaking than individuals low in public speaking anxiety, and the latter report more positive thoughts than the former as they anticipate delivery of a speech (Buhr, Pryor, & Sullivan, 1991; Daly, Vangelisti, Neel, & Cavanaugh, 1989).

Perhaps the most striking feature of the body of research based on the communication apprehension framework is that the outcomes of communication apprehension and avoidance are solely negative. Researchers have found that individuals who are low on emotional maturity, adventurousness, self-control, self-esteem, and tolerance for ambiguity are more inclined to exhibit communication apprehension (McCroskey, Richmond, Daly, & Falcione, 1977). Individuals with high levels of CA were perceived as less competent, less attractive, less sociable, and less composed than those with lower levels (McCroskey, Daly, Richmond, & Cox, 1975). There is also evidence that others' negative perceptions have a further impact in that teachers tend to have lower expectations of communication-apprehensive students, which lead to lower achievement (McCroskey & Daly, 1976).

Needless to say, the picture of persons with a high level of communication avoidance that emerges from prior studies is generally a negative one. Such persons might be described as typically introverted individuals who lack self-esteem and are resistant to change, have a low tolerance for ambiguity, and are lacking in self-control and emotional maturity. Persons at the other end of the CA continuum, on the other hand, might be described as typically adventurous, extroverted, confident, emotionally mature individuals with high self-esteem, tolerance for ambiguity, and willingness or even eagerness to accept change in their environment. Based upon profiles such as these, many hypotheses have been tested involving the behaviors and attitudes of people with different levels of CA and concerning other people's perceptions of such individuals (see McCroskey, 1977).

These propositions and research supporting them may not apply to people of different cultural orientations. In the predominantly individualistic culture (i.e., mainstream United States), talk is regarded in a positive manner and is generally rewarded. As stated previously, some other cultures do not place as high a premium on the amount or frequency of talk. It has been shown that culture or national origin influences the level of students' communication apprehension (Klopf, 1984; Olaniran & Roach, 1994).

Communication avoidance in the United States has been associated with deficiency. It is easy to find explicit references in the literature to support the view that communication approach is more desirable than communication avoidance. For instance, Richmond and McCroskey (1985) argue that high CA individuals tend to "suffer from general anxiety, to have a low tolerance for ambiguity, to lack self-control, to not be adventurous, to lack emotional maturity, to be introverted, to have low self-esteem, to not be innovative, to have a low tolerance for disagreement, and to not be assertive" (p. 45). Individuals high in communication apprehension also have been known (a) to score lower than average on academic tests (McCroskey, Andersen, Richmond, & Wheeless, 1981), (b) to either avoid or fail to participate meaningfully in classroom communication with teachers and peers (Comadena & Prusank, 1988), (c) to cause teachers to have more negative expectations of them than of those low in CA (McCroskey & Daly, 1976), and (d) to need clinical attention to fix the so-called deficiency (Comadena & Prusank, 1988). The association of these constructs with communication avoidance misrepresents the sources of communication avoidance as defects or inadequacies.

However, the value placed on oral communication skills in the North American culture may not be shared by many other cultures. Elliot, Scott, Jensen, and McDonough (1982) found that perceptions of verbal activity differ substantially between American and Korean subjects. Whereas the more highly verbal individual is more positively perceived within the mainstream U.S. culture, the less verbal individual is more positively perceived within the Korean culture. Communication approach (e.g., assertiveness) is generally linked to healthy personality adjustment in the mainstream U.S. context. However, there is a danger in assuming communication avoidance (e.g., nonassertiveness, communication apprehension) as merely maladaptive. When socialization of the people rewards conformity, humility, and the maintenance of harmonious relations (the characteristics of a nonassertive person), it is expected that interdependent persons are actively discouraged from asserting themselves as individuals.

Although extreme forms of communication avoidance and lack of verbal assertiveness can be a handicap in any culture, I am critical of the ethnocentric preoccupation with the Western view of the self that sees communication avoidance solely as a deficiency. Clearly, viewed from an individualistic standpoint, avoidance of communication becomes anything but a deficiency. I will discuss the necessity of reformulating theories in this and related areas. Conceptualizations and interpretations of results have been flawed or incomplete because of the individualistic bias of work in this area.

Numerous studies have linked high communication apprehension and a low willingness to communicate to a wide variety of social, organizational, academic, and communicative problems (e.g., Daly & Stafford, 1984; Richmond & Roach, 1992). If one assumes that the individual should be a bounded, autonomous, self-sufficient social unit independent of others, then nonassertiveness and shyness become a deficiency. That is, being silent or avoiding argument becomes an indicator of anxiety or one's lack of social confidence.

The individualistic view coincides with Sampson's (1988) notion of a centralized, equilibrium concept of personhood (i.e., individualism), which holds that only through mastery and personal control can one prevent chaos while maintaining order and coherence. This notion of personhood is typically true of Western cultures. Given the general assumption of the desirability of direct confrontation stemming from independent view of the self, it is not surprising that researchers have conceptualized the avoidant communication styles as a deficiency. I propose that differing degrees of verbal communication motivations may stem from (a) the strength of one's idealized role-identity (as bounded and separate) in interaction and (b) the sensitivity to others' evaluations as the interaction unfolds, depending on the degree to which one's identity is entwined with and dependent on others.

❖ TRADITIONAL VIEW: COMMUNICATION AVOIDANCE AS A DEFICIENCY

Traditionally, communication anxiety or reticence has been attributed to a weak sense of the independent self. From an individualistic point of view, an individual who has low communication motivation is thought to have an unstable or uncertain sense of her or his own role-identity as bounded and separate from others. It has been claimed that this fragile sense of role-identity is inherently vulnerable to threats during interaction, which causes communication anxiety. The hyper-sensitivity to evaluation is related to an uncertain sense of self and the accompanying fear of negative evaluations. This represents the deficit model of verbal communication avoidance.

Numerous scholars have noted the propensity for the Western cultural value of individualism to shape theorists' view of psychological functioning (see Gilligan, 1982; Markus & Kitayama, 1991; Sampson, 1988; Sharkey & Singelis, 1995). If one assumes that the individual should be separate and unique from others, then non-assertiveness and shyness become a deficiency. That is, being silent or avoiding argument does not help the individual to positively distinguish herself or himself from others. Rather than viewing communication avoidance as a personal deficiency, it is possible to view it as a sensitivity to the social context.

In the West, the Chomskyan notion of communicative competence consists mainly of the grammatical knowledge displayed in most communicative processes but, for Japanese, communicative competence means "the ability to send and receive subtle, unstated messages" (Lebra, 1991, p. 14). Among individuals with highly independent self-construals, "elaborated talk" (Hall, 1976) is necessary to establish identity—to make oneself stand out in the crowd. Thus, it should be expected that the highly verbal person will be perceived in a positive light because she or he is more successful at establishing "identity" (see Elliot et al., 1982).

Independents should be motivated to seek out, exert greater effort in, and derive greater satisfaction from situations allowing personal control. Thus, an individual's oral communication skills are valued abilities, and people are far more likely to be attracted to the ideas of individuals blessed with the gift of gab than to those with less proclivity to speak their mind (see Elliot et al., 1982).

In individualistic societies, the development of strong interpersonal relationships is heavily dependent on the amount of communication in which interactants are willing to engage. Hence, other things being equal, the more a person is willing to talk and to be nonverbally expressive, the more likely that person is to develop positive interpersonal relationships. Although research in the mainstream American culture strongly supports this conclusion, its generalizability to other cultures is questionable.

❖ COMMUNICATION AVOIDANCE STEMMING FROM A SENSITIVITY TO SOCIAL CONTEXTS

The deficit view is ethnocentric in its conceptualization of the self as a bounded, independent, and autonomous entity. A second way in which one's social role is threatened also involves others' evaluations. In this case, rather than arising from insecurity about the idealized role-identity as an independent self that one brings to an interaction, a heightened awareness of evaluations can result from a more generalized sensitivity to social context (Sharkey & Singelis, 1995). All else being equal, people who are closely in touch with the social identity that surrounds them might be more anxious because their perceptions of what takes place in the social context are heightened. A generalized sensitivity to others' evaluations and fitting in is one of the central characteristics of the collectivistic self.

Avoidance of verbal expression can help the individual to control the emotion and may at times also allow the passive expression of discontentment without the dangers of a direct challenge. Just as messages of silence (extreme forms of indirectness) might be evaluated differently within different relationship contexts (see Tannen, 1985), avoidant styles (or withdrawal) can be seen as positive or negative by members of different cultural orientations (as they are measured against what is expected in that context). In individualistic contexts, there often appears to be a demand to interact that characterizes much of dyadic communication—a built-in assumption that when people are engaged in focused conversation, it is their responsibility to keep verbal communication active. Silence or avoidant communication styles might, at times, represent a threat to this responsibility. Specifically, just like inferences regarding silences, avoidant styles (i.e., low verbal output) among interdependents can be seen as negative politeness—being nice to others by not imposing (for similar arguments regarding cultural differences in perceptions of silence, see Tannen, 1985). Low motivation for verbal output among independents may be seen as the failure of positive politeness—the need to be involved with others. This failure can occur in any culture but seems to be especially common in cultures that may be characterized as relatively individualistic.

Kim, Shin, and Cai (1998), in their study using participants from Korea, Hawaii, and the mainland United States, found that the higher one's independent cultural orientations, the less one is prone to remain silent in both first- and second-attempt requests. The benefits of low verbal output among interdependents comes from being understood without putting one's meaning on record, so understanding is seen not as the result of putting meaning into words, but rather as the greater understanding of shared perspective, expectations, and intimacy.

Sharkey and Singelis (1995) found that interdependence was positively correlated with embarrassability. This relationship was attributed to the sensitivity toward social contexts among high interdependents. They proposed that a sensitivity to the social context and the associated embarrassability could be viewed as positive characteristics that contribute to one's ability to adapt and fit into a social system, especially one that emphasizes groups and cooperative effort (i.e., collectivistic cultures). In individualistic cultures, a sensitivity to the social context can be useful, even though it is not emphasized. The disruption of an interaction would certainly have stronger effects on a presentation of self that emphasizes fitting in and being sensitive to the social contexts (see Sharkey & Singelis, 1995).

The field of communication is still dominated by a Euro-American perspective and is somewhat oblivious to its ethnocentrism. It has consistently been presumed that high communication avoidance is a pathology that visits disagreeable consequences on people unfortunate enough to be so afflicted. Recently, the construct of compulsive communication and a measure of this orientation, the Talkaholic Scale, were introduced into the literature (Hackman, Johnson, & Barthel-Hackman, 1995). McCroskey and Richmond (1993) refer to extremely low CAs as "talkaholics" and indicate that this propensity for communication may cause problems for these individuals. They define compulsive communicators as "individuals who are aware of their tendencies to over-communicate in a consistent and compulsive manner" (p. 107).

Although we now know a great deal about the correlates and effects of communication avoidance in the U.S. context, there is still much we do not know, particularly about the effects of unusually high levels of communication approach. Just as a certain degree of communication approach tendencies is essential for competent interpersonal communication in some situations, too much approach or aggressive styles could be a problem. Future research should focus more on (a) the potentially negative consequences of "talkaholism" (McCroskey & Richmond, 1995) and (b) the causes of excessive communication approach and avoidance, and the development of treatments from a cultural perspective.

Different degrees of communication approach and avoidance may be generated by differing concepts of self, which in part stem from individuals' different cultural backgrounds. Obtaining knowledge about the preferred levels of verbal communication can help to avoid misinterpreting the communication behaviors of people from other cultures. The idea that verbal communication motivation may function differently across cultures offers a useful framework for explaining intercultural misunderstanding. The prevailing culture determines what level of verbal communication will be seen as normal; who will be required to adapt to whose level of verbal communicativeness; and whose verbal style will be seen as deviant, irrational, or inferior. The implications of these relationships for cross-cultural communication are far-reaching. Interdependent (i.e., less verbal) individuals interacting within the independent social group are potentially at a disadvantage socially and are perceived as less attractive than other potential communication partners. Independent individuals operating within interdependent social groups may encounter a similar reversal regarding the perception of their verbal behavior (see Kim, 1999, for further discussion of this issue).

❖ IMPLICATIONS

In any kind of employment in the U.S. context, an employee's speaking capabilities are the key to success, promotion, and higher pay

(Klopf, 1995). Many jobs rely on the ability to speak well—for example, sales positions, managerial posts, teaching positions, service jobs, and so on. For the highly apprehensive businessperson, negative economic and social consequences can be expected. According to Richmond and McCroskey (1992), those who are highly apprehensive are characterized by the following:

- They are perceived by employers as being less attractive to work with and less socially adept.
- They are thought to be less satisfied in their jobs and to have poorer relationships with their fellow employees and supervisors.
- They are less likely to advance to higher-paying positions.
- They interact less with peers and strangers socially.
- They often are considered maladaptive even though they may be psychologically normal in other aspects of their behavior.

Because of their different implicit theories about conversational styles, cultural groups may disagree about appropriate choices of conversational strategies. According to Koester and Olebe (1988), as cultures vary, so do the specific behaviors that represent the underlying components of effectiveness. Individuals form impressions of others' communicative behavior and then use these expectations as guidelines to judge their own and others' behaviors.

Projections of cultural diversity clearly indicate the need to adapt to a rapidly changing workforce. To enhance productivity, employers must incorporate new strategies to work with employees from different cultures and backgrounds who emphasize varying levels of independence and interdependence. People from different cultural backgrounds bring different meanings, value assumptions, and discourse styles into the workplace conversation. Such differences can lead to communication breakdown and can threaten a common orientation to organizational goals (Fine, 1991).

Understanding people's attitudes toward verbal communication will help individuals to appreciate the complexity of communication in multicultural business organizations. The pace and intensity of change in today's business organizations are unprecedented, making tremendous demands on the individual's ability to adjust. The consequences of failing to understand others' sociolinguistic systems may well result in communication breakdown, position stagnation, failure to achieve organizational goals, social isolation, negative sanctions, a loss of self-esteem, a negative effect on work performance, and/or the loss of a job (Fine, 1991). As the world becomes more interculturally integrated, understanding the importance of the communication approach and avoidance motivations will contribute to a better understanding of the complexity of communication in multicultural business organizations. In the past, many organizational communication theorists painted a picture of organizations and organizational communication as being governed by the value of clarity in communication or "ambiguity control" (e.g., Conrad, 1991).

Thomas (1983) introduced the notion of "cross-cultural pragmatic failure" and argued that in different cultures, different pragmatic ground rules may be invoked. Pragmatic failure stems from cross-culturally different perceptions of what constitutes appropriate linguistic behavior that leads to perceptions of communication competence. Cultural stereotypes of the direct (or even blunt) American, or the roundabout Korean or Japanese, in business interactions may be anchored in people's cultural knowledge about the verbal communicativeness used within their respective cultures where independent or interdependent self-construals are valued.

Systematic desensitization (SD) is the primary technique that has been used to help people cope with the unpleasant feelings associated with public speaking anxiety (McCroskey, 1972). Cognitive-based interventions are designed to change the way one thinks about giving a speech (Ayers & Hopf, 1993). In the past, several cognitive interventions for oral CA have been reported in the literature, employing methods borrowed from various clinical schools of thought. A considerable amount of time has been spent trying to prove that one intervention is superior to another in reducing communication apprehension (Allen, Hunter, & Donohue, 1989). These interventions attempt a cognitive restructuring of exclusively high trait CA individuals. However, exclusive focus on high CA individuals (and cultural bias in the treatment of high CA) without a clear model of the cognitions that stimulate oral CA, therapists have to spend time identifying cognitions that increase CA for specific individuals. In contrast, a cultural model of communication motivation might identify cognitive patterns that contribute to high trait CA in many individuals, and thus guide more culturally sensitive interventions that target those patterns.

One needs to recognize that the central components of communication motivation are cultural value orientations. I criticize this line of research on conceptual grounds for its ethnocentric biases, noting that in some situations and cultural contexts, an avoidant style can have adaptive consequences.

The challenge of understanding communicative behaviors across cultures should include questions concerning individuals' predispositions toward talking and the reactions of others to the manifestations of such predispositions. Because predispositional communication motivation is a relational phenomenon and those susceptible to anxiety may be more relationally aware and connected, further studies should focus on relational orientations and their effect on communication anxiety and avoidance. Further, I believe that those with a predominantly interdependent self will be particularly susceptible to what can be termed *other-face communication anxiety*. An identity that encompasses the other will be more likely to share in the desire to save others' face. This area of research needs to move toward the construction of a truly universal theory of communication motivation through the empirical and theoretical understanding of cultural diversity.

5

Motivation to Approach Verbal Communication

Is Communication Approach Always Healthy?

❖ ❖ ❖

Stand up for your own rights.

— American expression

Once you preach, the point is gone.

— Zen phrase

❖ ASSERTIVENESS: STANDING UP FOR YOUR OWN RIGHTS

Assertiveness is defined as behaviors that enable one to act in her best interest or to stand up for herself without undue anxiety, and to express her rights without denying the rights of others (Alberti & Emmons, 1970). At least within the U.S. context, assertiveness has been viewed as a measure of social competence or as an indicator of interpersonal communication competence. In the United States, assertive behaviors are perceived as more competent and attractive than unassertive behaviors (Henderson & Furnham, 1982; Zakahi, 1985). In sum, people perceived as high in assertiveness are considered competitive, risk takers, fast to take action, take-charge individuals, and directive. People perceived as low in assertiveness are characterized as cooperative, risk avoiders, slow to take action, "go-along" persons, and nondirective.

Previous research in cross-cultural differences in assertiveness has focused on comparing the assertiveness of other cultures to the U.S. culture. For example, studies have documented the difference in assertiveness between Chilean and U.S. subjects (Carmona & Lorr, 1992); between Israeli, Portuguese, and U.S. respondents (McIntyre, Mauger, Margalit, & Figueiredo, 1989); and between Japanese and Americans (Klopf, Thompson, & Sallinen-Kuparinen, 1991; Prunty, Klopf, & Ishii, 1990). Cross-cultural studies have reported that Asians are less assertive than Caucasians (Fukuyama & Greenfield, 1983; Johnson & Marsella, 1978). Fukuyama and Greenfield (1983) compared the responses of Asian American and Caucasian American students on the College Self-Expression Scale and found that the Asian American students had significantly lower assertion scores on the following items: expressing feelings or making difficult requests in public, disagreeing with parents, and expressing annoyance to the opposite sex. Nagao (1991) found a significant difference in assertive behaviors among Americans and Japanese. Specifically, she found that a higher percentage of Japanese students than American students would perceive it to be inappropriate to question a professor if they disagreed with a professor's statement. The results are consistent with Thompson and Ishii's (1990) study of students from Japan, Korea, Finland, and the United States. The Japanese proved to be similar to the Finns; each held a moderate level of assertiveness that was not significantly different from the other. However, Thompson and Ishii found that American students are more assertive than Japanese students in their behaviors. The Koreans and Americans showed a high degree of assertiveness, with mean scores above 34. The Koreans, however, were significantly different than the Americans, with the Americans being the more assertive. Comparing the four cultures' men and women, the men were significantly more assertive than the women in three of the cultures. The exception was Finland; when the Finnish men were compared with the Finnish women, the women displayed a significantly higher degree of assertiveness. Except for the Finnish men, the other cultures' men confirm McCroskey, Richmond, and Stewart's (1986) claim that assertiveness is a masculine trait. The male stereotype pictures men as leaders who are forceful, strong, dominant, and independent, and the results from Japan, Korea and the United States support this notion. Because assertiveness is generally perceived as a masculine trait (Galassi, Delo, Galassi, & Bastien, 1974), women are often less positively evaluated for similar assertive behaviors than men are. Thus, assertiveness is considered to be a sex-role violation for women (Gervasio & Crawford, 1989).

Assertiveness has typically been treated as a unidimensional construct, but different types of assertiveness may play varied roles in different situational contexts. Recent evidence by Goldberg and Botvin (1993) supports the concept of assertiveness as a multidimensional construct and provides evidence for situation-specific assertive skills. Individuals of high interdependence may demonstrate a clear pattern of avoidance of communication, particularly during such threatening communication experiences as public speaking and interviewing with an influential person. This may not be the case among individuals of high independence.

Compared with Japanese parents, U.S. parents place greater value on their children's social initiative and verbal assertiveness as hallmarks of individuation and maturity (Azuma, 1986). In the United States, parents reinforce assertiveness by speaking with pride about their willful children and by fostering children's self-esteem; Japanese parents are more inclined to encourage self-effacement, which is incompatible with assertiveness (Rothbaum, Pott, Azuma, Miyake, & Weisz, 2000).

Perceptions of assertiveness are influenced by level of assertion, gender of the person, culture, and situational context (Cook & St. Lawrence, 1990). Assertiveness is often regarded as an individualistic interpersonal-oriented behavior in contrast to a collectivistic interpersonal-oriented behavior. People who exhibit assertive behaviors value individual events, beliefs, and feelings above those of groups. This would suggest that people from individualistic cultures are generally more assertive than people from collectivistic cultures.

Consistent personality profiles of assertive and nonassertive individuals has emerged in the literature. Assertive individuals stand up for their rights and are able to freely, directly, and honestly express their thoughts, feelings, and beliefs. Nonassertive persons are characterized, on the other hand, as inhibited, submissive, self-deprecating, self-denying, and conforming. In addition, assertive people are more gregarious, adaptable, sensitive, rational, and extroverted, and less subservient, defensive, self-protecting, and anxious (Ramanaiah & Deniston, 1993).

❖ ARGUMENTATIVENESS: A SUBSET OF ASSERTIVENESS

Argumentativeness is another predisposition toward verbal communication that has been extensively studied (Dowling & Flint, 1990; Infante & Wigley, 1986). Argumentativeness is considered a subset of assertiveness (Infante & Rancer, 1996); not all assertive behavior entails argument. Specifically, *argumentativeness* is defined as "a generally stable trait that predisposes the individualism communication situations to advocate positions on controversial issues and to attack verbally the positions which other people take on these issues" (Infante & Rancer, 1982, p. 72). The highly argumentative perceive the activity as an intellectual challenge. Through it, persons who defend a position well can win others over to that position. The highly argumentative feel pleasantly excited before an argument, and after the argument they feel satisfied and refreshed. Persons with low tendencies to argue try to avoid arguments and prefer that arguments not happen. Recognizing these emotional reactions, Infante and Rancer (1982) conceptualized argumentation as an approach-avoidance or excitation-inhibition conflict. They theorized that a communicator's argumentativeness is the propensity to approach an argument minus the tendency to avoid one. The highly argumentative would register high on approach and low on avoidance, whereas those with a low desire to argue would register high on avoidance and low on approach.

Argumentativeness and verbal aggressiveness are similar in that both are aggressive and attacking forms of communication (Infante & Rancer, 1996). However, they can be distinguished from each other according to the locus of attack: Argumentativeness attacks the positions taken by others on the issues, and verbal aggressiveness attacks the self-concept of other people instead of, or in addition to, their positions on issues (Infante & Rancer, 1996). In individualistic cultures (e.g., mainland United States), argumentativeness has been found to be a constructive form and verbal aggressiveness a counterproductive form of aggressive communication. Research in the organizational context has shown that argumentativeness is positively related to job satisfaction (Infante & Gordon, 1985). Research in the marital context has shown that argumentativeness is negatively related to individuals' involvement in interspousal violence (Infante, Chandler, & Rudd, 1989). As these studies indicate, in individualistic cultures, argumentativeness is a valued predisposition that can help people manage conflict constructively.

Argumentativeness is characterized by at least two people advocating positions on controversial issues and attempting to refute the positions of one another (Infante & Gordon, 1985). Because of these inherent attack-and-defend characteristics, attention is compellingly drawn to such communication behavior. It has been closely associated with constructive conflict over a difference of opinion and is often perceived as enhancing the image of the communication(s) (Rancer, Baukus, & Infante, 1985). Further, some claim that arguing produces learning, reasoning, and problem-solving benefits for the individual. For instance, Infante (1981) found that argumentativeness is related positively to learning, intellectual development, and communication. Yet it is far from omnipresent and probably is a negative influence upon learning and intellectual development in many parts of the world. Prunty et al. (1990) found that the Japanese were significantly less inclined to approach argument situations and had a significantly weaker argumentativeness trait than Americans did. Researchers report that, compared with Americans, typical Japanese are more apprehensive, speak less frequently, are less predisposed to talk, are less fluent (Klopf & Ishii, 1976), are less willing to self-disclose (Barnlund, 1975), are less assertive and less responsive (Prunty et al., 1990), are more anxious and are more prone to attain unanimous agreement on any matter (Doi, 1973), and are more inclined to silence (Ishii & Bruneau, 1988)—all qualities that are antithetic to argumentative behavior.

Researchers have observed that cultures of high-context communication are characterized by fewer cases of verbal aggression (Ma, 1990) and arguments or argumentation (Barnlund, 1975; Becker, 1986) than cultures of low-context communication. Assuming that these culture-level generalizations are generally consistent with an individual's self-concept, views of argumentativeness among people of highly interdependent self-construals may possibly be different from those high in independent self-construals.

Some authors have suggested that low argumentative individuals may avoid rather than engage in conflict or may use control tactics rather than solution-oriented choices. Persons high in argumentativeness perceive arguing "as an exciting intellectual challenge, a competitive situation which entails defending a position and winning points" (Infante & Rancer, 1982, p. 72). As a result, for such an individual, "feelings of excitement and anticipation precede an argument. Following an argument the individual feels invigorated, satisfied, and experiences a sense of accomplishment" (Infante & Rancer, 1982, p. 72).

In the mainstream U.S. culture, the tendency to avoid arguments is seen as a debilitating factor; the anxiety associated with arguing weakens the tendency to approach arguments (Infante & Rancer, 1982). It is easy to find explicit references in the literature supporting the view that high argumentativeness is more desirable than low argumentativeness. For example, Infante (1982) found that highly argumentative subjects reported higher grade point averages. Along with such research findings, improving argumentativeness is considered a worthy goal of speech communication teachers.

According to Prunty et al. (1990), argumentativeness is a Western practice—both impractical and inconceivable to the Japanese. Although arguments may disrupt interpersonal relationships, Americans, because they perceive argumentation positively, can try to revive relationships and usually succeed. Because the Japanese consider argumentation negatively, friendships disrupted by argument are rarely repaired (Barnlund, 1989). Interdependents' tendency to avoid arguments can be explained by their desire to preserve relational harmony and their motivation to save others' face.

It is likely that high interdependents tend to discourage aggressive communication, regardless of its locus of attack, because it is regarded as negative and disruptive behavior (Suzuki & Rancer, 1994). Accordingly, people with highly interdependent self-construals may want to avoid aggressive forms of communication and may feel anxious if they have to be aggressive in communication situations. To people with highly interdependent self-construals, taking an opposing side in an argument (argumentativeness) necessarily means becoming a personal rival and antagonist of the one who hold the other side (see Becker, 1986). Thus, argumentativeness may be seen negatively among high interdependents, but this is not the case among high independents.

Thus, research has shown that reticent (quiet) individuals are perceived less positively than more verbal individuals in individualistic societies (Elliot, Scott, Jensen, & McDonough, 1982). Some studies suggest that although more highly verbal individuals appear to be more positively perceived within the American culture, less verbal individuals are more positively perceived within the Korean culture. Thus, the value placed on oral communication skills in individualistic cultures may not be shared by other cultures.

Infante (1982) also found that more males than females were highly argumentative. Based on a median split, 58% of males and 41% of females were high on argumentativeness. Interdependence (focused on relationality, interdependence, and connection) corresponds to the female qualities conceptualized by Chodorow (1989), Gilligan (1982), and Lykes (1985). The individualistic self-orientation, with its emphasis on separation, independence, individuation, and self-creation, corresponds to the masculine culture identified by these theorists. The general findings on gender differences point to similar contrasts in gender culture. Rancer and Baukus (1987), utilizing the beliefs framework, concluded that males and females differ in belief structures about arguing, with females holding more negative beliefs about arguing than males. Burroughs and Marie (1990) found that males perceive themselves as more competent and prone to initiate communication, and they are less introverted than female respondents. Individuals (regardless of their biological gender) classified as masculine were significantly higher in argumentativeness than those classified as feminine, androgynous, or undifferentiated (Rancer & Dierks-Stewart, 1985). Rancer and Baukus (1987) concluded that males and females differ in their belief structures about arguing. A larger percentage of females than males believes that arguing is a communication behavior used for dominating and controlling another individual. Similarly, Nicotera (1989) found that women rated the items on the Argumentativeness Scale to be less socially desirable than men did.

❖ CRITIQUE AND SUMMARY

Research on verbal communication approach (i.e., assertiveness and argumentativeness) has been conducted primarily in the United States; cross-cultural studies on that topic are comparatively few. The outcomes and perceptions of assertiveness or argumentativeness are mostly based on research involving predominantly Anglo-Saxon subjects in the United States whose self-identity is autonomous and bounded. An assertive person is able to make requests, actively disagree with another's opinions, and express her or his personal rights and feelings. Wheeless (1975) views assertiveness as the task-oriented dimension of interpersonal communication. By being assertive, communicators can get things done. It would be imprudent to generalize the description of high versus low argumentative or assertive individuals (based on studies using subjects from the United States) to people belonging to other cultures.

Previous studies have reported that Asians are less assertive than Caucasians. The general conclusion that can be drawn from these results is that people from individualistic cultures are generally more assertive than people from collectivistic cultures. Although assertiveness is generally linked to healthy personality adjustment in Western psychology, there is a danger in assuming that nonassertiveness is maladaptive. From the interdependent standpoint, people are expected to be deferent to authority and are actively discouraged from asserting themselves as individuals.

Sue, Ino, and Sue (1983) proposed the concept of "situational assertiveness" to explain the assertive behavior of Asian Americans. They pointed out that "Asian Americans may be assertive in some situations (with friends, in informal settings, or with members of their own race) and deferential in others (with authority figures, in classroom settings or in counseling situations)" (pp. 581-582). They suggested that assessment should involve helping the client to determine which situations require culturally appropriate deference and which situations require assertiveness. For instance, Sue et al. (1983) found that Chinese American men were as behaviorally assertive as white men in many situations. However, Chinese American men experienced more difficulty in a situation that involved an authority figure (a professor) than did white men, which suggests a situation-specific response pattern. It is clear that one must avoid attributing an interdependent individual's lack of assertiveness to a stable trait such as shyness.

Assertive interpersonal skills are a basic necessity for effective functioning in many aspects of life in the United States. The nonassertive pattern common among ethnic minorities has been judged by some to be psychologically dysfunctional and has become a target for intervention. Because the lack of assertive skills can be a source of much unhappiness, it is not surprising that assertiveness training is one of the most frequently prescribed therapeutic interventions (Masters, Burish, Hollon, & Rimm, 1987). Members of many ethnic minority groups have values about assertive responding that differ markedly from those of the dominant culture.

Cultural sensitivity is crucial not only to the success of the intervention but also to the development of rapport between client and counselor. For example, misunderstandings arising from cultural variations in values or communication patterns may lead to a client's difficulty in developing trust and rapport with a therapist (Sue & Sue, 1981). In fact, teaching assertiveness (or argumentativeness) skills is a value-laden process based on an individualistic value orientation. The dominant culture and the culture of psychology have deemed certain assertive (or argumentative) behaviors to be appropriate. This valuing of assertive and argumentative behaviors may lead therapists to adopt a "let's fix the minority" approach that blinds them to other possible alternatives—including the alternative in which the client rejects the values of the dominant culture (Wood & Mallinckrodt, 1990). In helping people to make choices in their communication styles, therapists must avoid implying that there is one best way to behave. Rather, there are more or less effective ways of behaving in different situations. It must be clear to clients that the goal of training is not to persuade them to reject their cultural values. Instead, the goal is to develop an understanding of assertive and argumentative behaviors in various cultural contexts, to recognize cues that distinguish these different situations, and to build an increased repertoire for responding effectively in each of these contexts (Ponterotto, Casas, Suzuki, & Alexander, 1995). The therapist's task is to help clients acquire a repertoire of culturally appropriate skills to give them the power of choice. The therapist's openness to clients' experiences and a genuine respect for the choices that they make are the most fundamental elements of cultural sensitivity (Wood & Mallinckrodt, 1990). Culturally appropriate counseling and the link between culture and forms of communication motivation are important frontiers of future research.

Today, more than ever before, schools in the United States contain a complex mix of students from many cultures. National and regional demographic changes and distributional shifts document an increase in the minority and international student population. The many languages, customs, religious affiliations, communication patterns, and cultural values that students now bring to the classroom have left educational institutions and instructors scrambling to accommodate this diversity. Many of the problems confronting both students and teachers in these culturally diverse classrooms can be traced to culture. In fact, interactions between teachers and pupils from different cultures are fundamentally problematic, and cross-cultural misunderstandings often occur because classroom interaction is an archetypal human phenomenon that is deeply rooted in the culture of a society (Hofstede, 1983). Thus, educators need to call upon appropriate intercultural communication skills to support the learning process.

Training students to argue effectively and constructively has been a central part of the Western communication discipline for more than 2,000 years (Infante & Rancer, 1996). The rather massive and unequivocal finding that argumentativeness is constructive upholds this tradition. Verbal communication has been considered extremely important in achieving educational goals. The school in the individualistic society is an oral environment in which the principal means of transmitting knowledge is speech. The more a person talks, unless the talk is overly negative or morally reprehensible, the more positively the person is perceived. In U.S. classrooms, the individual is expected to be an active participant in class discussion, and speech is essential (Klopf et al., 1976). Instructional approaches offer short-term relief from what are considered the debilitating effects of communication avoidance, and therapeutic approaches offer long-term so-called cures for the problem.

As was shown by the review, one of the most significant influences on the development of communication motivation seems to be cultural orientation. Many authors researching verbal communication motivation end with the following pedagogical recommendation: Students should be encouraged to recognize the favorable, demonstrable, and pragmatic outcomes associated with motivation to argue and argumentative ability. One specific goal would be to stimulate individuals low in argumentativeness to enhance their motivation to argue and to develop their argumentative skills. However, therapists must be sensitive to cultural differences in values regarding assertiveness and must try to understand the client's frame of reference. A more culturally sensitive approach may include sensitizing educators to the problems associated with grading on participation, providing alternatives to some oral assignments, and removing the stereotype that quietness signifies ignorance or disinterest (McCroskey & Richmond, 1987).

Perceptions of verbal activity seem to differ substantially between people of different cultural orientations. Continued research in this area will enhance our understanding of the classroom consequences of low levels of verbal communicativeness among students and will provide specific instructional practices that teachers may use to create a learning environment that is sensitive to cultural influences.

6

Conflict Management Styles

Is Avoidance Really a Lose-Lose?

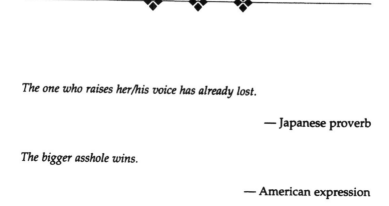

The one who raises her/his voice has already lost.

— Japanese proverb

The bigger asshole wins.

— American expression

Some of the most severe problems in intercultural relations arise as a consequence of interpersonal conflicts. Miller and Steinberg (1975) distinguish between pseudo conflicts and simple conflicts. Simple conflicts stem from incompatible goals, whereas pseudo conflicts arise from a communicative misunderstanding between parties. Given that intercultural communication is generally characterized by many ostensible differences between interactants, such as different expectations, the potential for pseudo conflicts is greater in intercultural relationships than in intracultural ones (see Lee & Rogan, 1991). Similarly, it is often not the content of conflict that creates tensions or frictions; rather, it is the cultural style that creates uncertainty and anxiety in the conflict encounter situation (Ting-Toomey, 1988).

Understanding the ways in which people from different cultures approach resolving conflicts is, therefore, of great importance. Inquiry into this culture dependency began in the 1980s with examinations of differences in conflict management styles used by members of different cultures. Researchers later began testing theory-based hypotheses in an attempt not only to describe but also to understand the differences in conflict handling between cultures (e.g., Chua & Gudykunst, 1987; Kim & Hunter, 1995; Trubisky, Ting-Toomey, & Lin, 1991). Some of these studies also introduced situational factors to examine the situational dependency of interpersonal conflict.

I begin this chapter with a review of cross-cultural studies on conflict management behaviors and their popularly adopted typologies of conflict management. Blake and Mouton's (1964) two-dimensional framework has been accepted without due caution among cross-cultural conflict management style theorists, who invariably cite the framework as the basis for their own work. Under scrutiny, I believe that the prior two-dimensional model of conflict management proves inadequate to be applied cross-culturally. In this chapter, I attempt to demonstrate how the individualistic orientation of American culture has led researchers to assume that confrontation is more desirable than avoidance. This assumption is faulty and is the result of neglecting the dialectic between confrontation and avoidance.

❖ PRIOR CONFLICT MANAGEMENT TYPOLOGIES

Interpersonal conflict may be handled with various styles of behavior. There have been many attempts to measure interpersonal conflict management styles (Kilmann & Thomas, 1975; Putman & Wilson, 1982; Rahim, 1983). Beginning with Blake and his associates (Blake & Mouton, 1964), five proposed conflict styles were organized on a two-dimensional grid (or Managerial Grid) to constitute a dual concern model. These styles and dimensions were then renamed several times, and several instruments were devised to measure the styles. One of the most popular of these has been Rahim and Bonoma's (1979) model, which consists of two orthogonal dimensions (*concern for self* and *concern for others*) and five styles (integrating, obliging, dominating, avoiding, and compromising). The five styles result from the combination of the two dimensions, as follows:

- The *integrating* style results from high concern for both self and others.
- The *obliging* style results from low concern for self and high concern for others.
- The *dominating* style results from high concern for self and low concern for others.
- The *avoiding* style results from low concern for both self and others.
- The *compromising* style results from intermediate concern for both self and others.

Thomas and Kilmann's Management Of Differences Exercise (MODE) (1978) has also been a popular instrument for conflict management studies. These researchers classified five conflict styles: competing, collaborating, compromising, avoiding, and accommodating. These styles are reflections of the two underlying cognitive/affective dimensions: *assertiveness* (attempting to satisfy one's own concerns) and *cooperation* (attempting to satisfy the other person's concerns). As interpreted by Thomas (1976),

- *Competing* is a power-oriented mode in which one pursues one's own concerns at the other person's expense in a manner that is both assertive and uncooperative.
- *Collaborating* is an assertive and cooperative approach where one party attempts to work with the other party in an effort to find an integrative and mutually satisfying solution.
- *Compromising*, which represents an intermediate position in terms of both assertiveness and cooperation, is a situation in which both parties satisfy at least some of their concerns.
- *Avoiding* occurs when one is both unassertive and uncooperative; interests are not articulated and the conflict is postponed to resurface at a later stage.

- *Accommodating* represents a mix of cooperativeness and un-assertiveness; it occurs when one neglects one's own concerns to satisfy the concerns of the other party.

For several decades, the dual concern model has been a popular method of organizing five conflict styles on a grid formed by the dimensions of seeking one's own concerns and seeking that of the other party. Ironically, although most conflict styles theorists have been profoundly influenced by the two-dimensional Managerial Grid, the factor structures of the instruments have been either disparate, inconsistent, or unclear. Conflict categories have been located within dimensional structures that are researcher-defined and researcher-salient (see Nicotera, 1993, for further discussion of this issue). Although the two-dimensional conceptualization may be useful in operationalizing the conflict styles in the U.S. context, it is unfortunate to impose it at the conceptual level. In the following section, I argue that the individualistic ideology in the mainstream American society has led researchers to assume that confrontation is more desirable than avoidance.

❖ INDIVIDUALISTIC BIAS IN PAST CONCEPTUALIZATIONS OF CONFLICT STYLES

As has been noted earlier, popular conflict management scales (e.g., Rahim, 1983; Thomas & Kilmann, 1978) rely heavily on Blake and Mouton's (1964) conceptualization of conflict management, which yields a five-style configuration based on *self-concern* versus *other-concern*. Although researchers vary in their terms, they generally assume the two-dimensional scheme. Regardless of whether researchers assume five styles (e.g., Hall, 1986; Rahim, 1983; Thomas & Kilmann, 1978), four styles (leaving out compromise, e.g., Pruitt & Rubin, 1986), or collapse to three styles (e.g., Canary & Spitzberg, 1987; Sillars, 1980), they are still influenced by the two assumed dimensions. Conflict styles based on the two assumed dimensions have been frequently adopted by communication researchers (Chua & Gudykunst, 1987; Putnam & Wilson, 1982; Ting-Toomey, 1988; Trubisky et al., 1991).

Several other models also assume two dimensions. Hall (1986) distinguishes between *concern for personal goals* and *concern for relationships*. Pruitt and Rubin (1986) characterizes the dimensions in terms of *concern for one's own outcome* and *concern for the other's outcome*. Thomas (1976) interprets the five-category scheme as combining two independent dimensions: *cooperation*, or attempting to satisfy the other party's concerns, and *assertiveness*, or attempting to satisfy one's own concerns. Brown, Yelsma and Keller (1981) propose two dimensions for distinguishing conflict styles: *feelings*, positive or negative, and *task energy*, high expension or low expension. Similarly, Chusmir and Mills (1989) break down conflict styles into two dimensions: *Assertiveness* involves the desire to fulfill the needs of the individual resolving conflict, and *cooperativeness* involves fulfilling the needs of others.

The models relying on Blake and Mouton's (1964) work conceptualize avoiding (or withdrawal style) as negative and/or destructive. According to Rahim (1983), avoiding styles reflect "low concern for self" and "low concern for others." Putnam and Wilson (1982) also consider avoidance or nonconfrontation as a lose-lose style. Thomas (1976) interprets avoiding as "unassertive" and "uncooperative." Brown et al. (1981) claim that withdrawing action means "negative feelings" and "low task energy." The flavor of these scales is that confrontation is more desirable than avoidance. Nicotera (1993) highlights possible logical flaws in existing taxonomic structures of conflict strategies. For instance, in the three dimension model (other's view, own view, and emotional/relational valence) inductively derived from the data set, Nicotera (1993) distinguishes "evasive" (which is not disruptive to personal relations) versus "estranged" (which is disruptive to personal relations).

Traditionally, within the U.S. context, it has been argued that "covert, or hidden, conflict also is destructive in that it leaves issues unresolved and may result in psychological and/or physical estrangement" (Comstock & Buller, 1991, p. 48). Galvin and Brommel (1986) claim that most conflict that is avoided leaves nagging tensions unresolved, creates a climate ripe for future overt destructive conflict, and fosters separation among family members. Furthermore, it has been argued that when people use integrative conflict strategies, constructive outcomes result, whereas use of avoidance strategies results in destructive outcomes (see Comstock & Buller, 1991). According to Filley and House (1969), in the lose-lose conflict situation, people are more likely to employ avoidance technique rather than personally confront the other party. In dealing with children's conflict resolution skills, Bryant (1992) claims that both anger/retaliation and withdrawal/ avoidance are potentially disruptive to social relationships.

Likewise, the work in this area has been biased by the individualistic assumption that confrontation is more desirable than avoidance, which limits a full understanding of the conflict phenomenon. This individualistic value became the basis for conceptualizing the avoidance styles as reflective of low concern for self as well as low concern for the other. This widely accepted assumption is now being recognized as a rather narrow and culturally conditioned view. Similarly, although some researchers consider argument (direct confrontation of matters) as a beneficial and prosocial mode of conflict resolution, they view avoidance as less socially acceptable (e.g., Infante, Trebing, Shepherd, & Seeds,, 1984; Rancer, Baukus, & Infante, 1985). Because of the individualistic bias, researchers have overlooked the potentially positive attributes of conflict avoidance and suppression. Furthermore, they have ignored the dialectic between conflict avoidance and confrontation and the complexity of avoidance as a conflict management strategy.

The benefits of using avoidance strategies among interdependents comes from being understood without putting one's meaning on record, so understanding is seen not as the result of putting meaning into words, but rather as the greater understanding of shared perspective, expectations, and intimacy. Likewise, although past literature (e.g., Canary & Spitzberg, 1987; Rahim, 1983) in interpersonal and organizational conflict tends to conceptualize the avoidance style as reflective of both low concern for self and other, the use of avoidance style in collectivistic cultures seems to be associated positively with the other-face concern dimension. The findings of Kim and Hunter's (1995) study clarify the issues regarding conceptualizations of conflict styles. According to their findings, there is a significant direct link between independence and dominating conflict styles. Expectedly, self-face concern directly influenced dominating style. The other-face concern goes with the two conflict management styles (obliging/avoiding and integrating/compromising).

Similar to these findings, Trubisky et al. (1991) found that members of the collectivistic culture use a higher level of compromising and integrating styles to handle conflict than members of the individualistic culture. Similarly, in Ting-Toomey et al.'s (1991) study, opposite to their predictions, members in collectivistic cultures opted for integrating styles more than members in individualistic cultures. Overall, the evidence suggests that members of individualistic cultures tend to prefer direct (dominating) conflict communication styles. Conversely, members of collectivistic cultures tend to prefer obliging, compromising, integrating, and conflict-avoidant styles. The latter four styles tend to emphasize to a certain degree the value placed on passive compliance and on maintaining relational harmony in conflict interactions (see Trubisky et al., 1991).

We need to reconsider the motivations that may underlie conflict avoidance and confrontation. Among high independents, control of one's autonomy, freedom, and individual boundary is of paramount importance to one's sense of self-respect and ego. The independent self-image places a higher priority on maintaining independence and asserting individual needs and goals. It is the individual's responsibility to say what's on her or his mind if she or he expects to be attended to or understood (Markus & Kitayama, 1991). The independents' communicative actions tend to be more self-focused and more self-expressive (Kim, 1993, 1994; Kim & Wilson, 1994). In general, conflict among high independents is viewed as functional when it provides an open opportunity for solving problematic issues. On the other hand, high interdependents may view conflict as primarily dysfunctional, interpersonally embarrassing, distressing, and as a forum for potential humiliation and loss of face (Ting-Toomey, 1994).

As also stated in Chapter 4, Kim, Shin, and Cai (1998), in their study using participants from Korea, Hawaii, and the mainland United States, found that the higher one's independent cultural orientations, the less one is prone to remain silent in both first- and second-attempt requests. Thus, for a person oriented toward the independent construal of self, the general tone of social interaction may be more concerned with expressing one's own needs and rights. Therefore, independent self-construal may systematically increase the importance of the self-face need in guiding choices of conflict strategies.

It has been suggested in the West that persons may focus on open communication because they believe that open discussion is the best way to deal with problems with their partners. Ting-Toomey (1991) contends that the norms and rules of intimacy expression and communication are differently perceived across cultures. For example, she found that whereas Americans openly discuss intimate issues with their partners, Japanese tend to use discreet and moderate communication modes in managing intimate issues and problems with their partners. Ting-Toomey states that collectivists tend to use the "flight" or "exit" approach to manage relational issues in romantic conflict situations. She suggests that collectivists tend to control revealing their own feelings and voicing their own opinions to their partners, whereas people from individualistic cultures (those who emphasize an independent self-construal) would tend to use the voice approach to deal with relational conflict issues—that is, they would probably engage in a greater degree of overt argument and disagreement when conflict occurs.

In the past, self-face maintenance was predicted to be associated strongly with variates dominated by the dominating and integrating styles (Ting-Toomey et al., 1991). Furthermore, members of individualistic cultures were predicted to typically prefer dominating and integrating (solution-oriented) styles. Although the finding on the use of competitive, controlling styles by individualists has been consistently supported by past cross-cultural conflict studies, previous research has found no clear evidence concerning the integrating and compromising styles. Overall, evidence lends strong support for the relationship between integrating/compromising styles and avoiding/obliging styles on the one hand, and other-face maintenance on the other (Kim & Hunter, 1995). Even though both integrating and compromising styles in the context of Rahim's (1983) scale reflect high self-concern and high other-concern, both styles seem to be strongly associated with other-face concern. Furthermore, although past literature in interpersonal and organizational conflict tends to conceptualize the avoidance style as reflective of low concern for both self and other, the avoiding style was strongly associated with other-face concern (Kim & Hunter, 1995; Ting-Toomey et al., 1991; Trubisky et al., 1991).

Markus and Kitayama (1991) posit that a normative imperative for members of interdependent cultures is internal self-control of one's private desires, emotions, or opinions that do not conform to that of the collective. In fact, to assert one's own agenda without regard for others would be considered immature. Cahn (1985) argues that such collectivistic needs lead people in collectivistic cultures (who are predominated by an interdependent construal of self) to use nonconfrontational communication modes in conflict or problem situations. Lebra (1984) describes several tendencies of collectivistic behavior in conflict situations that can be characterized as an emphasis on interdependent self-construals: (a) anticipatory management, or the use of management to prevent a conflict before it happens; (b) negative communication, which refers to the expression of conflict emotions in a negative manner (such as the expression of anger or frustration by noncommunication, such as ignorance and silence); (c) situational code switching, which refers to the pretense of being harmonious in peoples' presence even though two parties in conflict are actually avoiding each other; (d) triadic management or displacement, which refers to the management of conflict situations between two parties by using a third party (go-between); and (e) self-aggression, which refers to the tendency of directing accusations against oneself (intropunitive behavior).

As opposed to individuals with independent self-construals, individuals with interdependent-self construals are intimately connected with their social context (Markus & Kitayama, 1991). Fitting in with others and maintaining harmony are key to their self-esteem. Because individuals with dominant interdependent self-construals are concerned with others' feelings and evaluations, they control and restrict negative emotional expressions, such as anger and frustration. Also they tend to express themselves more discreetly and implicitly in their verbal strategies—that is, they prefer indirectness in communication. Thus, individuals with highly developed interdependent self-construals will avoid expressing negative emotions and voicing their opinions and disagreements directly and overtly in conflict situations.

It can be assumed that individuals with a highly developed interdependent self-construal are unlikely to express negative emotions (such as anger), to confront each other, and to use verbal aggressiveness and open discussion in conflict situations. They may even avoid reactions to their relational problems that can potentially cause further conflict. Among interdependents, the stress is not so much upon the individual and her interests, but on the maintenance of the collectivity and the continuation of harmonious relationships. In general, among interdependents, conflict is viewed as damaging to social face and relational harmony, so it should be avoided as much as possible (Ting-Toomey, 1994). These ideas, as applied to face maintenance dimensions, would mean that individuals with an interdependent self-view have, as an overall goal, the desire to avoid loss of face and to be accepted by in-group members, which strengthens their preference for other-face needs in achieving conflict goals. The requirement is to read the other's mind and thus to know what the other is thinking or feeling (Kim, Sharkey, & Singelis, 1994). It is likely that the interdependents' value patterns associated with relational harmony and saving the other's face will lead them to seek avoidance of conflict and maintenance of harmony in maintaining compromises (see Ho, 1976).

People attempt to maintain face in nearly all interactions. In all cultures, we seek to save face, but the concept has different referents in individualistic and collectivistic cultures. In an individualistic culture, the focus of face is primarily the *I*, who is concerned that her or his positive qualities be seen and her or his negative qualities be hidden or excused (i.e., self-face protection) (see Smith & Bond, 1998). In collectivistic cultural groups, where there is a danger of conflict, the danger is not that the *I* specifically would be embarrassed, but that *we* need to ward off that danger by reading the indirect communication cues sufficiently early that the untoward situation may be averted (i.e., other-face concern) (Smith & Bond, 1998). Thus, face is a concept that has universal applicability and significance (Brown & Levinson, 1978), but it seems to have particular salience for the collectivists.

In sum, I suggest that interdependents are less openly assertive and emotional in conflict situations because of their heightened sensitivity to others' face needs. Thus, they naturally lead to the adoption of high compromising and avoiding behaviors and a relatively low preference for competing and assertive postures. The interdependents' imperative toward group mindedness, relationship centeredness, and the need to maintain interpersonal equilibrium may militate against the adoption of open confrontation and overtly competitive styles of behavior (Kirkbride, Tang, & Westwood, 1991). Avoiding and compromising styles may serve to work to dilute antagonisms that might otherwise surface in the immediate situation. The fear of shame as a result of damaging or ruffling the social fabric or damaging someone else's face would also lead interdependents to avoid assertive or direct styles of handling conflicts. These arguments all suggest a likely preference among high interdependents for saving the other's face in conflict management. It may seem better to avoid the possibility of losing the other's face by engaging in avoidance behavior.

In view of the growing interconnectedness of societies and economies around the world, human civilization is now entering an age of intercultural mixing on a scale not previously witnessed. As a result, the possibility for conflict—often substantial within cultures—is even more probable between members of different cultures. Research has begun and should be continued to better understand the ways in which people prefer to handle interpersonal conflicts and how that preference varies depending on cultural and other variables. Such knowledge of conflict-related behavioral tendencies might help in the development of strategies for interpersonal, intercultural conflict resolution or prevention.

The ability to resolve social conflicts successfully depends in large measure on being able to accurately predict the effectiveness of conflict management strategies. Much-abused terms such as "communication breakdown" or "cross-cultural miscommunication" (Coupland, Giles, & Wiemann, 1991) can often be attributed to different perceptions regarding the choices of conflict tactics. For instance, communication breakdown in conflict situations typically occurs because interactants disagree about the effectiveness or social appropriateness of one another's conflict strategies. Individuals' beliefs about the appropriateness of conflict strategies are apt to affect what conflict tactics and strategies they choose and what inferences they make about their own and others' conflict-handling behavior. The current review implies that different cultural orientations seem to cause one to have drastically different ideas about what constitutes an appropriate conflict strategy or tactic.

To summarize, a main limitation of the past research on cross-cultural conflict styles stems from confusions regarding conceptualizations of conflict management styles. The majority of the literature has relied on conflict typologies created in the U.S. context, and the generalizability of these typologies to intercultural contexts is unclear. In typical studies of cross-cultural conflict styles, researchers rely heavily on either three, four, or five styles of conflict inventories, which are based on two dimensions (commonly called *concern for production* and *concern for people* or *concern for self* and *concern for others*) (Blake & Mouton, 1964). The conceptualization of conflict styles based on these two dimensions may not be generalizable across cultures. For instance, although past literature in interpersonal and organizational conflict tends to view the avoidance style as the least desirable option (reflective of both low concern for self and low concern for the other), the use of avoiding style in collectivistic cultures can be seen as mutually beneficial for both parties. (see Kim & Hunter, 1995; Ting-Toomey, 1989). Such validity problems indicate that the dimensions used to conceptualize and operationalize styles in the U.S. context may *not* be the generative mechanisms of behavioral choices in different cultures.

Given that cross-cultural interactions are burgeoning, there has never been such a sore need for knowledge about conflict styles in different cultures (Ting-Toomey, 1988). Theories on cross-cultural conflict styles are still in their infancy. Continuous conceptual refinement and diverse means of testing theories should yield further understanding of cross-cultural conflict communication processes.

7

Cognitive Consistency

A Cultural Assumption?

A foolish consistency is the hobgoblin of little minds.

— Emerson (quoted in Bartlett, 2000)

I loathe inconstancy—I loathe, detest
Abhor, condemn, abjure the mortal made
Of such quicksilver clay that in his breast
No permanent foundation can be laid;

— Byron, *Don Juan*, Canto ii, St. 209

The idea that people are motivated toward a resolution of cognitive inconsistencies has a long and respectable history in social psychology and communication. Although the tendency toward cognitive consistency is often described as a marker of human rationality and therefore might be expected to be widespread or even universal, a cultural perspective suggests that social psychological notions of consistency may be more or less culturally relative. Festinger (1957) contended that cognitive dissonance is the uncomfortable and disturbing state of mind in which people feel they "find themselves doing things that don't fit with what they know, or having opinions that do not fit with other opinions they hold"(p. 4). Although this may easily be the most common and consensually endorsed assumption, the vast majority of research hinging on this assumption has been conducted in North America within a context of Western philosophical thought. The tendencies toward cognitive consistency may not be basic to humankind but may depend in large part on significant aspects of contemporary North American culture.

❖ FUNDAMENTAL ASSUMPTIONS OF COGNITIVE DISSONANCE THEORY

Dissonance theory has spawned more than 1,000 studies, making it one of the most important and fecund theories in social psychology and human communication in general (Cooper & Fazio, 1984). Festinger (1957) theorized that people will persuade themselves to believe in something with which they initially disagree if they publicly advocate a position counter to their initial belief. Festinger held that the counterattitudinal advocacy would arouse cognitive dissonance. The theory predicts that the state of dissonant arousal would be relieved in one of the following two ways:

- The dissonance would cause people to change their attitude to match their behavior (i.e., attitude change toward the position advocated) if the inducement given for them to comply with the request to advocate a counter-attitudinal position was not great enough to justify their lie.
- The dissonance would be attributed to some inducement, which in the advocator's mind would justify the lie, thus allowing the original attitude to be retained.

Festinger (1957) posits that cognitive dissonance is the uncomfortable inconsistency between two or more elements—typically, between an individual's attitudes and behaviors. Theoretical revisions have led to an ego-based view of dissonance, in which the disturbing inconsistency is seen to lie between the individual's positive view of herself and the cognition that she has done something potentially foolish or bad (see Thibodeau & Aronson, 1992). By changing their original attitudes, individuals can make their behavior appear more in line with what would be expected from competent and adequate people, thereby reducing or eliminating the distressing dissonance.

Under this theoretical perspective, one could attempt to persuade another to hold a certain belief by getting that person to counter-attitudinally advocate the position desired. The persuader should only provide inducements of enough strength to just achieve compliance so that the strength of the justification would not prevent attitude change. The persuadee would then persuade herself to believe in the counter-attitudinal position if the incentive is not sufficient enough to justify her lie.

In one of the earliest experimental tests of the theory of cognitive dissonance, Festinger and Carlsmith (1959) had subjects perform a task that involved placing a large number of spools on pegs on a board, turning each spool a quarter turn, taking the spools off the pegs, and then putting them back on. As you can imagine, subjects' attitudes toward this task were highly negative. The subjects were then induced to tell a female "subject," who was actually an accomplice of the experimenter, that this boring task she would be performing was really interesting and enjoyable. Some of the subjects were offered $20 to tell this falsehood; others were offered only $1. Almost all of the subjects agreed to walk into the waiting room and persuade the subject accomplice that the boring experiment would be fun. Obviously, there is a discrepancy here between attitudes and behavior. Although the task was boring, subjects tried to convince another person it was fun. Why? To the subjects who received $20, the reason was clear—they wanted the money. The larger payment provided an important external justification consistent with the counter-attitudinal behavior. There was no dissonance, and the subjects experienced no need to change their attitudes. But for the subjects who received only $1, there was much less external justification and more dissonance. How could subjects reduce the dissonance? They could do so by changing their attitude toward the task. This is exactly what happened. When the subjects were asked to evaluate the experiment, the subjects who were paid only $1 rated the tedious task as more fun and enjoyable than did both the subjects who were paid $20 to lie and the subjects in a control group who were not required to lie about the task. Because the external justification—the $1 payment—was too low to justify the counter-attitudinal behavior, the subjects simply changed their attitudes to make them consistent with their behavior.

❖ IS COGNITIVE DISSONANCE A CULTURE-BOUND CONCEPT?

One of the powerful motives assumed to fuel the behavior of Westerners is the need to avoid or reduce cognitive conflict or dissonance. Classic dissonance occurs when a person says one thing publicly and yet feels another. One might argue, however, that the state of cognitive dissonance arising from counter-attitudinal behavior is not likely to be experienced by those with interdependent selves (Markus & Kitayama, 1991). It is likely that independent individuals have less tolerance for cognitive inconsistency than interdependent individuals because independent individuals are accustomed to behaving according to their own attitudes and beliefs, whereas interdependent individuals may be more accustomed to acting at the direction of social demands. Therefore, the procedure previously described to produce attitude change through counter-attitudinal advocacy and dissonance would not work as well with interdependent individuals as it might for independent individuals.

Several writers (Festinger, 1957; Miller, 1983) have suggested that certain personality factors may influence an individual's tolerance for cognitive inconsistency. Generally, discussion of such personality variables has emphasized the possibility of systematic differences in the extent to which persons can endure or live with inconsistency. However, we know virtually nothing about its cultural boundaries (see Heine & Lehman, 1997b). Miller (1983) reviewed studies that pointed to empirical support that individual differences were found among people in regard to tolerance for inconsistency (i.e., cognitive dissonance), specifically in terms of dogmatism and authoritarianism. If individual differences can be found within a culture, surely differences can be found between cultures as well. The more than 50 years of research on cognitive dissonance has demonstrated its robustness as a phenomenon. It is difficult to ascertain whether similar results would be obtained with non-Western samples.

In the theory of cognitive dissonance, conflicts are viewed as disruptive. Cognitive dissonance theory postulates the need for intrapersonally uniform or consistent states. However, a person may accept and tolerate dissonance as natural. Then, one needs to question the basic notion of a need or drive for consonance, a need being postulated as a part of human nature. This question has not been asked because the whole research tradition on cognitive dissonance is anchored in an implicit idea of human nature. These implicit assumptions, which are presupposed, can be found in almost all social scientific theories. They delimit the type of theoretical conceptualization one can arrive at. In a seminal paper, Gergen (1973) argued that social psychologists were engaged in examining contemporary historical developments rather than in discovering behavioral principles that would remain valid across time and place. Regarding the theory of cognitive dissonance, its fundamental tenet of people wishing to avoid (or reduce) dissonance seems to be a historically driven disposition that could be altered by time and circumstances.

Markus and Kitayama (1991) describe the interdependent self as having a flexible and variable structure, the self-schemata of which can vary in salience according to the social context in order to appropriately attend to the needs, desires, and goals of the significant other(s) with whom they are currently interacting. Studies provide direct evidence for the context-contingent nature of the self. For instance, Campbell et al. (1996) proposed the notion of *self-concept clarity (SCC)*, which references a structural aspect of the self-concept: the extent to which self-beliefs are clearly and confidently defined, internally consistent, and stable. Thus, self-concept clarity references an independent self-construal that is predominant in Western cultures; the self is viewed as an autonomous inviolate entity containing a unique and articulated set of internal attributes that remain stable across situations (Markus & Kitayama, 1991). The Eastern self, in contrast, is sustained and formed by its social environment (Markus & Kitayama, 1991), suggesting that situational changes would be associated with changes in the self. Inconsistency in the self, then, should not challenge the normative view of the Eastern self. Consistent with this speculation, Japanese participants exhibited lower levels of SCC and lower correlations between SCC and self-esteem than did a Canadian sample

(Campbell et al., 1996). Theorists who study the Japanese self refer to the self as indeterminate, multiple, and moving, and all of these characterizations are consistent with the absence of a constant or fixed *I* or *you* (Lebra, 1991).

Markus and Kitayama (1991) noted that the interdependent self tends to make behavior conform to changing situations to achieve the cultural mandate of connection with others, thereby suggesting less cross-situational consistency among the Japanese. Situational variability, however, does not necessarily imply a past self that lacks continuity with the present self. Campbell et al. (1996) found that the Japanese participants perceived the self to be less consistent across situations. The clarity construct was developed within the context of Western culture, in which the habitual point of focus is the individual, and different descriptive sentences were selected to reflect the clarity of individuals' self-beliefs. However, in Japanese culture, individuals look to the social environment to define the self (Cousins, 1989), suggesting that the apparent inconsistency and instability in Japanese self-concepts probably result from their interdependence and contextual nature (see Campbell et al., 1996).

These studies suggest that selves in interdependent cultural contexts are, for the most part, constructed in a relatively context-specific fashion (Markus & Kitayama, 1998). Selves in Asian cultures are mainly context-dependent, perhaps because they are integrated with and experienced within social roles, positions, and relationships. This mode of personality organization is very distinct from the Western mode, where the person is constructed to be a coherent, stable, and consistent being that is organized by an assortment of essence or traitlike attributes (Markus & Kitayama, 1998). Reflecting Western biases, in the West, the self-concepts of people said to have low self-esteem were characterized by relatively high levels of uncertainty, instability, and inconsistency (i.e., low clarity). On the other hand, those who exhibit a high level of self-concept clarity (e.g., internal consistency, and temporal stability of their self-description) were regarded as high in self-esteem (see Campbell et al., 1996).

Markus and Kitayama (1991) maintain that different psychological processes are often observed between cultures because pronounced cultural differences exist in the way that the self is typically construed. Because the identity of the independent self rests on a foundation of internal attributes, such as an individual's attitudes and opinions, any dissonance that is experienced involving these attributes is likely to be directed to the core of the self (Heine & Lehman, 1997b). Viewing one's attitudes as inconsistent with one's behaviors or viewing one's decisions as unsound, then, may pose a significant threat to independent individuals' self-integrity. Such inconsistencies are not likely to be easily compromised, and independent individuals should be motivated to go to great lengths to reduce dissonance (Markus & Kitayama, 1991).

In contrast, the core of the identity of the interdependent self lies more within the individual's roles, positions, and relationships. Internal attributes are patently less relevant to such persons' identities. Hence, inconsistencies between one's attitudes, or thoughts that one may have made a poor decision, are likely to be relatively tangential to such an individual's self-identity. Thus, interdependents should be less perturbed when their behavior does not follow from a particular belief and therefore might not show the standard cognitive dissonance effects. A recent study by Heine and Lehman (1997b) provided initial support for such a possibility by using a free-choice paradigm of cognitive consistency. Respondents were given a choice between two equally attractive CDs. After such a choice, some cognitive inconsistencies were likely to arise because the chosen CD may have had certain negative features and the unchosen CD may have had certain desirable features. Hence, there should arise a motivation to eliminate such a dissonant state by changing some of the cognitions involved. Heine and Lehman found that among the North American participants, there was a considerable spread of preference after the choice, such that liking for the chosen CD increased and liking for the unchosen CD decreased. However, the comparable effect was not found among the Japanese respondents. This result supports the idea that the requirement of internal consistency may be much weaker for people operating with an interdependent model of the self than for people operating with an independent model of the self.

Despite the formidable presence of dissonance theory in the literature, very little research has addressed whether dissonance reduction exists at a comparable level across cultures. Markus and Kitayama (1991) raised the possibility that those with an interdependent view of self might not feel threatened when their behavior is inconsistent with their attitudes, thereby suggesting that dissonance would not be experienced. Similar to this prediction, Sadana and Norbeck (1975) observed a doomsday cult in Japan both before and after the earthquake prophesied by their leader failed to materialize. They did not observe that the fact that the prophecy was proved false led to deeper faith and proselytizing among cult members as a means of dissonance reduction. In fact, the Japanese leader of this cult responded to his failed prediction by unsuccessfully attempting to commit suicide and then later by disbanding the sect.

Steele (1988) contends that rationalizing one's decisions is a tactic to affirm one's competence and adequacy—a goal that is arguably more important within Western cultures, in which cultural ideals require individuals to be independent and self-sufficient. Clearly, in future studies, it will be important to investigate explicitly how people from Eastern cultures respond to threats to the interdependent self. Such efforts would no doubt prove fruitful for deepening our understanding of the nature and motivations of the interdependent self. It is reasonable to suppose that differences in self-construals may be useful predictors of differential tolerance for inconsistency. I propose that, similar to other communication phenomena shown to be influenced and shaped by cultural identity, the need for consistency does not exist within a cultural vacuum.

To summarize, the idea of consistency in behavior has often been invoked as the key criterion of personality coherence. Nevertheless, cross-cultural research in recent years (Heine & Lehman, 1997b; Kitayama & Markus, 1999) has indicated that people in many cultures often disagree with Leon Festinger (1957) and many of his followers in North American social psychology, who have claimed that consistency among one's personal attributes centrally defines one's integrity. It is possible that the consistency view of personality is more pervasive, better accepted, better appreciated, and more highly valued in North America than in other parts of the world.

8

Attitude-Behavior Consistency

Cultural Ideal of Individualistic Society?

Suit the action to the word, the word to the action.

— Shakespeare, *Hamlet, a Tragedy*
(III, ii, 20), 1600/1818

Divines do not always practise what they preach.

— Dickens, *The Old Curiosity Shop*, 1880, ch. 37

Traditionally, social influence research, including the field of persuasion, has been conducted from a limited, monocultural perspective. The current analysis is relevant to one of the central problems in Western social influence literature—the inconsistency between attitude and behavior. The belief in consistency between attitude and behavior has been the focus of an extremely active domain of research concerning social influence. Ever since Gordon Allport (1935) described the attitude concept as the primary building block in the edifice of social psychology, many researchers have attempted to clarify the attitude-behavior relationship. The concept of attitude, typically viewed as a stable underlying disposition, has played a central role in explaining communication phenomena, particularly the effects of persuasive messages.

Most research in the area of communication and persuasion has centered on attempts to change attitudes toward some object or target, seeking to build theories that accurately explain and predict patterns of complex communication behaviors. Underlying these efforts has been the implicit assumption that behavior toward the object will change automatically with the attitude. Evidence has not always supported this assumption, however, and the difficulty in finding a strong, predictive relationship between attitudes and behavioral tendencies has turned into one of the greatest controversies in the social sciences.

Attitude-behavior relationships have been an interdisciplinary concern. Many theorists argued for the hypothesized links between attitude and behavior (see Kim & Hunter, 1993a, 1993b). The underlying assumptions and corresponding empirical findings are crucial not only to the theoretical development of human communication studies but also to other fields of applied social science, including consumer behavior, social policy, and public campaigns.

The issue of how much relation exists between attitudes and action has been widely debated (for reviews, see Kim & Hunter, 1993a). At present, there appear to be two rather distinct views. One set of authors claims that attitude is weakly and inconsistently related to behavior. In general, this line of researchers indicates that attitude is only one of numerous variables that must be considered in attempts to predict overt behavior. They point to other variables or conditions as determinants of behavior: (a) *individual characteristics,* such as cognitive complexity, self-monitoring, private self-consciousness, involvement, and self-awareness; (b) *attitudinal qualities,* such as direct experience with the attitude object, attitude accessibility, and the consistency between affective and cognitive responses; and (c) *situational normative factors,* such as social constraints, norms, reference group norms, and social support.

A second set of researchers has suggested that attitudes and overt behavior are closely related to each other, whatever the causal direction might be. Bem (1968) proposed that when internal cues are weak or ambiguous, situationally determined behaviors will lead to attitudes. The second directional assumption comes from the consistency theory, which holds that whereas attitudes may sometimes direct behavior, tendencies to reach consistency between behavior and attitude will act in both directions. The most commonly evoked directional position, however, has been a causal link from attitude to behavior. The assumptions of causal priority of attitudes over behaviors gave rise to several prominent models explaining the attitude-behavior relationship.

Although different theories contain different forms and conceptualizations of attitudes, it is not difficult to trace the common thread running through these diverse approaches. As early as 1934, LaPiere published evidence contrary to the implicit assumption that attitudes and behavior are closely related. Since then, empirical researchers all too frequently have found weak and inconsistent relations between the attitudes expressed by individuals and their actions in relevant life situations (see Ajzen and Fishbein, 1980).

According to Deutscher (1966), most researchers on attitude-behavior consistency lament once in their career that "we tackle the messy world as we knew it to exist, a world where the same people will make different utterances under different conditions and will behave differently in different situations and will say one thing while doing another" (p. 242). Deutscher further wrote, "We still do not know much about the relationship between what people say and what they do—attitudes and behavior, sentiments and acts, verbalizations and interactions, words and deeds" (p. 242). Under what conditions will people behave as they talk? Under what conditions is there no relationship? And under what conditions do they say one thing and behave exactly the opposite?

Deutscher (1966) challenged the assumption made by researchers: the notion that what people *say* is a predictor of what they will *do*. He concluded that "man is constrained to behave in ways which are contrary to his supposed nature; . . . the dialectic between man's private self and his social self must create occasional and sometimes radical inconsistencies between what he says and what he does . . ." (p. 253). (For readability's sake, I have reprinted this quote in its original, gendered, form.)

Models of the self and the collective could also provide an alternative view of one of psychologists' oldest problems—the inconsistency between attitudes and behaviors. From an interdependent perspective, such inconsistencies do not have to be framed negatively and do not have to give rise to great theoretical consternation. Interdependent selves do not prescribe or require consistency between one's internal attributes and one's actions. In fact, such consistency may reflect not authenticity but, rather, rigidity (a lack of flexibility) or even immaturity (Markus & Kitayama, 1994). Consequently, the pressure for consistency should be much weaker than is the case with independents, and if consistency is not observed, it should be much less bemoaned.

Iwao (1988) offers some suggestive evidence that people in collectivistic cultures often sacrifice consistency for the sake of interpersonal accommodation. Iwao asked American and Japanese respondents what they would prefer to do when confronted by various disagreements—try to change the other person's view, change their own view, or feign agreement. Americans preferred to try to change the other person's view more than did Japanese, whereas Japanese were much more likely to prefer to feign agreement. The latter type of behavior among Japanese might seem hypocritical to holders of the independent view of the self because the Japanese prefer to behave in ways that differ from what they truly believe. Given the interdependent view, however, maintaining a good relationship may be much more important than attempting to settle the disagreement, and thus it would be uncouth and insensitive to contradict or argue (Fiske, Kitayama, Markus, & Nisbett, 1998).

Doi (1986) argued that Americans are decidedly more concerned with consistency between feelings and actions than Japanese. He discusses the difference between the Japanese public self and private self. He suggests that, in the United States, it is extremely important for these two selves to remain consistent. When the public self deviates from the private self, an individual is considered a hypocrite. In Japan, being polite and maintaining harmony is what is important. An individual's actual feelings about an action are unimportant (Triandis, 1989). One's internal attributes (i.e., private attitudes or opinions) are not regarded as the significant attributes of the self. Furthermore, one's private feelings are to be regulated in accordance with the requirements of the situation. Restraint over the inner self is assigned a much higher value than is the expression of the inner self (Markus & Kitayama, 1991). On the other hand, many American children are socialized to be true to themselves and to stick by their convictions or principles. To do otherwise would be to risk inconsistency and inauthenticity.

One piece of evidence consistent with the current analysis comes from research by Triandis (1995). He summarizes evidence that in Asia, social norms are bound to be relatively more important than attitudes in predicting behavior. Although a fine attunement between the self and the social surrounding is not always attainable, psychological processes are likely to be established in such a way that actions that are seemingly unrelated or even incongruous with internal attitudes are readily reinterpreted to maintain the sense of the self as fully embedded or encompassed in the context (Kitayama & Markus, 1999). From the Western perspective, in which the disposition (e.g., attitude) is the core of the person, doing something because of obligations to others or because of the situational needs or constraints can be seen as passive and as sacrificing one's autonomy and control. For example, Kitayama and Markus (1999, p. 265), wrote that "when North Americans are thanked for doing things for others, it is not uncommon to hear them say, 'Oh, I like to do these kinds of things; it was fun,' or 'It was my pleasure.'" Revealing that one was merely responding to social pressure or to the appeals of others can indicate weakness and a lack of personal integrity (e.g., inconsistency between attitude and behavior). Yet, given an interdependent view of the person, it is one's social embeddedness, rather than internal attributes, that gives meaning to existence.

Cultures that emphasize the importance of the individual place great value on the expression of personal desires and the pursuit of personal goals. In such cultures, people regard it as hypocritical when others fail to act in accord with personal attitudes, although acting in accord with those attitudes might damage personal relationships. To accommodate others may seem to involve giving in to external constraints and failing to be true to oneself. In line with this possibility, Kashima, Siegel, Tanaka, & Kashima (1992) examined the strength of the cultural belief that attitudes should normally be consistent with behaviors and found that this view is much more strongly held by Australians than by Japanese. For interdependent individuals, it may be regarded as selfish, immature, or disloyal to act in accord with personal attitudes or even to express such attitudes if they conflict with the maintenance of a smooth social equilibrium (Fiske et al., 1998). A predominant feature of the self in European-American contexts is the persistent need for consistency and stability. Empirical research on the self reveals that evidence of malleability or variability in the self is often downplayed or actively discouraged. The psychological tendency toward consistency is extremely robust and well-documented and has been discussed as a universal human motive (Markus, Mullally, & Kitayama, 1997). The desire for a consistent self is tied to the notion that the self, by cultural definition, is whole, stable, and integrated rather than fragmented and distributed. Further, individuals should not be bound to particular situations, and personal attributes should transcend particular interpersonal relationships.

Tripathi (1988) points out that the most important distinction between Indian and Western minds lies in the ways boundaries are laid down that define mental structures. In the Western mind, boundaries appear to be more stable and fixed—self and environment, mind and matter, subjective and objective, material and spiritual, secular and religious, and so on. The Indian mind, on the other hand, is governed by boundaries that are constantly shifting and variable. The action or behavior by itself is not to be judged; it is the context in which it is made that determines the ethical meaning. Thus, correct behavior is much more oriented toward what is expected in specific contexts of a variety of roles and relationships.

According to Markus and Kitayama (1998), the good, authentic, or genuine personality in Western culture is one in which the attributes are unified or integrated into a system or a whole with strong boundaries, one that is stable over time, and one that can resist influence from others and situations. The idea of a bounded individual who is separate from others and who should not be unduly influenced by them also leads to a powerful consistency ethic in which the good or authentic self is the same relatively unchanging self across different situations. Behavior that changes with the situation is more likely to be viewed as waffling, hypocritical, or even pathological rather than as flexible or responsive.

In European-American contexts, the person has often been imagined as a machine—most recently as a computer—that carries its basic operating instructions on the inside, that controls behavior, and that functions the same way no matter where it is located or what it stores. In many Asian contexts, the self is visualized not as a machine, but as something from nature, such as a plant. The plant metaphor suggests that a person is open, rather than bounded, and it blurs the inside-outside, self-society distinctions that are deeply embedded in European-American understanding (Markus, Mullally, & Kitayama, 1997).

❖ PREDICTING BEHAVIORS: DE-EMPHASIZING SITUATIONS OVER ATTITUDES

For the most part, human communication has been deeply wedded to an individualistic model of the person, in which a separate, bounded individual is seen as the primary fact. The assumption is that there exist certain stable internal qualities of the person—dispositions or traits—that manifest themselves across different situations.

In numerous studies conducted with European and American respondents, there seems to be a pervasive bias to favor explanations of social behavior in terms of relevant internal or dispositional attitudes of a person. Choi, Nisbett and Norenzayan (1999) note that "one of the greatest and most remarkable misunderstandings we have about people, one that gives rise to many other inferential failings, is the belief that behavior is usually best regarded as reflecting personality traits or other internal attributes" (p. 47). Because of the robustness of this bias in European-American cultures, Gilbert and Malone (1995) half-jokingly suggested that perhaps some extraterrestrials may be free from the bias! Yet there are reasons to suspect that this *lay dispositionism* may not be so universal.

Ethnographers, philosophers, and historians of science have observed that lay theory in the modern West locates the responsibility for behavior primarily in the individual, a tendency that may be described as *dispositionism* (Choi, Nisbett, & Norenzayan, 1999). This is in contrast to the lay theory in East Asia focusing on the whole context of behavior, which may be called *situationism* or *contextualism* (Fiske et al., 1998). According to Choi et al., "Whereas Westerners focus on the individual, Easterners focus on the social situation" (p. 48). Similarly, the psychologist Chiu (1972) observed that "Chinese are situation-centered. They are obligated to be sensitive to their environment. Americans are individual-centered. They expect their environment to be sensitive to them" (p. 236).

Challenges to traditional communication theories must confront the pervasive Euro-American belief in the autonomous individual and, for instance, the tacit assumption that emphasizing the situation in a significant way somehow denies individual freedom and agency and casts the person as a pawn or mindless robot (see Markus & Kitayama, 1998). The individual is the locus of action—at least that is the impression conveyed by a host of theorists, including cognitive psychologists, constructivists, social cognition researchers, and many students of human communication (see Hewes & Planalp, 1987). Although all these theorists recognize the importance of the social contexts of individual choice, an increasing number of voices from widely diverse perspectives have challenged the extent to which the individual holds a favored position in their theorizing (Hewes & Planalp, 1987).

Hewes and Planalp (1987) discussed *trait* approaches to communication, which place the locus of action in the predispositions of individuals to initiate action or to react to behavior. Specifically, trait approaches to human communication place the individual as central and offer a very simplified version of the capacities the individual brings to bear in social interaction. As Hewes and Planalp put it:

> These characteristics of the trait approach arise from the very definition of a trait—a stable predisposition to behavior . . . . Thus human beings are conceived of primarily as bundles of predispositions, and these predispositions are relatively stable across time and across specified contexts. These dispositions are, for the most part, taken as givens. (p. 150)

Cultures may be said to have overall tendencies to idealize and think in terms of either the context-free or the context-sensitive kinds of rules. What is focal in an interdependent self is not the protagonist herself but, rather, her relationships to other actors (Hamaguchi, 1985). Singelis and Brown (1995) also note that being connected to others and fitting in is a primary source of self-esteem for the interdependent individual. Whereas independent individuals cultivate their own self-esteem through self-actualization, the self-esteem of interdependent individuals hinges upon their harmonious functioning within the social network. It is important to note that although interdependent selves derive the most meaning from being a part of social relationships, they are still able to possess invariant individual attributes and abilities (Kim, 1995; Markus & Kitayama, 1991). Individual attributes and abilities are just less salient to the interdependent person. The self in relation to others is the major focal point.

It has been claimed that people from collectivistic cultures view the person not as an autonomous being with abstract qualities but in terms of specific relationships to significant others, which Schweder and Bourne (1984) labeled "sociocentrism." The focus is on specific, situation-bound behaviors and social categories rather than on abstract personality traits because the persona may change across social contexts (Miller, 1984). People from collectivistic cultures do describe personal attributes, such as abilities, opinions, judgments, and personality characteristics, and yet these attributes are understood as situation-specific, sometimes elusive and unreliable, and not particularly diagnostic (Rhee, Uleman, Lee, & Roman, 1995).

In 1977, Sampson argued that the dominance of the cognitive perspective reinforced the individualistic and subjective biases in American social thought, thereby distracting thinkers from assessing the objective social situation in which we all act. America, of course, is an individualistic cultural system, and theories about individualistic cultural logic underscore its de-emphasis of external factors in controlling behavior. Recently, Seeman (1997) addressed the neglect of the situation in social psychology. As he pointed out, there have been some attempts to characterize situations, but given psychology's cognitive orientation, it is not surprising that the result has been individual-centered modes of situational description. Bond (1998) argues that what is striking is the extent to which situations are defined in terms of affects (e.g., cooperative-competitive, intense-superficial). Bond claims that we must define the situation in ways that are independent of the response of the person experiencing, remembering, or imagining the experience of that event. Otherwise, we are using the situation as a projective test for personality processes and fail to examine the independent contribution of the situation toward predicting behavior (see Bond, 1998).

To summarize, exactly how attitudes can predict behavior is hotly debated in Western social sciences (including communications). European-American researchers believe that attitudes cause changes in intentions leading to actions (in other words, that A leads to B). European-American researchers puzzle over how attitudes can cause behaviors because they generally think they do. Other cultures might vary from this European-American folk belief (and the views of other Western cultures) regarding the attitude to behavior causation. For example, behaviors might be attributed to other causes in other cultures (see Lillard, 1998).

❖ EMPHASIZING OTHER SOURCES OF BEHAVIOR

Situational, External, or Relational Causes. Independent individuals may often view actions as attributable to traits (e.g., attitudes) of the person. This attribution pattern is often in error because situations are much more responsible for behaviors than the average European-American person is likely to acknowledge. Still, it is part of Western folk theory (Lillard, 1998). Collectivistic cultures have been shown to be much more attentive to situations in discussing the reasons behind others' actions. According to Lillard, various levels of group cohesion might influence what really causes actions. In collectivistic or interdependent cultures, individuals' attitudes are not especially important predictors of behavior because people subsume their desires to externally imposed norms. Ochs (1988) discussed this issue: "The emphasis on personal intentions in Western white middle-class society and scholarship is tied to a cultural ideology in which persons are viewed as individuals, who have control over and are responsible for their utterances and actions" (p. 144). Paul (1995) suggested that talking about others' attitudes and mental states might disrupt group harmony. Group cohesion among collectivistic individuals is a reason to conceptualize actions as caused by the collective: If one views others' acts as being caused by collective influences, it maintains group harmony more than if one sees others' behavior as being caused by individual desires or attitudes (see Lillard, 1998).

Another external factor that seems to contribute to differences in the attitude-behavior link is the degree to which one considers other people to be the cause of one's action. For the American Cheyenne, behavior is seen as motivated by relationships more than by individual wills (Straus, 1977). One's actions are generally explained by reference to someone else's actions or to one's relationship with some other—for example, "I hit him because he hit her. . . . I drank with him because he is my cousin" (p. 333). Straus described a social worker's frustration that the Cheyenne do not take responsibility for their actions but instead make excuses. However, Straus emphasized that these are not excuses to the Cheyenne; they truly are causes.

Ethereal Causes. The previous examples indicate differences in emphasis, with interdependent individuals placing more weight than independent individuals on situations and on other people as possible sources of action. According to Lillard (1998), in some cultures, even more radical ideas than situations are embraced as causes of actions. These stem from different conceptions of reality in which ethereal entities are held to be part of everyday existence. As Parish (1994) put it, people live in the world that they imagine. If they imagine spirits are real, then the spirits are part of their real world. For example, like many other cultures, the Newar of Nepal see behavior as being caused by a god rather than by a person's self. Unlike the ancient Greeks, the Newar locate this god within one's own heart rather than externally (Parish, 1994). Admittedly, some people within contemporary Western culture would claim that unusual acts (e.g., lifting a car to save a child who is pinned underneath) are the work of God, but such thinking is not in the social science model of how people explain behavior (Lillard, 1998). It appears, then, that the traditional attitude-behavior research undoubtedly fails to include some external or ethereal causes.

To summarize, cultures appear to hold various views of what causes actions. Whereas the Europeans and Americans attribute actions to the self, including attitudes and mental states, some cultures see spirits, situations, and other people as more central causes of action (Lillard, 1998). Some of these other causes (situations, other people) are within the realm of possibility but are simply not as emphasized in the Western A-B research. Attention to internal traits and attitudes, the idea of a private person, and the notion that attitudes cause behavior are all optional, and such options seem to be influenced by cultural conceptions of self. It appears that the independents' tendency to attribute behaviors to attitudes is at least in part a cultural acquisition.

9

Susceptibility to Social Influence

Conformity or Tact?

Whoso would be a man, must be a Non-conformist.

— Emerson, "Self-Reliance," 1841, p. 41

The opinion of one man is not as good as that of a thousand.

— Doolittle, *Chinese Vocabulary*, ii. 682, 1872
(quoted in Stevenson, p. 1719)

Communication researchers and other social scientists have long been interested in social influence and conformity. Kiesler and Kiesler (1969) defined conformity as a change in belief or behavior in the direction of the common interests of a group as a result of real or imagined pressure from the group. Similarly, Moscovici (1980) argued that when majorities exert social influence, they produce compliance. That is, individuals will publicly accept the majority view while privately retaining their initial view, motivated by a desire not to appear deviant or not to risk possible negative sanctions from the majority, such as ostracism or ridicule. The body of experimental research in this area has spanned more than half a century, dating back to the Sherif's (1935) pioneering research on the autokinetic effect. Since then, researchers have established that a wide range of personality and situational variables affect conformity, including group size (e.g., Asch, 1956), fear (Darley, 1966), unanimity (Asch, 1956), group cohesiveness (Back, 1951), and judgment difficulty (Deutsch & Gerard, 1955), to name a few.

It has been widely discussed that some national groups are stereotyped as conforming and passive, whereas other groups are viewed as independent and assertive (Peabody, 1985). Asch (1952), who conducted seminal research on conformity to group pressure, considered a conformist to be someone who has failed to develop (or has lost) the capacity to rise above group passion and prejudice and has instead subjected herself or himself to the "slavish submission to group forces" (1952, pp. 2-3). He also felt that conformity can "pollute" the social process and that it is important for a society to foster values of independence in its citizens. Reflecting the individualistic bias, Asch was primarily interested in factors that enabled individuals to resist group pressure and factors that he saw as rooted in a society's values and socialization practices (see Bond & Smith, 1996). As Asch (1956) put it,

> That we have found the tendency to conformity in our society so strong that reasonably intelligent and well-meaning young people are willing to call White Black is a matter of concern. It raises questions about our ways of educating and about the values that guide our conduct. (p. 34)

The acts of rejecting or following norms do not carry any inherent valence; it is the cultural context that provides the connotation and determines whether an act will be understood and experienced as good or bad. In a cultural context other than that of mainstream America, uniqueness and conformity may well hold connotations opposite to those in the American cultural context (Kim & Markus, 1999). Smith and Bond (1998) correctly point out that the concept of conformity has a negative overtone in Western societies. Independence of judgment is valued highly, and conformity is thought of as weak or supine. This connotation was confirmed in a U.S. study by Kane and Tedeshi (1973), who found that within the format of the Asch experiment (in which participants were asked to name which of three comparison lines was the same length as a standard), subjects who acted independently were rated more positively by judges than those who conformed. Similarly, Kim and Markus (1999) argued that the term *unique* has positive connotations of freedom and independence in European-American cultural contexts, whereas the term *conformity* has positive connotations of connectedness and harmony in East Asian cultural contexts. Four studies examined how these divergent cultural values and individual preferences for uniqueness and conformity influence each other. Studies 1 and 2 used abstract figures to measure East Asian and European-American preferences for uniqueness. Study 3 examined the choice of pens by East Asians, Europeans, and Americans as a function of whether or not the pen appeared unique. Study 4 analyzed Korean and American magazine ads, focusing on themes of conformity and uniqueness. In all these studies, East Asians preferred targets that represent conformity, whereas Europeans and Americans preferred targets that represent uniqueness. Their results highlight the relationship between individual preference and the adoption and perpetuation of cultural values.

The cultural conditions underpinning conformity have been a long-standing concern and are important for theories of social influence. Yet cultural aspects of conformity have been relatively neglected; only three previous reviews exist (Bond & Smith, 1996; Furnham, 1984; Mann, 1988).

The lack of understanding about possibly different values placed on conformity would lead one to misunderstand or misinterpret others' behavior. Understanding why and in what situations certain characteristics of people conform will certainly be an essential requirement for successful intercultural interactions.

❖ AN ECO-CULTURAL EXPLANATION OF CONFORMITY

Berry (1967) has achieved some success in predicting conformity levels on the basis of the type of environment within which societies are located. Almost exclusively, Berry (1974) has been the one to gather information about comparisons of subsistence economies; he proposed a link between the mode of subsistence and a society's values and social behavior. He built on work by Barry, Child, and Bacon (1959), who found that the socialization practices of high food-accumulating societies (pastoral or agricultural people) emphasized obedience and responsibility, whereas those of low food-accumulating societies (hunting and fishing peoples) emphasized independence, self-reliance, and individual achievement.

Berry (1967) argued that this difference resulted from the different needs of these two types of economies: High food-accumulating societies need individuals who are conscientious and compliant, whereas low food-accumulating societies need individuals who are individualistic and assertive. He further argued that these differences should also be reflected in conformity behavior and, consistent with this hypothesis, he found higher rates of conformity among the Temne of Sierra Leone, a high food-accumulating society with strict disciplinarian socialization practices, than he did among the Eskimo of Baffin Island, a low food-accumulating society whose socialization practices are lenient and encourage individualism (see Bond & Smith, 1996, for further review of this issue).

In sum, the eco-cultural model offers a theory of group behavior from which, given information about the ecology and food-gathering habits of a community, it is possible to predict how its members will respond to conformity pressures. This model could be extended by distinguishing between the values held by individualistic and collectivistic societies.

Moving beyond the subsistence economies, several studies report cross-cultural differences that had been anticipated from the relative value attached to conformity in the societies concerned. Compared with Americans, there is evidence for greater conformity among the Chinese (Huang & Harris, 1973) and among Brazilians (Sistrunk & Clement, 1970). Studies conducted in Japan have been inconclusive. Frager (1970) replicated Deutsch and Gerard's (1955) study with Japanese students and found a lower level of conformity compared with the U.S. results and even some evidence for anticonformity (i.e., deliberate nonconformity). This may have been because the majority were strangers; Williams and Sogon (1984) found a much higher level of conformity when the majority of participants were friends than when they were strangers.

Recently, Bond and Smith (1996) conducted a meta-analysis on cross-cultural studies on conformity. Including only studies that used an Asch-type line judgment task, they collected a total of 68 reports involving 133 separate experiments with a total of 4,627 participants. Analyses using measures of cultural values derived from Hofstede (1980, 1983), Schwartz (1990), and Trompenaars (1993) revealed significant relationships confirming the general hypothesis that conformity would be higher in collectivistic cultures than in individualistic cultures. That all three sets of measures gave similar results despite differences in the samples and instruments used provides strong support for the hypothesis. Moreover, the impact of the cultural variables was greater than any other type of variable, including those moderator variables (such as majority size) typically identified as being important factors. In general, people from collectivistic cultures tend to conform more to group pressure than their counterparts from individualistic cultures. The researchers concluded that cultural values are significant mediators of response in group pressure experiments.

❖ CONFORMITY AS SOCIAL SENSITIVITY AND INDEPENDENCE AS INSENSITIVITY

Bond and Smith (1996) state that whereas the Asch-type method appears to be a reliable means of assessing responsiveness to group pressure across cultures, it is questionable whether that behavior is best described as conformity, given that term's negative connotations (yielding, submissive, and so forth). They note that such connotations stem from Western values, which stress the importance of self-expression and of stating one's opinion in the face of disagreement with others. In other cultures, however, harmony with others may be valued more highly; agreement in public while privately disagreeing may be regarded, for example, as properly displaying tact or sensitivity. Viewed from this perspective, conformity in the Asch (1952) paradigm may be better described as tactfulness or social sensitivity, and independence can be characterized as tactlessness or insensitivity. Thus, the Asch paradigm may be a fair way of assessing across cultures how people respond to a discrepant group judgment, but its description as conformity may not be cross-culturally appropriate.

Smith and Bond (1998) argue,

Consider how the Asch experiment might be interpreted in one of
the nations where higher effect sizes were found. The naive subject
finds him or herself in a situation where fellow subjects in the
experiment are evidently making a lot of incorrect judgments.
Anticipating that the experimenter will later reveal who has made
errors, they may choose also to give incorrect judgments in order to
save later embarrassment of their peers. In one culture, the giving
of correct answers may be most highly valued, while in another it
may be more important to avoid embarrassment. Thus, a behavior
that we choose to think of as conformity may have a different
meaning when it is located within a different context. Looked at
this way, the naive subject's behavior might be considered not so
much as conformity but more as tact or sensitivity. (p. 17)

The negative value put upon conformity in Western societies is
illustrated in another way. The Asch experiment is almost invariably
described as a study of conformity even though the original study
showed that two-thirds of the judgements made by subjects were
independent of the pressure upon them to give the wrong judgment.
Friend, Rafferty, and Bramel (1990) examined the reports of the Asch
studies in 99 U.S. social psychology texts. They found an increasing
trend over time to concentrate upon the fact that one-third of the judgments were erroneous and to use this as evidence of how widespread
the process of conformity is in society. Because many Americans highly
value independence and initiative, we might expect that any evidence
of conformity would be interpreted negatively.

Among conformity researchers, there has been an assumption that
individuals who are exposed to social influence pressures (e.g., disagreement with others) are subjected to conflicting pressures. Several
forces encourage them to resist social influence—for example, self-trust
and desire for independence. At the same time, other pressures encourage them to accept social influence—trust in the shared group opinion
(i.e., informational social influence) and group power (i.e., normative
social influence). Varying the strength of these forces is thought to
affect the degree to which social influence is accepted by the individual
(Deutsch & Gerard, 1955). In the Asch paradigm involving judgments
of line length, participants are concerned not just with being correct,

but also with, for example, not wanting to break ranks and not wishing to stand out or be ridiculed (Bond & Smith, 1996).

Keeping in mind this conflict model, consider how self-construals might affect social influence on conformity pressures. Selves, as well as theories of selves, that have been constructed within a European-American cultural frame show the influence of one powerful notion—the idea that people are independent, bounded, autonomous entities who must strive to remain unshackled by the influences of various groups and collectives (Markus & Kitayama, 1994). This individualistic ideal is characterized by a desire not to be defined by others and is accompanied by a deep-seated wariness, in some instances even a fear, of the influence of the generalized other, of the social, and of the collective (Markus & Kitayama, 1994).

The increase in noncompliance is seen by many U.S. investigators as an important milestone in the development of individuation which, in turn, is regarded as a foundation of maturity (Rothbaum, Pott, Azuma, Miyake, & Weisz, 2000). Kim and Markus (1999) point out that for the most part, in American social psychological research reflecting the general American cultural ideals, the notion of conformity as a willing change of the individual to accommodate the group is virtually non-existent. If it occurs at all, it is cast somewhat pejoratively as passive coping or secondary control. Groups are most often discussed in terms of pressure, coercion, irrationality, and their power to deindividuate and to distort reality.

From the perspective of an independent self, there is an abiding concern that the social group will somehow overwhelm or disempower the autonomous, free self. Social conformity is very often presented as a troublesome aspect of social behavior, as being in opposition to individual behavior, and as compromising individual rights and preferences (Markus & Kitayama, 1994). This perspective follows directly from a culturally held view of the self as distinctly separate from the collective. But many other cultures—indeed, most—place a higher value on interdependence and fostering empathic connections with others. In these cultures, people may gladly emulate their associates and may be responsive to others' wishes in order to sustain smooth social relationships (see Fiske, Kitayama, Markus, & Nisbett, 1998). Thus, conformity may not reflect an inability to stick by one's own perceptions, attitudes, and beliefs (the defining features of the self) in the face of social pressure. Instead, conformity to particular others with whom the other is interdependent can be a highly valued end state. It can signify a willingness to be responsive to others and to adjust one's own demands and desires to maintain the ever-important relationship.

Indeed, in Japan, giving in to another is typically not a sign of weakness; rather, it can reflect tolerance, self-control, and maturity (Markus & Kitayama, 1994). It is possible that independent individuals may view conforming individuals as weak, and interdependent individuals may view nonconformity as a threat to group harmony. In an independent perspective, the mature self tends to be portrayed as a firmly bounded entity, capable of functioning autonomously and of resisting social pressures and other contextual influences. Thus, the lack of knowledge about possibly different values placed on conformity would lead one to misunderstand or misinterpret others' behavior. Although conformity is obviously a necessary integrative mechanism, it is often viewed as yielding to the collective, and investigators work to explain why individuals feel the need to give in. This same behavior could be seen as the mutual negotiation of social reality or as attunement with the other.

Bond and Smith (1996) expected differences between individualistic and collectivistic cultures in susceptibility to social influence to be even greater when the task was, for example, an opinion issue. Indeed, the effects of group pressure have been found to vary between tasks requiring physical judgments, and it is likely that this distinction would be important for conformity across cultures. As noted by Furnham (1984), even though cultural influence as an independent variable has not been totally ignored, there is a relative paucity of research in this field compared with other areas of research in conformity behavior. In fact, the current theoretical preoccupation with the constraints on the self provided by others and the desire to resist them may be a product of the European-American cultural view that the self is experienced as separate and autonomous from others. The nature of the relationship between cultural values and conformity requires further elaboration and investigation.

Classic sociological theories suggest that ideas about what to feel and how to feel with respect to a certain event are among the most significant cultural meanings and practices that distinguish cultural contexts. To feel good about one's choice in East Asia, one has to have the sense that the preference expressed is agreed on and approved of by others. However, to feel good about one's choice in the United States, one has to have the sense that the choice has expressed a particular or individuated preference, even though one is also following the norm of not following the norm (Kim & Markus, 1999). The norm to be unique is just as real as the norm to conform. As long as these norms exist, being different from the norm or conforming to the norm is likely to be labeled and culturally marked in different ways.

10

Internal Control Ideology and Interpersonal Communication

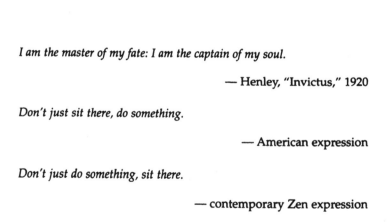

I am the master of my fate: I am the captain of my soul.

— Henley, "Invictus," 1920

Don't just sit there, do something.

— American expression

Don't just do something, sit there.

— contemporary Zen expression

*L*ocus of control (LOC) refers to the individual's perception of where the causal agent of an observed environmental change is located. The concept was originally developed in the context of Rotter's (1954) social learning theory as a variable representing people's beliefs about whether or not reinforcement is contingent on their behavior. Indeed, the original investigators of the LOC construct at Ohio State University were clinical-personality psychologists with social learning orientations and sociologists sympathetic to that orientation (Lefcourt, 1992).

Since its conceptualization, the construct of locus of control—and like terms such as *perceived control, self-efficacy, personal causation,* and *causal attribution,* just to name of few—has reached a venerable age (Lefcourt, 1992) as scholars across the various disciplines of academia apply it (and its derivatives) to their theories and studies. Each of these constructs deals with aspects of perceived causality and control, which have much overlap and commonality with the LOC construct itself. LOC has been used to interpret human behaviors, one of which is communication styles.

Internal locus of control refers to the perception of positive and negative events as consequences of one's own behavior and as being under one's personal control. In contrast, external locus of control refers to the perception that these events are not contingent on one's behavior but are reliant upon factors such as fate, luck, or chance (Ward & Kennedy, 1992, p. 178).

The locus of control construct presents a significant body of literature concerning how expectancies for control influence human behavior. Specifically, this literature focuses on theory and research related to the concept of locus of control and its implications on interpersonal communication. The work in this area has been biased by the assumption, explicit or implicit, that internality is more desirable than externality. The dominant concept of personhood in the area of locus of control is a Western ideal: a centralized, equilibrium-based conception. In this view, the individual is the architect of order and coherence through personal control and mastery.

A belief in external control exists when a reinforcement is perceived by the subject as following some action of her own but as not being entirely contingent upon her action. Internal control is defined as the individual's perception that the event is contingent upon her own behavior or her own relatively permanent characteristics (Rotter, 1966). The individual in this perspective seeks to control her environment by influencing others to adopt her own views so that control and harmony is maintained. This climate of control has profound implications on the meaning of personhood or self. Western values place high merit on personal control. In this worldview, it is the goal of individuals to be the master of their lives and to achieve self-actualization. There is also a strict boundary between the self and others. Sampson (1988) refers to this as a self that is exclusionary, wherein independence from others and self-governing is placed in high regard. In this perspective, locus of control ultimately lies within the individual. A belief in internal control appears in those societies that value and emphasize individual independence, self-reliance, and personal initiative, as is the case in the United States (see Chiu, 1986).

❖ INTERNAL CONTROL IDEOLOGY

It is easy to find explicit references in the literature supporting the view that internal locus of control is more desirable than external locus of control. Both theory and research point to internal control as the more effective model of functioning (Lefcourt, 1966). Internality has been positively related to perseverance (Weiss & Sherman, 1973), creativity (Ducette, Wolk, & Friedman, 1972), self-esteem (Heaton & Duerfeldt, 1973), and a favorable outlook toward the future (Smith, Steinke, & Distefano, 1973). A burgeoning body of research has been undertaken relating internality (as a personality dimension) to various indices of psychological well-being, including self-esteem, mood states, neurotic and psychosomatic disorders, and general life satisfaction (Chiu, 1986; Crittenden, 1991). The internals are believed to be more interpersonally flexible (Brenders, 1987), are more socially composed, report higher levels of social experience, suffer less anxiety than externals (Hamilton, 1991; Rubin, 1993), and display high levels of verbal aggression (Avtgis & Rancer, 1997). According to Ward and Kennedy (1992), the assumption that LOC may predict psychological adjustment has been investigated in the studies of acculturation, and evidence has emerged from their study to support the link between an external orientation and psychological distress.

According to Ward and Kennedy's (1992) study, people with an internal LOC orientation feel they control events in their lives and expect to control a situation. Further, internals are assertive, extroverted, and self-directed; they feel powerful and take responsibility for the outcomes of their actions and interactions (Lefcourt, 1992). Thus, internally focused individuals have been described as having a tendency toward prosocial and competent behavior, such as achievement and relationship development. On the other end of the spectrum, externals have been portrayed as viewing life events as dependent on luck, change, or powerful others; externals have been described as feeling powerless and fatalistic. Therefore, externals need affiliation and are more dependent on others than are internals. Lefcourt (1966) has indicated that because internal control is a more desirable social and personal orientation, it is important to investigate means by which individuals may gain this orientation.

In reviewing the relation of locus of control to personality, Joe (1971) concluded that "the findings depict externals, in contrast to internals, as being relatively more anxious, aggressive, dogmatic, less trustful and more suspicious of others, lacking in self-confidence and insight . . . and having a greater tendency to use sensitizing modes of defenses" (p. 623). Given this general assumption of the desirability of internal locus of control, it is not surprising that researchers have examined the necessary conditions for decreasing external and increasing internal locus of control (see Furby, 1979).

Rotter (1975) referred to this tendency in the literature as "the intrusion of the 'good guy—bad guy' dichotomy." He stated that "in spite of fears, and even warnings to the contrary, some psychologists quickly assume that it is good to be internal and bad to be external" (p. 60). Furby (1979) further points out that rather than rejecting this basic assumption, Rotter endorsed it and warned only against its extreme form. Rotter stated, "Of course, in some senses this [assumption that it is good to be internal] is true, but the problem lies in assuming that all good things are characteristic of internals and all bad things are characteristic of externals" (p. 60).

According to the independent view of the self, individuals are reinforced as a result of the perceived positive effect of their acts on themselves. A high reinforcement value is placed on the individual's subjective experience. The sense of autonomy, self-direction, and freedom of thought, rather than interdependence and behavioral and ideological conformity, are valued (Schooler, 1990). Because individuals are viewed as autonomous, self-directed entities, they can legitimately be seen as responsible for their own actions and performances.

All in all, the definition of individualism implies that persons in individualistic societies typically wish to be self-directed and highly value the phenomenological experience of freedom of choice. Personal efficacy is valued not only because individuals value their independence but also because they see themselves as primarily responsible for what happens to them. Sampson (1988) discusses a self-contained individualism in which firm self-other boundaries indicate a sharp distinction between a region belonging to the person and a region intrinsic to others. He suggests that the egocentric and sociocentric metaphors reflect different ways of understanding how the world can be maintained in an orderly and coherent manner. The dominant view in Western culture maintains that order and coherence are achieved by means of seeking control and mastery over the world through the model of the ideal person designed to achieve control, which is thereby characterized as a centralized, equilibrium-preserving structure. Although all cultures are concerned with issues of order and coherence, an apparently unique feature of the Western worldview is its insistence that the individual be the main architect of this achievement. Sampson (1988) suggested that this burden requires that people attain the ideal of the centralized, equilibrium personhood structure to achieve coherence and hold chaos at bay. In terms of personal control, mature persons are governed internally, and self boundaries firmly exclude others.

As Markus and Kitayama (1991) state, most of what psychologists know about human nature is based on one view—the Western view of the individual as an independent, self-contained, and autonomous entity. The contrasting view of the sociocentric ideal maintains that the individual seeks order and coherence by seeking to fit into the ongoing scheme of things and to minimize self-other distinction (Sampson, 1988). Markus and Kitayama argue that the independent and interdependent construals of self are among the most general and over-arching schemata of the individual's self-system because they encompass and organize the more specific self-regulatory schemata. These very general cultural self-schemata (independence and interdependence) may determine the process of lending meaning and coherence to the world. For example, one of the significant themes that appears repeatedly throughout Western psychology reflects a variation among individuals in how their actions are perceived to control the changes in the environment. The internal/external locus of control reflects this difference (Rotter, 1975). Both the psychological and communication literature have contributed significantly to the body of research into behavioral differences between the internal and the external LOC.

❖ RELATIONSHIP BETWEEN LOCUS OF
CONTROL AND COMMUNICATION IDEOLOGY

According to Miller and Steinberg (1975), the basic function of all communication is to control the environment so as to realize certain physical, economic, or social rewards from it. This view of communication typifies a view that has dominated the study of communication for many years. Although some scholars disagree with this notion, the study of how people attain this control through communicative means has evolved into an extremely popular area of research. Persuasion has also been defined in different ways by different communication scholars, each emphasizing the notion of control. Thus, persuasion becomes an attempt to extend control over others, which is the final frontier in one's realm of control over environment. Obviously, struggle is inherent in this context, where two independent individuals are vying for dominance.

Communication researchers have been studying goal-oriented behaviors as they relate to psychological traits (e.g., needs and desires). The assumption is that to communicate effectively, communicators will actively formulate goals and fulfill needs for their social interaction (Rubin & Rubin, 1992). In other words, eager communicators are self-motivated individuals seeking rewards from interpersonal interaction.

Then what is the nature of interaction between locus of control and communication motivation? Rubin and Rubin (1992) found that locus of control is an antecedent to interpersonal communication motivation, especially in communicating to control others. They claim that those who believe that chance and powerful others control their lives communicate because of a desire to be included and for escape from objective reality. Specifically, they found that (a) external locus of control related positively to interpersonal inclusion motivation, and (b) there is a positive link between internal locus of control and interpersonal control motivation (Rubin & Rubin, 1992). In a separate study, Rubin (1993) found that externals tend to be more anxious when communicating with others, and they tend to find interaction less rewarding and less satisfying than internals. Orientations toward locus of control have been found to influence assertive behaviors. Rajecki, Ickes, and Tanford (1981) found that externals were more assertive in eliciting information when faced with an intruding stranger than in an unstructured setting.

Several studies have examined the role of locus of control in dyadic social-influence processes. In an organizational simulation, Goodstadt and Hjelle (1973) found that internals were more likely to use personal persuasion tactics (such as encouragement) and were less likely to use coercion. In interpersonal conflict situations, internality was positively associated with integrative tactics, whereas externality was positively associated with avoidance and sarcasm strategies (see Canary, Cunningham, & Cody, 1988). In marital interactions, internals were more assertive and persistent than externals (Doherty & Ryder, 1979), whereas in other conversations, externals seemed to use more assertive tactics but to lack confident intonation (Bugental, Henker, & Whalen, 1976). In a study of goals and locus of control, Canary, Cody and Marston (1986) noted that high internals reported a greater likelihood of using positive feelings of target, referent influence (i.e., appeals to the relationship), and rationality (i.e., giving reasons); what they called "powerless actors" (externals) relied more on direct requests, manipulation of both positive feelings and negative feelings (i.e., showing disappointment, pouting, etc.), and avoidance. Furthermore, Avtgis and Rancer (1997) contended that externals tend to avoid or withdraw from interpersonally aversive situations and that externals exhibit higher levels of verbal aggressiveness than internals. They claim that this finding is also consistent with research that suggests that externals exhibit other avoidance tendencies, such as greater communication anxiety and esteem protection behaviors (Avtgis & Brenders, 1994).

To summarize, it has been claimed that people who expect to control a situation often find themselves in control; they are assertive, self-disclosive, and extroverted. Internals are known to be more persuasive and to use fewer coercive strategies than externals (Goodstadt & Hjelle, 1973). Further, Patterson (1983) hypothesized that the internally controlled "may be more sensitive (than externals) to interpersonal and environmental changes that require deliberation and management in interpersonal behavior" (p. 178). Rubin and Rubin (1992) also claimed that people with fatalistic or helpless expectations act in ways that confirm their expectations; they tend to attribute their state to luck, chance, powerful others, fate, or an unjust, difficult, or politically unresponsive world.

According to Brenders (1987), externals may have a different interpersonal agenda than internals, seeking to capitalize on so-called lucky breaks and the help of powerful others, and working on "developing defense explanations for potential social failures, or otherwise pursuing interpersonal strategies that permit some limited mastery of the situation" (p. 109). Furthermore, Brenders suggests that the socially helpless (externals) will become withdrawn and less satisfied with life. Rubin and Rubin, however, did not find lower life-satisfaction levels for externals. According to Berger and Metzger (1984), compared with externals, internals have more communicative strategies and are more sensitive to others. Furthermore, they argue that the number of relationships one establishes with others (externals would have fewer) and resistance to social influence (internals would have more) are social consequences of locus of control.

Research concerning assertiveness and locus of control suggests that externals will use more coercive tactics when in interactive situations than will internals (Bugental et al., 1976). The lack of perceived control over the communicative encounter suggests that externals may lash out due to the lack of confidence in interpersonal encounters (Brenders, 1987). Brenders (1987) argued that control is essential for competent interpersonal communication, although too much control could be a problem: "At one extreme, those with grandiose control beliefs may be personally effective but socially irritating. On the other end of the continuum, those experiencing a sense of social helplessness will be both psychologically depressed or socially withdrawn" (p. 88).

Why might people develop different control orientations? Culturally, society reinforces a certain value system and expects roles to be followed. The assumption that internals are better adjusted may be true in one culture but not necessarily true in another culture. According to Furby (1979), internal ideology consists essentially of the Protestant ethic: the belief that hard work, effort, skill, and ability are the important determinants of success in life. Hsieh, Shybut, and Lotsof (1969) captured the essence of this individualistic ideology in describing American society as "a culture that emphasizes the uniqueness, independence, and self-reliance of each individual. It, among other things, places a high value on personal output of energy for solving all problems; pragmatic ingenuity; individualism, that is, self-reliance and status achieved through one's efforts . . . ." (p. 122).

Without cultural bias, we can look carefully at these statements and recognize the large number that are influenced by ideology. Why is it that internal locus of control has generally been assumed to be desirable? The answer lies in an examination of the social context of our knowledge of locus of control. Gurin, Gurin, Lao, and Beattie (1969) distinguished between "control ideology"'—(the generally accepted view in the culture about the degree to which individuals control their own lives) and "sense of personal control"—(the degree to which an individual feels she has control over her own life). Control ideology corresponds to the naive psychological knowledge in the culture with respect to locus of control (Furby, 1979). Academic researchers grow up, do research, and develop theories in a society where the ideology of internal control is prevalent. They are as subject to native knowledge as everyone else in their society. Thus, it is not surprising that this ideology might influence what they regard as their academic knowledge (Furby, 1979).

In broad terms, research findings have pointed to a link between external locus of control and psychological and emotional disturbances (Dyal, 1984) as well as so-called dysfunctional or incompetent communication behaviors. However, there is possible ethnocentrism in conceptual and empirical approaches to locus of control, mental health, and communication styles. A number of cross-cultural scholars have criticized locus of control research on conceptual grounds for its ethnocentric biases, noting that in some situations and cultural contexts an external LOC can have adaptive consequences (Ward & Kennedy, 1992). Wortman and Brehm (1975) suggested that "when an organism is confronted by outcomes that are truly uncontrollable, the most adaptive response may be to give up" (p. 330). Dyal (1984) has suggested that in Asian countries with Karmic philosophies, such a problem-solving approach might diminish the stress of life changes. These conceptual criticisms and the empirical research highlight the importance of cultural sensitivity in interpretations of control orientations.

The cultural differences in the self-system challenge much current thinking about cognition, emotion, and behavior. For example, the preferred strategies of personal control and coping may vary with the nature of the self-construals. In an insightful integration of Japanese and American research, Weisz, Rothbaum, and Blackburn (1984) argue that the control attempts of individuals from collectivistic cultures differ importantly from those of members of individualistic cultures. They suggest that in individualistic cultures, where uniqueness and self-expression are stressed, taking direct action, confronting others, and speaking up on one's own behalf are the normative and preferred means of addressing a problem or difficulty. They label these direct attempts to influence the existing situation through the individual's own efforts as *primary* control strategies; the term *direct* is substituted in discussion of primary coping strategies in this chapter. Individuals with an interdependent self-control, who prefer close alignment or harmony with others, attempt to adjust to social situations through strategies that focus on changing the self rather than on changing the situation or others' opinions (Cross, 1995). Examples of these indirect strategies include reinterpreting a situation so as to derive meaning from it, accepting the situation and changing one's expectations or desires, and vicariously experiencing control by closely identifying with a more powerful other. Weisz et al. (1984) label these indirect attempts to regulate the self and psychological responses to a situation as *secondary* control strategies. In collectivistic cultures, in which individual wishes and goals are subordinated to in-group goals, direct coping strategies may be viewed as immature or selfish and can threaten harmony in relationships (Cross, 1995). Secondary or indirect coping strategies may be adaptive or effective in a collectivistic culture.

Communication and psychological theories and research on locus of control have been developed in a social and cultural context. Cultural context has influenced the kinds of facts discovered and their theoretical interpretation. I have demonstrated how the individualistic orientation of the mainstream U.S. culture led researchers to assume that internal locus of control is more desirable because it leads to what they consider more effective responding (e.g., control communication strategy) in one's environment than does external locus of control. The discussion here has touched only the surface of potentially fruitful analyses in this area; I hope it will stimulate others to continue in this vein.

11

Deceptive Communication

Moral Choice or Social Necessity?

One should speak the truth; one should speak what is pleasant; and one should not speak the truth if it happens to be unpleasant.

— Ancient Sanskrit saying

This above all: to thine own self be true
And it must follow, as the night the day,
Thou canst not then be false to any man

— Shakespeare, *Hamlet, a Tragedy*
(I, iii, 78-80), 1600/1818)

A defendant perjures herself in court; a student cheats on a final exam; a well-wisher offers an insincere compliment. Although the moralist would condemn the actions of each, there can be little doubt that deceptive communication pervades daily discourse and spans the spectrum from consequential to trivial and from blatant to inadvertent (Miller & Stiff, 1993). Deception can be encoded to achieve a variety of communication goals; some of these goals serve the communicator and some serve the target. However, when individuals in daily life use words such as *lie, liar,* and *deceptive,* they are not merely referring to the content of the message but also to the *motives* of communicators. Interest in lying transcends most disciplinary, cultural, and historical boundaries. Analyses of lying appear in religious treatises, staid textbooks, and irreverent tabloids (DePaulo, Kashy, Kirkendol, Wyer, & Epstein, 1996). Perspectives on lying are as diverse as their sources. Lying has been described as both a threat to the moral fabric of society (Bok, 1978) and a social skill (DePaulo et al., 1996).

This chapter discusses what is considered to be truthful and deceitful communication in different cultures. Communication researchers and other social scientists have evinced keen interest in the variables influencing the practice and outcomes of deceptive communication (Miller, 1983). Deceptive communication refers to "message distortion resulting from deliberate falsification or omission of information by a communicator with the intent of stimulating in another, or others, a belief that the communicator himself or herself does not believe" (Miller, 1983, pp. 92-93).

Just as an inclination to deceive and injunctions against deception are universal, a value for the truth also crosses national lines. In a 1981 survey conducted in 10 Western European countries, parents in 9 nations ranked honesty as the most important quality to be passed on to children (Harding & Phillips, 1986). Perhaps this ideal does translate into action, for as one social theorist asserted, "Pretty much all of the truth telling in the world is done by children" (Alexander, 1987, p. 197). More likely, the young are unskilled in what seems to be a behavior that increases with maturity, for although adults claim to value honesty, they appear to cultivate what John Locke (1894) calls a "love of deceit" (p. 146). Paradoxically, most people would verbalize allegiance to the principle of honesty because they recognize that some degree of veracity is necessary for the maintenance of an orderly society; however, when utilitarian motives conflict with abstract ideals, principle yields to pragmatism and deceit replaces truth.

Society and most conversations rest on an assumption of veracity in information exchange—that is, the information presented in a message and its intended meaning are assumed to be truthful

(Goffman, 1959). In actual practice, though, communicators frequently decide that honesty is not the best strategy. Instead, they conclude that some measure of dishonesty will best achieve their desired communication outcomes. Many people, therefore, find the ability to successfully deceive others an indispensable strategy for acquiring goods and services, developing and managing satisfying social relationships, and creating and managing a desired image (Buller & Burgoon, 1994).

❖ DECEPTION AS A MORAL ISSUE: INDEPENDENT PERSPECTIVE

In his 1972 book, *Sincerity and Authenticity*, Trilling notes that the ideal of sincerity as a state or quality of the self is a kind of moral mutation in Western culture. Sincerity as an ideal emerges with Western individualism. Trilling traces the concept of sincerity—the sincerity of an intact selfhood in which actions and words correspond to inner feelings and convictions—through its literary transformations to our present dilemmas, when we are so acutely aware of the erosion of selfhood under the assault of society.

According to Smith and Bond (1998), a universalistic characteristic of independent cultures is that truth is thought of as an absolute state, just as laws are thought of, in principle, as equally applicable to all citizens. In more collectivistic cultures, communication is always thought of as occurring within a social context. Social sensitivity and tact are required in determining what it is appropriate to say in a given setting. Even in individualistic cultures, the telling of so-called white lies (untrue statements designed to preserve social harmony) is widely condoned. We may expect, however, the frequency of such statements to be higher in collectivistic cultures.

In related work, deception detection research has demonstrated a phenomenon that has come to be known as a "truth bias" among individuals asked to make veracity determinations (Koper, 1994). Unless participants were alerted to the possibility that a message was a lie, they reported that people tell the truth. The truth bias demonstrated by members of individualistic cultures represents the assumption that people should be honest in their communication with others, regardless of the circumstances.

Regarding the truth bias in the United States, Miller (1983) wrote,

> The social and political agonies occasioned by the Vietnam War and the Watergate episode, the appeal for truth in advertising and lending, the frequently uttered plea for a return to personal authenticity, and a host of similar events have emphasized the extent to which deceptive communicative practices pervade late Twentieth Century American society and have reminded us that the fabric of a functional, compassionate society is woven from candid discourse. As a result, most socially concerned students of communication realize that fuller understanding of how deceptive communication works—or, to put it differently, a greater awareness of the variables underlying the rhetorical and persuasive force of deceptive messages—represents a first line of defense for a citizenry bombarded with false and misleading statements. (p. 92)

Independent individuals may be more likely to see deception as an ethical issue and to have a truth bias in their dealings with others. They are taught to tell the truth at all times, regardless of the consequences, and they assume that others are being honest with them, stimulating trust and openness. This cultural value is pervasive in Western culture and, as such, potentially creates an image of naivete that Westerners ought to consider (Koper, 1994). In the popular U.S. press, as well as in the literature on ethics, lying often is described as a selfish act. It is assumed that people lie to get jobs, promotions, raises, good grades, and better commissions. In the Western context, lies are more often told to serve the self rather than to benefit others (DePaulo et al., 1996).

The act of deceiving often does not mesh with the direct communication styles that individualists prefer and value. Lying, for example, is contradictory to individualists' value for expressing true feelings and internal attributes. Further, anxiety about deceiving others is expected to be greater for people of independent self-construals than for people of interdependent self-construals. Ebesu and Miller (1994) argue that there is usually some guilt and negative affect associated with engaging in deception and fear of getting caught. Because independent self-construals work against false information, independents are expected to have lower motivation for deception than interdependent individuals. Similarly, Miller (1983) argued that reliance upon ingratiation strategies, such as insincere opinion agreement or false flattery, is typically perceived as a morally objectionable method of currying favor with others, with the deceptive communicator frequently falling heir to the pejorative label "apple polisher" or "yes-man."

Aune and Waters (1994), in one of the few studies of deception across cultures, compared motivations for deception in Samoan and North American subjects. They found that people in Samoa, who are considered to be more collectivistic than North Americans, are more motivated to deceive another for the sake of their own family or group or to please an authority figure rather than to serve the self. They also found that North Americans are motivated to deceive when they feel an issue is private or to protect the target person's feelings. This implies that individuals with highly interdependent self-construals may differ from individuals with highly independent self-construals in their motivations for deception.

Kim, Kam, Singelis, Wilson, and Sharkey (1998) predicted that self-construals would significantly impact one's likelihood of using certain deceptive strategies, one's perceptions of what constitutes deceptive communication, as well as one's perceptions of the relevance of particular message response strategies. Not surprisingly, they found that independents were highly unwilling to use the lie message response strategy. Again, this finding is consistent with prior research on the individualistic bias for truth telling (Gilbert, Krull, & Malone, 1990; Koper, 1994). In the United States, outright lying is generally viewed as a reprehensible act, and individuals are discouraged from substituting deceit in place of truth. Additionally, individuals of independent construals thrive on being true to the self. That is, they prefer to speak what they truly feel to emphasize their own uniqueness. Thus, it is understandable that independents would be less likely to use the lie message response because not only is lying viewed negatively among independents, but it also does not allow the independent to express her or his true self.

Kim, Kam, et al.'s (1998) data also strongly support the notion that individuals of different self-construals may possess different perceptions of what communication strategy is considered to be deceptive. In their study, as compared with interdependents, independents perceived the lie message response strategy to be very deceptive in nature. According to Doi (1986), in the United States, it is extremely important for the public and private selves to remain consistent. When the public and private selves are discrepant, an individual is considered duplicitous, two-faced, and hypocritical. Thus, for independents, consistency between thoughts and actions is highly essential. Lies are essentially discrepancies between what is truly felt and what one says. Hence, it is comprehensible that independents may perceive lies as extremely deceptive in nature. Consistent with previous arguments, unequivocal lies may be more anxiety producing for the independent self (which is concerned about the consistency of beliefs and their expression) than they are for the interdependent self.

In addition, Kim, Kam, et al. (1998) found that independent construals perceived the irrelevant assertion message response to be highly deceptive in nature and that they were highly unwilling to use the irrelevant assertion response to carry out their deceptions, especially in an other-benefit situation. (The irrelevant message response strategy seeks to avoid addressing the topic at hand altogether. It is a diversionary response in which attention is drawn away from the topic at issue). These findings seem to suggest the possibility that independents' need to be direct in communication is what causes them to render irrelevant message responses as faulty, indirect and, thus, deceptive. Gudykunst and Ting-Toomey (1988) have claimed that communication in the United States affords little room for the cultivation of ambiguity and that the value orientation of individualism propels North Americans to speak their minds freely by using direct utterances. Furthermore, individualistic values foster the norms of honesty and openness, and these norms are achieved through the use of precise, straightforward language behaviors.

❖ DECEPTION AS A SOCIAL NECESSITY:
   INTERDEPENDENT PERSPECTIVE

Although ethicists might bemoan this trend away from truth, many theorists argue that deceptive communication is an indication of neither ethical laxity nor moral corruption but is actually a necessary tool for the management of interpersonal relationships (Barnes, 1994). In this line of thinking, rather than being regarded as a mark of defective character, successful deceptive communication is a sign of a well-developed coping mechanism because constantly speaking the cold, hard, brutal, unsparing truth would hardly seem to make for congenial interaction.

The communicator may assert that a boring, uneventful evening qualified as "a nice time," that a particularly unpalatable dinner was "a delicious meal," or that an unbecoming tie or blouse is "quite attractive" (Miller, 1983). Of course, such misrepresentations of self-feelings are usually considered harmless in most cultures and are even sanctioned as fulfilling accepted norms of social acceptability and responsibility. As Bok (1978) puts it:

> In the eyes of many, such white lies do no harm, provide needed support and cheer, and help dispel gloom and boredom. They preserve the equilibrium and often the humanness of social relationships, and are usually accepted as excusable so long as they do not become excessive. Many argue, moreover, that such deception is so helpful and at times so necessary that it must be tolerated as an exception to the general policy against lying. (pp. 58-59)

However, deception may be seen among interdependent individuals as a more acceptable mode of communication, especially if it benefits others and protects others' face. This would seem to promote the perception of collectivists as inscrutable and, at least potentially, as untrustworthy by those outside of the culture. The significance of the connectedness with social contexts among interdependent individuals leads them to be more situation specific than independent individuals, who are separate from social contexts (Singelis & Brown, 1995). For example, Miller (1984) found that Hindu adults in India (collectivists) used more contextual references (e.g., "she is loyal to her employer") than did Americans (individualists) when they were asked to explain certain types of behaviors.

Moreover, the interdependent individuals' great concern for avoiding negative evaluations and desire not to hurt others' feelings make them emphasize what they consider to be appropriate social communication styles (Kim & Sharkey, 1995). Thus, in an other-benefit situation, in which the perceiver is expected to benefit from the deception (e.g., saving face by appraisal), interdependents may be willing to use deceptive strategies. Independent individuals, on the other hand, may value the truthfulness of a message unconditionally, regardless of situational contingencies.

Perhaps the most intriguing finding of Kim, Kam, et al.'s (1998) study was that interdependents did not perceive the blatant lie message response as deceptive, and they were highly willing to use this message response strategy in the other-benefit situation. They also perceived the lie strategy to be a very relevant message response. Furthermore, interdependent individuals were more likely to use irrelevant assertions as a possible message response strategy. Taken together, these findings seem to indicate that perhaps the altering or rejection of truthful information is not considered to be deception in collectivistic cultures. Rather, this manipulation of the pure, unsparing truth is a necessary means by which harmony is maintained and preserved.

How does the ever-present need to attend to others and gain acceptance influence the form of deception motivation? As with other areas of communication behavior, I propose that the motivational processes of deception depend on the nature of the self-system. One important motivation associated with different levels of self-construal is a change in the basic goals of social interaction. There is a fundamental difference between social motives derived from personal self-interest and those derived from concern for the interests of others (McClintock, 1972). Both Markus and Kitayama (1991) and Baumeister and Leary (1995) stressed that interdependent relationships are characterized by mutual concern for the interests and outcomes of the other. Batson (1994) defined this concern as the basis for altruistic motivation, which is the motivation to benefit the other. (He stressed that altruistic motivation is not to be confused with self-sacrifice, which concerns costs to the self.) At the collective level, group welfare becomes an end unto itself.

Psychologists have assumed that it is universally true that people are motivated to maintain a positive view of the self (Tesser, 1986). What constitutes a positive view of the self depends, however, on one's construal of the self. If we assume that *others* will be relatively more focal in the motivation of those with interdependent selves, various implications follow. Those with interdependent selves are receptive to others, adjusting to their needs and demands. Interdependents restrain their own inner needs and desires to serve others' needs. For those with independent selves, feeling good about oneself typically requires fulfilling the tasks associated with being an independent self—that is, being unique and expressing one's true inner feelings. Feeling good about one's interdependent self may be instrumental to the ability to flexibly adjust to social contingencies, which is often regarded as an important sign of the moral maturity of a person (Markus & Kitayama, 1991).

In Japan, there is a virtue in controlling the expression of one's innermost feelings; no virtue accrues from expressing them. Triandis (1989), for example, reported a study by Iwao (1988), who gave respondents a series of scenarios and asked them to judge which responses would be appropriate for the person described in the scenario. In one scenario, the daughter brings home a person from another race. One of the possible responses given was that the daughter's father "would never allow them to marry but told them [he] was in favor of their marriage." This answer was rated as best by only 2% of the Americans. In sharp contrast, however, it was rated as best by 44% of the Japanese. Among the Americans, 48% thought it was the worst response, whereas only 7% of the Japanese rated it as the worst.

The title of Imai's 1981 book, *16 Ways to Avoid Saying No*, is fairly indicative of the nature of this work. Stemming from Imai's personal experiences as a businessman and consultant in Japan, it assesses how Japanese businesspeople respond to requests, specifically those they cannot or will not fulfill. Imai (1981) suggests a number of alternatives to the explicit word *no*, including answers that sound similar to those deemed deceptive by Western standards (Lapinski, 1996). Hence, among people of highly interdependent self-construals, there may not be a strong emphasis on maintaining consistency between what one feels and what is said. Among individuals of highly independent self-construals, consistency between thoughts and actions is essential. One might argue, therefore, that the state of anxiety arising from so-called deceptive remarks is not likely to be experienced by those with interdependent selves.

Those with highly developed interdependent self-construals are connected with their social context (Markus & Kitayama, 1991). Because these individuals are concerned with others' feelings and evaluations, they control and restrict the expression of their true inner feelings if the expression of those feelings would be detrimental to the social relationship. Thus, individuals with highly developed interdependent self-construals tend to avoid expressing negative emotions, voicing their true (negative or damaging) opinions, or expressing disagreements directly and overtly in communication situations. Direct deceit is the most effective way to avoid these expressions, which are potentially damaging to others or to relational harmony. By being direct in their deception, even the suspicion of misrepresentation that might accompany a more indirect strategy is averted, and the others' face is most strongly supported.

The works of several authors seem to indicate that what is considered deceptive may vary considerably among people of different self-construals. Taken together, this literature suggests that self-oriented motivation for deception is associated with the independent self-construal because its source of esteem is embedded in expressing and establishing the uniqueness of the self. Furthermore, the individualistic moral preoccupation with deception seems to indicate that individuals of this cultural orientation are biased toward truth telling. For those with independent self-construals, voicing one's true feelings is paramount to establishing the singleness and originality of the self. The interdependent self-construal is associated with the use of deception for other-oriented motivation because this type of self focuses on maintaining relational harmony and on meeting the needs and desires of others. For the interdependent self, the need to maintain harmony overrides the need to be entirely truthful or to express one's true inner feelings, and deception may be seen as an entirely acceptable mode of communication if it means preserving a healthy relationship with others.

Exploring information manipulation theory, Lapinski (1996) found that the higher an individual's interdependent self-construal, the more generally honest she or he viewed deceptive messages. People of interdependent self-construals usually take an other-oriented approach to communication, which places the responsibility of reading the others' minds on the hearer (Kim & Sharkey, 1995). This reduces the responsibility of the deceiver for the accuracy of the message and allows interdependent individuals to be direct and clear in deception when saving others' face. Thus, overall, interdependent individuals may rate direct deceptive strategies as more likely to be used than independent individuals.

In summary, when speakers from different cultural backgrounds interact, the communication problems that develop can in part be attributed to the differing perceptions that individuals have of what deceptive communication fully entails. Additionally, communication difficulties can also be attributed to the notion that individuals of different self-construals possess dissimilar motivations toward deceptive communication. Whereas independents may engage in interaction with a bias toward being truthful, interdependents may take part in an interaction with self- and other-face needs foremost in mind, and this may cause them to assume that deception will inevitably occur in conversation.

Nishiyama (1993) discussed deception in a cultural framework from a business perspective. Nishiyama suggested that there are a number of strategies and behaviors that are considered everyday business practice in Japan, yet these behaviors may be misinterpreted as deception by American businesspeople. Some of these misinterpretations may stem from cultural misperceptions regarding what constitutes a deceptive message. Message responses that are considered to be deceptive by independents may not be viewed as deceptive by interdependents, and vice versa. Examining deception from a cultural standpoint enables a more profound understanding of individual motives for deception. Future research in the realm of deceptive communication should not neglect to take cultural influences into account because they may have a significant impact on deceptive communication.

This chapter has shown that independent and interdependent construals may be strong predictors of one's motivation to deceive as well as of one's perceptions of what constitutes deceptive communication. If individuals are made aware of the differing motivations for and perceptions of deceptive communication, they may become more understanding and accommodating of the conversational styles of others and, thus, communication misunderstandings may be avoided.

This chapter also examined the influence of the cultural self-concept on motivations for deception as well as on perceptions of deceptive communication. A review of previous literature on deceptive communication has revealed that few works have examined the impact of culture on perceptions of deceptive messages. This review has shown that one's cultural self-concept may have substantive effects on one's motivations for, as well as perceptions of, deceptive communication.

12

Self-Disclosure

Bragging vs. Negative Self-Disclosure

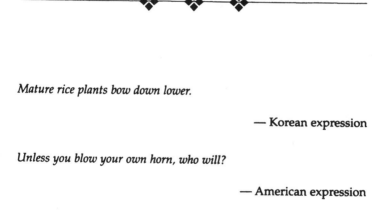

Mature rice plants bow down lower.

— Korean expression

Unless you blow your own horn, who will?

— American expression

Self-presentation is one of the fundamental and important processes by which people negotiate identities for themselves in their social worlds (Tice, Butler, Muraven, & Stillwell, 1995). Self-presentation researchers have long remarked on how people are adept at modifying and tailoring their self-disclosures to produce the optimal, desired effects on their listeners. In the privacy of one's own mind, perhaps, one may be relatively free to imagine oneself as having any sort of identity; however, serious identity claims generally require social validation by other people, so the construction of identity requires persuading others to see one as having desired traits and qualities (e.g., Baumeister, 1982). The importance of self-presentation is reflected in how pervasive the motivations are. It appears that there is a strong and pervasive desire to make a positive impression on others (Tice et al., 1995). However, *how* one creates a positive impression may vary depending on many factors, including how one construes self-views. In this chapter, I will illustrate the process whereby cultural views of self are transformed into psychological tendencies and then into communication styles (i.e., independence to self-enhancement to bragging, interdependence to self-criticism to negative self-disclosure).

❖ MOTIVATIONAL INFLUENCES
ON STYLES OF SELF-DISCLOSURE

Prior research has shown a marked tendency for those in North America to assert and enhance an overall evaluation of the self (i.e., self-enhancing communication) (Greenwald, 1980; Tesser, 1986). Myers (1987) found that more than 50 percent of a sample of American college undergraduates reported that they perceived themselves to be in the top 10 percent in interpersonal sensitivity.

In a highly influential article, Taylor and Brown (1988) surveyed the social-psychological literature on the accuracy of social perception (including self-perception). In this survey, mental health was operationalized in most studies by the absence of low self-esteem or depression. Taylor and Brown (1988) arrived at the conclusion that mentally healthy individuals show unrealistically positive self-evaluations (self-enhancement), exaggerated perceptions of control or mastery, and unrealistic optimism. They provided the evidence that supported their conclusion: Most people (mostly university students in the United States) show the illusion of, for example, self-enhancement.

This conclusion is anchored in an individualistic approach to the self. From a different orientation, one in which the individual is cast not as an independent entity but as one fundamentally interdependent with others, the self-enhancement or bragging could be understood differently. Kitayama, Markus, Matsumoto, and Norasakkunkit (1997) have suggested with initial evidence that a Japanese tendency to appraise the self in a critical light is in the service of improving the self vis-à-vis socially shared standards of excellence. Indeed, clear evidence exists that self-criticism in Japan is often a spontaneous, genuinely felt, personal response, although under certain conditions it can also be motivated by a self-presentational concern not to stand out in public (Kitayama et al., 1997).

Findings from a number of social psychological domains suggest that Americans show a general sensitivity to positive self-relevant information, which Kitayama et al. (1997) refer to as *self-enhancement*. Several studies have illustrated various manifestations of self-enhancement in the United States. For example, most Americans studied perceived themselves as being above average on a wide variety of desirable traits (Brown, 1990; Taylor & Brown, 1988). Thus, the existence of a strong self-enhancement motive in Western society is well documented.

The idea of the free, separate, and unique individual is also pervasively represented and reproduced in a vast array of culturally significant social representations, including images, proverbs, and stories of people who are masters of their fates and captains of their destinies, lone cowboys, people who pull themselves up by their own bootstraps, squeaky wheels that get the grease, and people going by the road less traveled (Heine, Lehman, Markus, & Kitayama, 1999). Although people are alike in being normatively guided in their actions, it matters that in the course of their actions, Americans feel they are charting their own courses, marching to the beat of a different drummer, or boldly going where no one has gone before (Kim & Markus, 1999).

Similarly, American children as young as age 4 believe themselves to be better than their peers. U.S. adults typically consider themselves to be more intelligent, friendlier, and more attractive than the average adult (Myers, 1987). There is a growing body of literature that indicates that the self-enhancement effect is reversed in non-Western groups. The predominant pattern is mainly to explain one's success in terms of effort or luck and one's failure in terms of one's lack of abilities or talents. This sensitivity to negative self-relevant information is referred to as *self-criticism* (Kitayama et al., 1997). Heine and Lehman (1997a) could not replicate the tendency for people to overemphasize the uniqueness of one's positive attributes in Japan, Thailand, or Korea. Kurman and Sriram (1997) examined whether the motive for self-enhancement exists in equal degree in a more collectivistic society.

Academic self-evaluation obtained from eighth graders in Singapore and Israel revealed that self-enhancement was evident in both cultures, but it was stronger in Israel. The authors suggest that the lower levels of self-enhancement in Singapore are driven by self-presentation norms and other cultural influences. This is consistent with findings of higher self-evaluation among Westerners (Bond & Cheung, 1983).

It is not likely that the Asian self-reports are due merely to impression management style because even when responses are recorded in a manner that maintains the anonymity of Japanese respondents, self-enhancement is still absent or reversed (Kitayama et al., 1997). Instead, it seems likely that the tendency not to self-enhance, or even to self-criticize, may reflect authentic subjective experience. Asian practices may paradoxically be comparable in function to Western tendencies toward self-enhancement. The inclination to self-criticize may be a way to affirm the identity of the self as interdependent by engaging in the process of self-improvement—an important element of the interdependent, Japanese sense of well-being (Fiske, Kitayama, Markus, & Nisbett, 1998). For Japanese interdependent selves, the perceived absence of negative features, rather than the perceived presence of positive features, might be crucial in the maintenance of well-being.

In a European-American middle-class context, the dominant modes of cultural participation involve discovering, confirming, and expressing the positive attributes of the self (Markus, Mullally, & Kitayama, 1997). A developmental study by Yoshida, Kojo, and Kaku (1982) documented that self-enhancement and self-promotion are perceived quite negatively in Japanese culture. Students at a Japanese elementary school were asked how their classmates (including themselves) would evaluate a hypothetical peer who commented on his own superb athletic performance either in a modest, self-restrained way or in a self-enhancing way. The evaluation was solicited on the dimension of personality ("Is he a good person?") and on the dimension of ability ("Is he good at [the relevant athletic domain]?"). The results showed that the personality of the modest peer was perceived much more positively than was that of the self-enhancing peer. Whereas the second graders took the comment of the peer at face value, perceiving the self-enhancing peer to be more competent than the modest peer, third graders viewed the two as equally competent, and the fifth graders believed that the modest peer was more competent than the self-enhancing peer. The same trend, of lower likability for self-enhancers, was described by Bond, Leung, & Wan (1982) in their study of Chinese subjects in Hong Kong. For the most part, the American prescription is to confidently display and express one's strengths, and those who do so are evaluated positively (e.g., Mullen & Riordan, 1988).

Markus et al. (1997) argued that within a Japanese cultural system that is rooted in the importance of maintaining, affirming, and becoming part of significant social relationships, sensitivity to negative self-relevant information is not an indicant of low self-esteem or something to be avoided or overcome. Rather, it has positive social and psychological consequences. Markus et al. (1997) also argued that when selfways emphasize being part of the group, standing out or being different even in a positive sense may not be valued. Instead, selfways may give rise to what from a Western perspective appears to be self-effacement (Tanaka, 1987).

Psychological tendencies involving the self, such as self-enhancement (the United States) and self-criticism (Japan) are afforded and sustained by the ways in which realities are constructed in each cultural context. On the basis of past research, it is evident that self-enhancement appears obvious and natural in those cultural contexts in which one is encouraged to create a distinct and objectified self. To the extent that the self is interdependent with others, it seems likely that there will be many fewer concerns with enhancing and actualizing one's identity because the need to create an autonomous self is not a cultural imperative (Kitayama et al., 1997).

The content of the disclosures appears crucial to the receipt of positive interpersonal evaluations. In the U.S. context, it was found that people tend to feel more attracted to, interested in, and positive toward positive disclosers as compared with negative disclosers (Gilbert & Horenstein, 1975; Jones & Gordon, 1972). Gilbert and Horenstein (1975) found that respondents in the United States best liked those male disclosers who disclosed positive rather than negative information about themselves. This is consistent with Kleinke and Kahn's (1980) finding that a man who reveals negative things about himself is especially likely to be perceived as weak and incompetent. Rudman (1998) also found that self-promoters were perceived as more competent than self-effacers. Thus, the content of the disclosures appears crucial to the receipt of positive interpersonal evaluations. Similarly, Miller, Cooke, Tsang, and Morgan (1992) asked American respondents to rate characters who disclosed in a boastful, positive, or negative fashion. Boasters and positive disclosers were viewed as more competent than negative disclosers. Compared with the boaster, the positive discloser was rated as more feminine (less masculine) and less competent. Thus, in the European-American context, if we would like to be perceived as competent and successful, boasting appears to be a better strategy than disclosing negatively.

Recently, Ellis and Wittenbaum (2000) found that American students were more likely to praise personal qualities rather than others' attributes when trying to appear qualified for the award of excellence. In fact, promoting others was rare; only an average of 2% of communicated thoughts were others-promoting. Despite the small amount of variability in others-promotion within the American sample, the researchers still found a strong positive association between inter-dependent self-construal and others-promotion. In the past, it was theorized that, to present an image of competence, individuals would promote personal attributes of the self. Although the Ellis and Wittenbaum study found this to be true, it also showed that individuals try to appear competent by praising significant others as well.

Because the self is construed differently across cultures, the participating psychological processes may take correspondingly different forms. Western cultures are organized according to meanings and practices that promote the independence and autonomy of a self that is separate from other similar selves and from social context. The self is made meaningful primarily in relation to a set of attributes that are internal to the bounded, separate self. European-American practices are often centered on distinguishing oneself and standing out from the rest, whereas Japanese practices are often framed in terms of *hitonami* (average as a person); to the extent that one is average, one is relieved. From a Japanese perspective, being different entails the risk of being excluded (Fiske et al., 1998).

Whereas many Europeans and Americans typically emphasize that they are unique, different, and better than others, people in many East Asian and other cultures typically emphasize that they are ordinary, quite similar to, or not different than others. Asian cultures do not highlight the explicit separation of each individual. These cultures are systematized according to meanings and practices that promote the fundamental connectedness among individuals within a significant relationship. The self is made meaningful primarily in reference to those social relations of which the self is a participating part (Fiske et al., 1998).

A very different interpretation of the cultural differences in self-enhancement is that they result from a methodological artifact. Given that cross-cultural studies of self-enhancement typically use a target of evaluation that is theoretically more meaningful to those from Western cultures (i.e., individualistic self), it is reasonable to be concerned that if a study demonstrates an absence of self-enhancing tendencies among Japanese, the result may be due to its evaluation of a target that is inconsequential to Japanese. That is, individualistic North Americans may be motivated to enhance their individual selves, whereas Japanese may be motivated to enhance their collective selves. This view suggests that past cultural differences in self-enhancement reflect differences in content (the target of the evaluation) rather than differences in process (the motivation to see the self, or one's group, in a positive light). Recently, Heine and Lehman (1997a) examined whether parallel differences emerge when the target of evaluation is the group. In two studies, group-serving biases were compared across European Canadian, Asian Canadian, and Japanese students. Study 1 revealed that Japanese students evaluated a family member less positively than did both groups of Canadian students. Study 2 replicated this pattern with students' evaluations of their universities. The data suggest that cultural differences in enhancement biases are robust, generalizing to individuals' evaluations of their group.

In a similar vein, Lee, Aaker, and Gardner (2000) distinguished between self-regulatory processes that focus on promotion and prevention strategies for goal pursuit. Promotion goals refer to the pursuit of gains and aspirations toward ideals. On the other hand, prevention goals refer to the avoidance of losses and the fulfillment of obligations. In a series of five studies, they found that individuals with a dominant independent self tend to exhibit a bias toward promotion focus, weighting gain-framed information (particularly happiness) as more important than loss-framed information. On the other hand, those with a dominant interdependent self tend to exhibit a bias toward prevention-focused negativity, weighting loss-framed information (particularly anxiety) as more important than gain-framed information. This study helps explain cultural differences in self-enhancement and self-improvement tendencies. Because interdependents are motivated to avoid failure, they may ruminate more on their negative features in an attempt to eradicate them. The tendency toward self-criticism in members of interdependent cultures is probably due to their greater motivation to avoid failure in the future—a clearly prevention-focused emotion. On the other hand, research by Kitayama and colleagues (1997) demonstrated that American individuals chose a greater number of success versus failure situations as relevant to their self-esteem. More generally, these differences may be derived from differences in regulatory focus.

Those in Western cultures may develop a variety of social psychological processes that enable them to maintain and increase their self-esteem. As a result, these individuals may be highly attuned to positive characteristics of the self. Those in Asian cultures may be motivated to adjust and fit themselves into meaningful social relationships. Thus, maintaining the positive overall evaluation of the self that is separate from the social context may not be the primary concern of these individuals.

Markus and Kitayama's (1991) work suggests that the inclination to maintain and bolster one's self-esteem may develop in individuals socialized in a cultural group in which an independent view of self is encouraged. However, the tendency to negatively evaluate the self may emerge in individuals socialized in a cultural group in which an interdependent view of self is valued.

This process implies that communication styles result from a collective process through which the views of the self are inscribed and embodied in the very ways in which social acts and situations are defined and experienced in each cultural context. Thus, situational definitions that compose the American mainstream cultural context are relatively more conducive to self-enhancement and bragging self-disclosure. Similarly, situational definitions that compose the Japanese cultural context may be relatively more conducive to negative self-disclosure. Thus, independent individuals should be more likely to engage in self-enhancing communication styles than in negative self-disclosing styles. Similarly, situational definitions among interdependent individuals should be relatively conducive to self-criticizing communication styles, and interdependents should be more likely to engage in negative self-disclosure than in self-enhancing communication.

❖ GENDER AND THE PREFERRED
    FORMS OF SELF-PRESENTATION

Past research on gender differences in self-enhancement and self-criticism has suggested that women tend to be more interdependent than men and that self-enhancement in the United States is weaker for women than for men. According to Kurman and Sririam's (1997) study of Singaporeans and Israelis, gender differences reveal a higher self-enhancement for males. Although females had higher grades than males, their self-evaluations were comparable to the self-evaluations of males. This trend of lower self-enhancement among females can be attributed to their higher sensitivity to negative feedback (Roberts, 1991).

This discussion seeks to stimulate further study of gender differences in self-disclosure tendencies. Recent efforts to acknowledge gender difference in self-presentational tactics have approached the problem intrapsychically (Kacmar & Carlson, 1994). It has been argued that women are unable to self-promote because of low self-esteem (i.e., a belief that "they have nothing about which to brag"; Kacmar & Carlson, 1994, p. 690). Similar negative attributions can be made about interdependent individuals who may be reluctant to self-promote for fear of violating their normative tasks, which in turn may limit their perceived suitability for many occupations in individualistic societies. Self-presentation strategies undoubtedly influence both career and interpersonal success. The present discussion highlights the normative pressures that may cause interdependents discomfort when they consider using self-promotion as a means to self-efficacy. Self-promotion may intuitively be more normative and acceptable for independents than for interdependents.

13

Silence

Is It Really Golden?

Words, words, words: Fluttering drizzle and snow.
Silence, silence, silence: A roaring thunderbolt.

— Zen expression

Speech is civilization itself. The word, even the most contradictious word,
preserves contact—it is silence which isolates.

— Mann, *The Magic Mountain*, 1927, p. 518

In this chapter, I focus on a relatively neglected component of human communication—silence. According to the Oxford English Dictionary, the term *silence* refers to "abstaining or forbearing from speech or utterance (sometimes with reference to a particular matter)"

(Simpson & Weiner, 1989, p. 465). Silence has typically been considered an out-of-awareness phenomenon—the ground against which the figure of talk is perceived (Tannen, 1985). The *silent* strategy is consistent with Brown and Levinson's (1978) *don't do FTA* strategies, which are the actions that are presumably the least face-threatening. Studies of communication from a Western perspective have tended to view silence as absence—an absence of sound and, therefore, an absence of communication (Scollon, 1985). Within a given speech community, social values and norms strongly influence the amount of talk and the amount of silence that is considered normal or appropriate.

Kincaid (1979) indicated epistemological biases that have hampered our thinking about human communication. One of the implicit biases has been a concentration on discrete messages and not on silence, rhythm, and timing. Reversing polarities and treating silence as the figure to be examined against the ground of talk may heighten awareness of this universal aspect of human communication while at the same time emphasizing its complex nature as a cultural phenomenon.

❖ SILENCE AS
    MALFUNCTIONING OF (HUMAN) MACHINES

Researchers still favor Descartes's metaphor of the machine as the model for both human cognition and interpersonal interaction. This perspective has consequences both for the ways in which we do research and in our interpersonal interactions with people whose understanding of communication does not employ the metaphor of the machine (Scollon, 1985). In the Western context, silence in a conversation appears to be a very negative quality. Thus, Feldstein, Alberti, and BenDebba (1979) find the results of their research intuitively reasonable. They write,

> It does not seem unduly strange that speakers take longer turns when talking with persons who are reserved, detached, and taciturn than with persons who are talkative, cheerful, and cooperative. Nor is it difficult to believe that persons who are reserved, cold, suspicious, insecure, and tense tend to produce longer pauses. (p. 85)

Scollon (1985) noted the implied direction of causation: The researchers have taken the personality characteristics as given and then assumed that those characteristics have caused the phenomenon of pausing. In their view, suspicious people pause longer than those who aren't suspicious. It seems difficult for either individuals or researchers to give up the idea of the humming conversational machine. Scollon (1985), in his essay "The Machine Stops: Silence in the Metaphor of Malfunction," argues that silence is typically heard as the malfunctioning of a machine (the industrial metaphor):

> The normal state of the machine is thought of as a steady hum or buzz, with hesitation or silences indicating trouble, difficulty, missing cogs, and so forth. We see the quality control engineer sitting at a window on the production line overlooking the production of the gross cognitive product as reflected in verbal outputs. (p. 26)

He further argues that changing the metaphor changes the meaning of silence. To increase our understanding of the meaning of silence in conversation, we must first examine the metaphors generating our research and our conversational stance.

Since the time of the ancient Greek philosophers, Western thought has emphasized bipolar values and concepts using opposing terms such as black versus white, good versus bad, life versus death, and yes versus no. Speech versus silence has been researched and taught from the same bipolar perspective: Speech has a positive connotation and silence has a negative one (Ishii & Bruneau, 1988). Saville-Troike (1985) states that "the important position of silence in the total framework of human communication has been largely overlooked" (p. xv). The importance of silence in intracultural and intercultural communication has recently been recognized in various studies (Tannen, 1985). Silence is no longer treated only as mere absence of sound, nor is it viewed as simply pauses within discourses or at turn-taking boundaries in conversation. Nevertheless, only a marginal amount of data is available on the communicative significance of silence. Silence, its functions, and its meanings in intercultural communication continue to be a largely unexplored area.

The negative connotation of silence in the Middle Eastern and Western context is exemplified in the original decree of male supremacy used to support the idea of the natural inferiority of women and to silence them, as shown in the following two excerpts from the Bible:

> Let the woman learn in silence with all subjection. But I suffer not a woman to teach or to usurp authority over the man, but to be in silence. For Adam was first formed and then Eve, and Adam was not deceived, but the woman being deceived was in the transgression. (1 Timothy 2:11-14, *Layman's Parallel Bible*)

> Let the women keep silence in the churches: for it is not permitted unto them to speak; but they are commanded to be under obedience, as also saith the law. And if they learn anything, let them ask their husbands at home; for it is a shame for women to speak in the church. (1 Corinthians 14: 34-35, *Layman's Parallel Bible*)

❖ SILENCE AS NEGLECTED COMPONENT
   OF HUMAN COMMUNICATION

The study of communication has focused on talk to the exclusion of silence. In some situations, silence is more acceptable than talk in many parts of the world, a fact that some U.S. scholars have not acknowledged. Ishii and Bruneau (1988) support this notion. They contend that today's U.S. communication scholars view the Western rhetorical tradition uncritically, assuming it is the only possible perspective. This tradition views silence and ambiguity negatively, especially in social and public relations. Ishii and Bruneau charge that Western scholars fall prey to a major misconception when they assume that silence is completely different than speech, its foreign opposite, its antagonist. Scholars from other cultures may view silence very differently. To them, silence may really be golden, a state to be encouraged. Giles, Coupland, and Wiemann (1992) compared the beliefs of Chinese and Americans about talking. The Americans described talking as pleasant, important, and a way of controlling what goes on. The Chinese were more tolerant of silence; they saw quietness as a way of controlling what goes on. According to Basso (1990), we must study when people speak *and* when they do not:

> An adequate ethnography of communication should not confine itself exclusively to the analysis of choice within verbal repertoires.

It should also ... specify those conditions under which members of the society regularly decide to refrain from verbal behavior altogether. (p. 305)

The study of silence is important for at least two reasons. First, the use of silence can be seen as one among a range of strategies or options that can itself be part of, or constitute, a way of speaking (see Braithwaite, 1990). Like talk, silence is another symbolic resource that can be used by any member of a culture. Second, one of the basic building blocks of communicative competence, both linguistic and cultural, is knowing when *not* to speak in a particular culture. Therefore, to know when, where, and how to be silent, and to understand the meanings attached to silence, is to gain a keen insight into the fundamental structure of communication in that society (Braithwaite, 1990). Silence is not just the absence of behavior. As Samarin (1965) noted, "Silence can have meaning. Like the zero in mathematics, it is an absence with a function" (p. 115).

Each culture maintains its own norms concerning acceptable as well as unacceptable or aberrant speech behavior in social interactions. Values regarding appropriate behavior are often reflected in proverbs or popular sayings. In Finland, for instance, some proverbs equate talkativeness with foolishness, such as "A loud voice shows an empty head" (Sallinen-Kuparinen, 1986, p. 23)

The Japanese, another culture that respects silence, similarly cautions against excessive speaking: "The cat that does not mew catches rats" (Klopf, 1995, p. 17). In many parts of the world, silence is power; in some cultures, it is even more powerful than the spoken word. Inagaki's (1985) survey revealed that, out of 3,600 Japanese participants, 82% agreed with the saying "Kuchi wa wazawai no moto" (i.e., "It is what people say that gets them into trouble."). One of the factors that has predisposed the Japanese people to be less positive toward verbal communication is their preference for not speaking unnecessarily. Since ancient times, Japanese people have believed in kotodama, which literally means "the sprit living in words" (see Hara, 2000). This folk belief creates the superstition that a soul dwelling in words has the supernatural power to make anything happen simply by verbalizing it. Even in modern Japan, meaningless or careless utterance is not respected and valued. Silence as sensitivity, which refers to the ability of reading others' minds intuitively, is indispensable to harmonious communication in Japan. In Ishii's (1984) *enryo-sasshi* (modesty-sharp guesswork) communication, this skill is characterized as an aspect of Zen philosophy and Confucianism. This model theorizes an interpersonal communication process in which two individuals (Japanese in particular) are not explicit or direct in their interaction but, rather, are empathetically reserved, cautious, and respectful of the other's inner worlds with empathy (Bruneau, 1995). As for Zen Buddhist practices, Tsujimura (1987) argues that the main characteristics of Japanese nonverbal communication are *ishin-denshin* (communicating mind to mind), taciturnity, and reading *kuuki* (constraint of mood), which are based on Zen philosophy. A skillful user of silence is regarded to be a mature and competent communicator in Japan.

According to Carbaugh (1993), talk is the major means for connecting people, but talk can also separate people who otherwise are naturally connected. In mainstream American culture, as in most Western cultures, connections between people are created and re-created through talk. Silence between strangers or between casual acquaintances can be perceived as embarrassing, even threatening. In some native American cultures, however, talk may be seen as a threat to the connection between human beings (Carbaugh, 1993).

Neither sociolinguistics nor the study of cognitive and strategic communication has so far ascribed much importance to subtle communication strategies such as remaining silent. Silence in communicative settings is often equated with inaction. Perceptual and/or cultural bias has led researchers to focus on more explicit communicative behaviors (e.g., verbal statements) while treating silence as merely background. The important position of silence in the total framework of human communication has been largely overlooked (see Saville-Troike, 1985). For instance, the list of requesting strategies studied to date is derived from the assumption that people will give some *overt* indication when they try to comply with a request. But some people commonly avoid direct requests if at all possible.

There is a large body of literature documenting cultural differences in communication (Gudykunst & Ting-Toomey, 1988) and beliefs about talk (Giles et al., 1992). Since the time of the Ancient Greeks, Westerners have tended to celebrate talk and rhetoric, construing them as vehicles for the discovery and expression of truth. In addition, there seems to be an aversion to silence because people find it awkward and embarrassing. Silence tends to be interpreted variously as any one of the following: a lack of interest; an unwillingness to communicate; a sign of hostility, rejection, or interpersonal incompatibility; anxiety or shyness; or a lack of verbal skills (Giles et al., 1992).

In contrast, the East Asian tradition appears to value preserving the harmony of the social group more highly than expressing individuals' inner thoughts and negative feelings (Barnlund, 1989). Moreover, an array of Taoist sayings, such as "To be always talking is against nature" and "One who speaks does not know," provide attitudinal and behavioral guidelines for conversational styles (see Giles et al., 1992). Because of the belief that meaning can be sensed but not phrased, a talkative person is often considered insincere or a showoff. The Korean term *noon-chi* (tact) and the Japanese term *haragei* (wordless communication) capture the essence of East Asians' positive feelings toward communication without words. Confucius opposed eloquent and clever speech, advocated hesitancy over brilliance, and grounded his criticism of speech deeply within his philosophy of the ideal person. This Confucian attitude still persists widely in East Asia.

According to Tannen (1985), silence is the extreme manifestation of indirectness. If indirectness is a matter of saying one thing and meaning another, silence can be a matter of saying nothing and meaning something. I speculate that silence among interdependents often comes from being understood without putting one's meaning on record. Thus, understanding may result from empathy rather than from putting one's meaning into words. Interdependent cultural orientations might make it less likely for silence to be interpreted as a failure to meet social norms or personal expectations. Among high interdependents, in requesting contexts (and probably even more in re-requesting contexts), silence would not be perceived as incompatible with interpersonal rapport. Independents, however, may perceive silence as the failure of positive politeness (i.e., the need to be involved with others). Thus, individuals with highly independent self-construals would attribute a low value to silence.

The significance of silence is derived by convention within particular speech communities and conveys some information on cultural norms for, and attitudes toward, loquacity (Saville-Troike, 1985). Attitudes toward silence and speech are among the internalized social and cultural standards by which people measure their own (and others') communicative performance. Such norms are used to interpret whether silence in requesting and re-requesting situations means agreement, denial, avoidance, or a violation of norms. Among interdependents, wordless communication can convey rich meaning—meaning may often be missed by independents.

Saville-Troike (1985) argues that children seem to talk more when they are being socialized into societies (e.g., America and Britain) that place a high value on individual achievement; they talk less when they are being raised in societies (e.g., China and Japan) in which family and group achievement are more valued. The latter perspective expects children to be seen but not heard. Special attention is needed to distinguish between and properly interpret the different meanings of silences. Stereotyping and misunderstanding occur when the characteristic uses of silence by members of one speech community are interpreted according to the norms and rules assumed by members of another. Thus, learning appropriate rules for silence is also part of the acculturation process for people attempting to develop communicative competence in a second language and culture (Saville-Troike, 1985).

An adequate description and interpretation of the process of communication requires that we understand the structure, meaning, and functions of silence as well as of verbal strategies. Recently, Kim, Shin, and Cai (1998) posed two hypotheses in their study:

1. For both first- and second-attempt requests, independents would perceive silent communicative acts as less effective than would interdependents.

2. For both first- and second-attempt requests, independents would perceive silent communicative acts as less likely to be used than would interdependents.

The researchers found that the more pronounced one's independent cultural orientations, the less prone one is to remain silent in either the first- or the second-attempt requests.

We should view silence as a valid object of investigation bounded by cultural orientations. Further, a total theory of communication should be concerned with the ways in which these two modes of behavior (verbal strategy and silence) are related to the culture and social organization of a speech community. Deep cultural differences affect our interpretations of silence and even our research agenda.

Intergroup communication is fraught with potential misattribution and intergroup miscommunication (Brislin, 1981). The source of misunderstanding can be silence just as often as it is speech, especially when those involved are unaware of differences in their beliefs (or implicit theories) about silence. Because the meaning of silence is derived by convention within particular speech communities, cross-cultural misunderstandings can result. Prior research on conversational strategy selection tended to ignore the fact that not saying anything (the opposite of speech) can be a legitimate conversational strategy. Neither sociolinguistics nor the study of cognitive/strategic communication has so far afforded much theoretical attention to silence.

One tends to use one's own norms in interpreting others' speech and deducing their intentions. Norms of interpretation are involved when a hearer infers whether a silence in a communication situation means agreement, denial, avoidance, or a violation of norms. Stereotyping and misunderstanding occur when the patterned use of silence by members of one speech community is interpreted according to the norms and rules held by members of another. Therefore, miscommunication arises among speakers of different backgrounds. Moreover, judgments are made not about how others speak but about their personalities (Tannen, 1985). Silence among interdependents can constitute a silent speech act and become the message itself or part of it. In many cases, it can be the silence itself that contains the most important cues (which independents can easily miss) for the meaning of the message. Special attention must be paid to the range of possible silences, and particular care is required to interpret them properly.

In reviewing past research on refusal strategies, Ifert (2000) argues that refusals may occur without any explicit verbal messages, as suggested by Burroughs, Kearney, and Plax's (1989) resistance strategy of avoidance, Alberts, Miller-Rassulo, & Hecht's (1991) leaving strategy, and Kim, Shin, et al.'s (1998) silence strategy. Other than limited mention in taxonomies such as those noted above, nonverbal or silent resistance methods have been largely ignored by communication scholars (Ifert, 2000).

To summarize, we need to focus attention on a relatively neglected component of human communication—silence. Silent communicative acts carry their own illocutionary force, so we need to consider silence as a communicative strategy in the analysis of speech events. Cultural differences affect the interpretations of silence in interaction and even affect our research agenda.

14

Models of Acculturative Communication Competence

Who Bears the Burden of Adaptation?

When in Rome, do as the Romans do.

— St. Ambrose, *Advice to St. Augustine*, 387 A.D.

Virtue and vice, happiness and misery, are much more equally distributed to nations than those are permitted to suppose who have never been from home, and who believe . . . that their residence is the center of the world, of light, of privilege, and of enjoyment.

— Delano, *Narratives of Voyages*, 1817, p. 256

There are two broad domains of interests in intercultural communication: (a) the comparative examination of communicative similarities and differences across cultures and (b) the communicative adaptations made by individuals when they move between cultures. The former, the preeminent line of inquiry in cross-cultural communication, attempts to link variations in communication behavior to cultural contexts; the latter, a relatively new area, seeks to understand changes in individual communication behavior that are related to the process of acculturation and communicative implications. It is the latter domain that I am concerned with in this chapter.

Immersion in a new culture often challenges one's beliefs, values, self-view, and worldview (Cross, 1995). Acculturation is a multifaceted process that refers to individual changes over time in identification, attitudes, values, and behavioral norms through contact with different cultures (Berry & Kim, 1988). At a fundamental level, acculturation involves alterations in the individual's sense of self. Even though cultural identity is an important aspect of acculturation, there are few studies on how it influences people's self-concepts and their styles of communication.

Individualism is typically analyzed as the critical element of Western society (Guisinger & Blatt, 1994; Markus & Kitayama, 1998). Lebra (1992) contends that individualism is a function of a Cartesian categorization system that draws a sharp distinction between the self and others. Similarly, in defining the self, self-identification is often dichotomized as either individualist or collectivist. Cross-cultural psychological research on the self has also commonly classified the self as either individualist— (the self as a bounded and unique object) or as collectivist—(the self as an ensembled object, merged into the common life of the nation group (see Oyserman, 1993).

The self-other dichotomy remains a highly influential paradigm in the West. Certainly, the polarization of categories such as self and other, autonomy and relationship, all contribute to a devaluation of connectedness, making it more difficult to find a way of connection that is empowering for all concerned (Klein, 1995). For instance, minorities have struggled to define and counter the polarized oppositions on which this marginalization is often based. The growing proportion of minority group members in the United States and other countries has resulted in an increasing concern with issues of pluralism, discrimination, and racism (Phinney, 1990).

Presumed unidimensionality of the self-construals is used to justify one-way adjustment, mostly on the part of the minority. Recently, Ryder, Alden, and Paulhus (2000) compared the unidimensional and bidimensional models of acculturation in the contexts of personality, self-identity, and adjustment. Two main predictions of the unidimensional model received little support—namely, that two separate measured dimensions would be (a) highly negatively correlated and (b) inversely related to other external variables. The results of their studies demonstrate that the bidimensional model constitutes a broader and more valid framework for understanding acculturation. They conclude that the unidimensional model offers an incomplete and often misleading rendering of the acculturation process. In an initial effort to exemplify the complexities faced by everyone in coming to terms with these multiple, sometimes competing cultural meanings and practices, I will explore the notions of cultural identity and acculturative communication competence. Because of lack of research in this area, my discussion of acculturative communication competence is speculative in nature. I have, however, been able to identify several characteristics that I hypothesize are central to being a socially competent person.

In the next section, I discuss the central role of communication processes in cross-cultural adaptations of individuals. First, I cover the assimilation theory, which states that identity acquisition is complete only after an individual becomes a member of the dominant group and acquires host communication competence. Next, I emphasize the alternation model, which posits that an individual is able to gain competence within two or more cultures without losing her or his cultural identity or having to choose one culture over the other. Finally, I contrast host communication competence with bicultural communication competence.

❖ ASSIMILATION MODEL: "MARGINAL MAN [*SIC*]" PERSPECTIVE

Assimilation refers to the process in which a member of one culture loses her or his original cultural identity as the person acquires a new identity in a second culture (LaFromboise, Coleman, & Gerton, 1993, p. 396). The English word *assimilate* comes from the Latin *assimulare*, meaning to make similar. The goal of the assimilation process is to complete absorption into the new culture. The assimilation model sees the acquisition of another cultural identity as a one-way process. In other words, if an individual embarks on the process of acquiring a new identity, she cannot go back to her previous cultural group. For instance, assimilation in America is often viewed as gaining membership into the mainstream Western group (Feagin & Feagin, 1996).

For nearly a century, the most prominent image of the incorporation of immigrants has been that of the melting pot. In 1925, playwright Israel Zangwill made an influential statement of this optimistic idea in *The Melting Pot* (I have reprinted this quote in its original, gendered, form):

> America is God's Crucible, the great Melting-pot where all races of Europe are melting and re-forming! Here you stand, good folks, think I, when I see them at Ellis Island, here you stand in your fifty groups, with your fifty languages and histories, and your fifty blood hatreds and rivalries. But you won't be long like that, brothers, for these are the fires of God. . . . A fig for your feuds and vendettas! Germans and Frenchmen, Irishmen and Englishmen, Jews and Russians—into the Crucible with you all! God is making the American. (p. 33)

Zangwill's idealistic image of a crucible that melts 50 divergent groups to form a truly new American blend symbolizes a mutual adaptation process in which old and new groups freely blend together on a more or less equal basis. Yet actual intergroup adaptation has often involved more conflict than Zangwill envisioned. Also conspicuously absent from this melting-pot image are Americans of color, such as African, Asian, Latino, and Native Americans (see Feagin & Feagin, 1996).

In America, assimilation theories of identity acquisition are often applied to subordinate groups attempting to fit into the dominant group. Assimilation does not allow for alternate identities but, rather, forces all to adhere to what the dominant group wants. When subordinate groups do not adhere to the dominant group's characteristics, the subordinate group is often blamed for not successfully assimilating and becoming American (Feagin & Feagin, 1996). Assimilationists have designated this identity as *marginality*.

The theory of marginality traces back to Stonequist's (1935) theory of the "marginal man [*sic*]." According to Stonequist, wherever there are cultural transitions and conflicts, there are marginal personalities. A marginal person is an individual living in two different cultures that are not merely different—they are antagonistic. This theory views identity in a linear sense. Either individuals attain group membership in the dominant group or they are left with nothing. When a marginal person participates in the dominant group culture and fails to assimilate, it is theorized that this person experiences an extreme type of marginality. This extreme marginality is characterized by social psychological problems, rendering the individual a delinquent in society. This dilemma leaves the marginal person angry at the original identity that she no longer identifies with while hating the dominant group because she was not accepted. In sum, marginality is a label that has been used to describe those who are unable to assimilate into the dominant culture.

According to Stonequist (1935), a marginal person is one who is poised in psychological uncertainty between two (or more) social worlds. Stonequist (1935) indicated that the marginal person is a product of the meeting of two races and/or cultures. The marginal person is one who becomes associated with both and yet does not wholly belong to either. The personality characteristics of marginal individuals include ambivalence, excessive self-consciousness, restlessness, irritability, moodiness, lack of self-confidence, and so on. Words have been derisively used to describe marginal people; terms such as "apple," "banana," "coconut," and "oreo" reflect the negative stereotype often applied to people who have intimate relationships with two or more cultures.

Assimilation assumes an ongoing process of absorption into the culture perceived as dominant or more desirable. Gordon (1964) proposed a unidimensional assimilation model to describe the cultural changes undergone by immigrants. Across their life spans, immigrants are portrayed moving along a continuum. At one pole is the maintenance of the immigrant culture; at the other pole is an adoption of the host culture, usually at the cost of losing the heritage culture.

Ruiz (1981) emphasized that the goal of the assimilation process is to become socially accepted by members of the target culture as a person moves along the continuum. In the United States, much social theorizing has emphasized assimilation, the more or less orderly adaptation of a migrating group to the ways and institutions of an established host group. The assimilation perspective, broadly defined, continues to be the primary theoretical framework for sociological research on racial and ethnic inequalities.

The assimilation model focuses on the acquisition of the majority group's culture by members of the minority group and assumes a hierarchical relationship between the two cultures. One of the distinguishing characteristics of the acculturation process is its involuntary nature. Most often, the member of the minority group is forced to learn the new culture (and its preferred communication styles) to survive economically. The assimilation ideology includes the expectation that immigrants will adopt the public values of the host country (Bourhis, Moise, Perreault, & Senecal, 1997). The assimilation ideology expects immigrants to abandon their own cultural and linguistic distinctiveness for the sake of adopting the culture and values of the dominant group, which constitutes the core of the nation state.

Up until the middle of the 20th century, the assimilation ideology prevailed in the United States; subsequent waves of immigrants were expected to lose their respective ethnocultural distinctiveness for the sake of adopting the mainstream values of the American way of life (e.g., rugged individualism, capitalistic entrepreneurship). According to LaFromboise et al. (1993), the following three dangers can make the assimilation process very stressful:

- It is possible that individuals attempting to assimilate will be rejected by the second culture.
- Individuals attempting to assimilate are likely to be rejected by members of their original group.
- A high amount of stress is associated with learning and becoming a member of the second group.

It is common to see oppressed individuals, especially members of indigenous groups, participating in the Western market system to survive economically. However, these members may ultimately be held back because of their ethnic and cultural membership.

The common assumption, exemplified by the positions of Park (1928) and Stonequist (1935), is that living in two cultures is psychologically undesirable because managing the complexity of dual reference points generates ambiguity, identity confusion, and normlessness. However, the progress of humankind depends on the interface of cultures. The marginal individual can be seen as the product of this interaction; such an individual can be described as a "cosmopile," a wiser person than those who are familiar with only one culture. In other words, even though the process toward bicultural identity is psychologically uncomfortable, it has long-term benefits for the individual and society and the achievement of human potential for individuals.

Stonequist (1935) contended that marginality has certain social and psychological properties. The social properties include factors of migration, racial difference, and situations in which two or more cultures share the same geographic area, with one culture maintaining a higher status than another. According to this view, the mulattos (people with one white and one black parent) or American Indian children are typically viewed as marginal individuals. However, this conceptualization stresses culture conflict as the basis of the personality characteristics of the marginal person. Group antagonisms, therefore, become the source of the personality difficulties noted.

❖ ALTERNATION MODEL:
   BICULTURAL PERSON PERSPECTIVE

A vital step in the development of an effective partnership among people involves moving away from the assumptions of the linear model of cultural identity. Ramirez (1983) defined *biculturalism* as an integration of the competencies and sensitivities associated with two cultures within a single person so that the person can identify with two or more cultures and participate in them without conflict or maladjustment. *Acculturation* refers to "changes in cultural patterns toward those of the host society" (Gordon, 1964, p. 71). The concept of biculturalism is closely related to the concept of acculturation, but biculturalism assumes that acculturation can take place without a corresponding loss in ancestral cultural patterns (Buriel, 1994).

Recently, Ryder et al. (2000) demonstrated that the bidimensional model constitutes a broader and more valid framework for understanding acculturation. The continued use of a unidimensional approach could provide an incomplete, even misleading, picture of acculturation and acculturative communication competence. Unidimensional models are based on the implicit assumption that change in cultural identity takes place along a single continuum over the course of time. More specifically, acculturating individuals are seen as being in a process of relinquishing the attitudes, values, and communication behaviors of their culture of origin while simultaneously adopting those of the new society. Unidimensional instruments of acculturative communication competence would be unable to distinguish a bicultural individual who strongly identifies with both reference groups and their communication behaviors from one who does not strongly identify with either group. Bicultural individuals with bicultural communication competence would end up at the midpoint of a unidimensional scale. In theoretical terms, the unidimensional perspective fails to consider alternatives to assimilation, such as the emergence of integrated or bicultural identities (Ryder et al., 2000).

Most researchers take for granted that Mexican Americans lose touch with their native Mexican culture more and more the longer they live in America. Some researchers, however, interpret this process of cultural erosion as corresponding with increasing integration with Euro-American culture. This line of reasoning assumes that Mexican American and Euro-American cultures are on opposite ends of a single cultural continuum (see Buriel, 1994, for further discussion of this issue). In the unidimensional model, movement away from the independent pole necessarily brings one closer to the interdependent pole. Consequently, the degree of integration with one cultural orientation is negatively related to the degree of integration with the other.

The alternation model assumes that it is possible for an individual to know and understand two different cultures (LaFromboise et al., 1993). It also supposes that an individual can alter her or his behavior to fit a particular social context. It is possible and acceptable to participate in two different cultures or to use two different languages, perhaps for different purposes, by alternating one's behavior according to the situation. Furthermore, the alternation model assumes that it is possible for an individual to have a sense of belonging in two cultures without compromising her sense of cultural identity.

The essential strength of the alternation model is that it focuses on the cognitive and affective processes that allow an individual to withstand the negative impact of acculturative stress. Several authors have noted the additive element of biculturality or multiculturality, suggesting that the acculturation process need not substitute new cultural values for old. Rather, acculturation may add new behaviors that allow for cultural-frame-of-reference shifting (Dyal & Dyal, 1981). Saltzman's (1986) "150 percent person" represents just such a culturally expanded individual. Bennett (1993) claims that two potential responses to living on cultural margins are *encapsulated marginality* and *constructive marginality*. The encapsulated (trapped) marginal is a person who is buffeted by conflicting cultural loyalties and who is unable to construct a unified identity. In contrast, by maintaining control of choice and control of the construction of boundaries, a person may become a constructive (bicultural) marginal. A constructive marginal is a person who is able to construct context intentionally and consciously for the purpose of creating her or his own identity. The goal of the next section is to develop a deeper understanding of the nature of bicultural and marginal identities by focusing on dimensional views of cultural identities and corresponding acculturative communication competence.

❖ HOST COMMUNICATION COMPETENCE:
ONE-WAY ASSIMILATION

Traditionally, it has been claimed that the power of individual strangers to change the host environment is minuscule when compared with the pervasive influence the host culture has on them. Clearly, a reason for the essentially one-sided change is the difference between the size of the population sharing a given stranger's original culture and that of the population sharing the host culture. To the extent the dominant power of the host culture controls the daily survival and functioning of strangers, it presents a coercive pressure on them to adapt (Gudykunst & Kim, 1997).

Consequently, according to Gudykunst and Kim (1997), strangers are almost exclusively the ones who make adjustments. Thus, the direction of acculturative change in strangers is toward assimilation—that is, a state of a high degree of acculturation into the host milieu and a high degree of deculturation of the original culture. It is a state that reflects (a) a maximum convergence of strangers' internal conditions with those of the natives and (b) a minimum maintenance of the original cultural habits. Indeed, studies of historical change in immigrant communities have demonstrated the long-term assimilative trend of the cross-cultural adaptation process, particularly across generations (e.g., Kim, 1988).

Strangers acquire and internalize new learning (acculturation) as well as suspend and unlearn some of the old practices (deculturation) so they can move in the direction of an increased functional fitness and ultimately into a state of assimilation in the host society (Gudykunst & Kim, 1997, p. 352). Consequently, the cross-cultural adaptation process is essentially a process of achieving the communication necessary for strangers to be functional in the host society (Kim, 1988). The assumption of most prior research in this area is that it is the strangers who need to become competent in the host communication systems (see Fox, 1997). The cross-cultural adaptation process was said to involve a continuous interplay of deculturation and acculturation that brings about change in strangers in the direction of assimilation, the highest degree of adaptation theoretically conceivable. It is by that one-way process that strangers are resocialized into a new culture so they can attain an increasing compatibility and functional fitness.

Underlying the assimilation process is the notion of host communication competence (HCC). HCC is used to describe the changes in communicative styles that immigrants make to adapt to the dominant host culture so that they will be considered a rightful member of the majority and will fit into the existing social structure of the host society (Gudykunst & Kim, 1997). Through this prism, communication problems are attributed to the immigrants themselves, who are held responsible for their failure or success in assimilating to the host society. This model implies a one-way change process in which the immigrants assimilate and are absorbed into the host society.

The assimilation theory and corresponding host communication competence state that identity acquisition is complete only after an individual becomes a member of the dominant group and acquires host communication competence. Just as natives have acquired their cultural patterns through interaction with others, strangers over time acquire the new communication patterns through participating in the host communication activities. Through prolonged and varied experiences in communication, strangers gradually learn and internalize some of the cognitive, affective, and behavioral communication patterns operating in the host society (Kim, 1988). The acquired host communication competence, in turn, facilitates their participation in the host social communication processes. The acquired communicative capabilities serve as a set of adaptive tools to assist strangers in satisfying their personal and social needs. Fox (1997) argues that "such an approach implies an orientation not to reaching a mutual understanding (two-way process), but rather to 'successful' change on the part of only one of the participants. This creates a disequilibrium in the relationship between participants" (pp. 91-92). Implicitly, the assimilation model and the corresponding HCC does situate immigrant groups within the lower echelons of the social hierarchy found in most stratified societies (Bourhis et al., 1997).

❖ BICULTURAL COMMUNICATION COMPETENCE: A FLUID CULTURAL ALTERNATION

Biculturalism and consequent bicultural communication competence (BCC) place less emphasis on assimilating and more emphasis on making choices between the communication patterns of two or more cultures or groups. The implications of a bicultural perspective in identity acquisition is that it allows for a more fluid cultural exchange between groups. Rather than placing groups in a hierarchy of dominance, the idea behind a bicultural viewpoint is that the characteristics of a group can be used in a positive way. Rather than dictating to an indigenous person or stranger what she or he needs to do to survive, a bicultural perspective begins by evaluating life from the indigenous group's perspective. Biculturalism allows culture to be a choice rather than something that requires purging old practices and beliefs from the self for individuals to survive.

Biculturalism or multiculturalism views identity acquisition among different cultures and ethnic groups as dynamic. Unlike assimilation, the bicultural perspective is a blending of lifestyles, values, and skills. Individuals keep their ethnic and cultural membership without having to assimilate completely into the dominant culture. Biculturalism views identity as a multifunctional choice. Identity becomes a dynamic entity, not a linear equation like assimilation. According to biculturalism, identity formation and corresponding communication styles in the context of contact between different groups are always changing to fit the needs of dual group membership.

As previously discussed in this chapter, a corresponding theory to the idea of bicultural communication competence is the alternation model of cultural identity (LaFromboise et al., 1993). This model states that an individual can alter her or his behavior to fit a particular social context. Based on the idea of the alternation model, bicultural individuals come to a deeper understanding and appreciation of their as well as others' communication styles. These theories also acknowledge that these groups will participate in dominant group activities while retaining positive self-concept (see Table 14.1).

The usefulness of a bicultural self-perspective has been noted by several authors (Bennett, 1993; Kim et al., 1996; Oyserman, 1993). A person who is simultaneously maintaining high independent as well as high interdependent self-construals (i.e., someone who is bicultural) may be able to modify her or his behavior appropriately and successfully when moving from one culture to another. This notion of adaptability seems to coincide with the "rhetorically sensitive person" (Hart & Burks, 1972), who tries to accept role taking as part of the human condition, attempts to avoid stylized verbal behavior, and is characteristically willing to undergo the strain of adaptation.

A vital step in the development of an equal partnership for minorities in the academia, social, and economic life of the United States involves moving away from assumptions of the linear model of cultural acquisition and corresponding host communication competence. In this chapter, I reviewed the literature on the psychological impact of being bicultural or multicultural. Obstacles of being bicultural or multicultural are reviewed and summarized to uncover their implications for bicultural communication competence.

The implications of the notion of different self-systems (e.g., independent and interdependent construals) are substantial. In this chapter, the manifestations of differing self-structures were examined in the areas of acculturation. Individuals who experience acculturation must deal with their new circumstances in some way. The traditional classification of acculturating groups (immigrants, refugees, sojourners, etc.) can be fruitfully reconceptualized in terms of changes in their self-system (self-construals). Changes in self-system (self-construals) among different acculturating groups can also provide new insights into the types of acculturating groups and their differing experiences of stress. We need to further investigate the specific ways in which self-construals may determine the flexibility in actual conversational strategy choices across different cultural settings.

Table 14.1   Two Models of Acculturative Communication Competence:
Host Communication Competence (HCC) vs. Bicultural
Communication Competence (BCC)

Focus	HCC	BCC
Model of Culture Acquisition	Linear, accommodation model: Maximum convergence of strangers' internal conditions with those of the hosts and a minimum maintenance of the original cultural habits.	Alternation model: Individuals keep their ethnic and cultural membership without having to assimilate completely into the dominant culture. Biculturalism views identity as a choice and as multifunctional. Identity becomes a dynamic entity, not a linear equation like assimilation.
Burden of successful communication	Strangers are almost exclusive bearers of the burden of making adjustments (one-sided change).	Both the host and the stranger share the burden of adjustment.
Perceived freedom of choice	Coercive pressure on strangers to adapt to the host culture	Self-conscious attempt to preserve and create ethnic identity
Ultimate goal in cultural identity	Remove oneself from the old culture and acquire the new to survive	Cultural identity as choice depending on situation and context
Assumptions about group status	Assumption of dominant and subordinate group. The power of an individual stranger to change the host environment is minuscule.	Potential for equal partnership
Nature of Communication Competence	Identity acquisition is complete only after an individual becomes a member of the dominant group and acquires host communication competence. Acquires new cultural patterns through participating in the host communication activities. Stranger is required to acquire the communicative capacity that enables her to carry out behaviors in accordance with the host cultural patterns.	Identity formation in the context of contact between different groups is constantly changing to fit the needs of dual group membership.

I would like to point out the desirability of integrating individuality and social relatedness (e.g., Guisinger & Blatt, 1994), an achievement actually realized by many people in American society. In summary, the way that identity change is conceptualized fundamentally affects the notion of acculturative communication competence and can ultimately hurt or enhance an individual's journey of adequate identity acquisition. Many of the previous models, such as assimilation and marginality, base their views on a Western dualistic perspective. A bicultural or multicultural model that allows for membership in two or more cultures and corresponding bicultural or multicultural communication competence represents a shift away from the traditional model of identity acquisition (assimilation and corresponding host communication competence). This model may seem merely Utopian. However, recent research and thinking show that such a synthesis may indeed become reality.

III

Toward a Bidimensional Model of Cultural Identity

At this point, readers will appreciate how strongly the development of human communication theory in the United States has been based on individualistic orientations and empirical research involving subjects representing the mainstream U.S. culture. There are common patterns underlying the preferred styles of human communication and functioning in the United States. The low external validity of such research and theory has been recognized by many researchers, but the proposed solution to the problem has frequently consisted only of recommendations to examine other samples of the population to test generalizability. According to Brokner and Chen (1996), in evaluating whether people from different cultures vary in their psychological make-up, researchers would be well advised to do more than perform simple cross-cultural comparisons of the mean level of the psychological dimensions in question. For instance, much work has been done to describe and explain cultural similarities and differences in individuals' verbal communication styles (e.g., cross-cultural comparisons of mean differences in communication apprehension). However, such inquiry is, in Kuhn's (1970) opinion, wholly within paradigm. That is, it primarily expands or elaborates on the accepted paradigm rather than providing a significant challenge to underlying assumptions. Greater scientific gain may lie in the breaking of a paradigm.

The evolution of a society is closely linked to changes in the value system that underlies all its manifestations. The values that a society lives by determine its worldview and its scientific enterprise. Once a collective set of values and goals has emerged, it constitutes the framework of the society' perceptions, insights, and choices for innovation and social adaptation. As the cultural value system changes, often in response to environmental challenges, new patterns of cultural evolution will emerge. For instance, the pluralistic cultural environment in many organizations today can be complicated by the myth of value-free organizational communication. According to Fine (1991),

> Theories about communicating in organizations have most often been based on the assumption of [cultural] homogeneity—an assumption that is generally left unstated. That assumption is not surprising, since organizations in the U.S. historically have been homogeneous, especially within the managerial rank. White males have dominated not only corporate life, but also academic ranks. Thus, organizational theories have generally been created by white men based on the experiences of other white men. (p. 260)

Consistent with the continuing emphasis on white male norms in organizational communication, American writers have traditionally defined miscommunication in organizations as failure to be understood; failure to be authentic, honest, and disclosive; or failure to establish an open and clear dialogue. Openness addresses the linguistic choices associated with being more or less open—that is, how clear or ambiguous a communication strategy may be (Eisenberg & Witten, 1987). Recently, however, some writers (Eisenberg, 1984; Eisenberg & Phillips, 1991; Eisenberg & Witten, 1987; Pascale & Athos, 1981) have pointed out that the ideology of openness might be a cultural assumption, possibly a Western (i.e., mainland United States) ideology.

Eisenberg (1984; Eisenberg & Witten, 1987) claims that one of the major reasons organizational participants and theorists uncritically endorse open communication is an implicit belief in the sharing metaphor. This metaphor "implies that effective communication requires the cultivation of shared cognitions and emotions between interactants" (Eisenberg & Phillips, 1991, p. 252). The tendency toward openness models of communication is uniquely associated with the mainland United States and reflects a desire to resolve differences rather than to learn to live with them (Eisenberg & Phillips, 1991). Many managers place excessive trust in increasing the clarity of communication between people (Pascale & Athos, 1981). This philosophy, however, may not lead to productive communication within a predominantly interdependent workforce. On the other hand, within a predominantly independent workforce, ambiguous and implicit messages may not be productive. In the end, any acceptable definition of effective communication must be relative to the social context—worldview, set of values, and point in time (Eisenberg & Phillips, 1991).

The study of values is thus of paramount importance for all social sciences, including human communication; there can be no such thing as a value-free social science. As Capra (1982) put it,

> Social scientists who consider the question of values "non-scientific" and think they are avoiding it are attempting the impossible. Any "value-free" analysis of social phenomena is based on the tacit assumption of an existing value system that is implicit in the selection and interpretation of data. By avoiding the issue of values, then, social scientists are not more scientific but, on the contrary, less scientific, because they neglect to state explicitly the assumptions underlying their theories (p. 190).

Capra (1982) also argues,

> In transcending the Cartesian division, modern physics has not only invalidated the classical ideal of an objective description of nature but has also challenged the myth of a value-free science. The patterns scientists observe in nature are intimately connected with the patterns of their minds; with their concepts, thoughts, and values. Thus the scientific results they obtain and the technological applications they investigate will be conditioned by their frame of mind. Although much of their detailed research will not depend explicitly on their value system, the larger paradigm within which this research is pursued will be never be value-free. (p. 87)

Theories of European-American communication behavior have been extremely influenced by the prevailing ideology of a unidimensional model of cultural identity. They have often viewed the self as in tension with, or even in opposition to, the collective. The source of all important behavior is typically found in the unique configuration of internal attributes—thoughts, feelings, motives, abilities—that form the bounded, autonomous whole. Because of this ideology, two areas that have been underanalyzed and undertheorized are (a) the ways in which the self is, in fact, quite interdependent with the collective and (b) the communicative consequences of this fact. It is necessary for theorists to go beyond theories that are directly shaped by the cultural ideal of individualism and to consider a broader view of the self (see Markus & Kitayama, 1994).

To underscore how cultural frameworks structure both everyday and scientific understandings of human communication, in the next two chapters, I will review the literature on the model of cultural identity. Emphasis is given to the bidimensional model, which posits that individuals are able to gain competence within two or more cultures without losing their cultural identity or having to choose one cultural identity over the other. Then, I present a model outlining bicultural or multicultural identities in contrast with culture-typed identities.

15

The Sources of Dualism

Mechanistic Cartesian Worldview

Thought has always worked through opposition. Through dual hierarchical oppositions.... Everywhere (where) an ordering intervenes, a law organizes what is thinkable by oppositions (dual, irreconcilable, or sublatable dialectical).

— Cixous, *Sorties*, 1997, p. 91

In Part II of this book, I reviewed literature that shows a dramatic divergence in psychological functioning and communicative behavior between independent and interdependent selves. I focused on some of the phenomena that communication theorists have been most concerned with and what they have regarded as universal. In my discussion, I take the approach of cultural psychology. This approach assumes that people's cognitive, emotional, motivational, and behavioral processes are shaped through their engagement in a cultural world. The psyche, then, is not a separate, autonomous set of processes; it exists and functions only in close conjunction with the culture (Fiske, Kitayama, Markus, & Nisbett, 1998). In this chapter, I discuss how the field itself has been influenced by dichotomous culture-typed identities. This has implications for individuals' identities as well as for scientific endeavor.

The use of dichotomies is a heuristic device popular in the West, especially in psychological descriptions of individuals. A host of exclusive descriptive categories, such as extroversion or introversion, emotion or cognition, speech or silence, have been used frequently in personality descriptions. Such dichotomous categories are also common in characterizations of nations, cultures, and cultural orientations. Although this device is convenient, it produces stereotypical and distorted pictures of complex social reality (see Sinha & Tripathi, 1994).

American (and Western) psychology, both reflecting and reinforcing the individualistic Western cultural ethos, has drawn a clear boundary between self and nonself. Further, because much work is actually done in cultural contexts that are extremely different from the West, sharp polarities predominate in the cross-cultural discourse on the self. When an entire culture or society is pigeonholed in dichotomous categories such as masculine/feminine, active/passive, or loose/tight, significant differences as well as subtle nuances are glossed over. Also, when cultures and individuals are presented in black-or-white terms, not only does this cloud our understanding, but it also inevitably leads to our making good/bad comparisons.

Western religious traditions have often supported or been used to support dualisms that pit (polarize) opposites against each other. The active-passive, reason-emotion, mind-body, and man-woman dyads are primary examples of these. Models that acknowledge differences without placing them in opposition are thus useful in overcoming various kinds of dualism. The dualistic impulse lies deep within the Western psyche. It stems in large measure from an unreflective reification of abstractions such as subject and object, self and other. Even the physical senses seem to be constructed along subject-object dichotomies, making dualistic perspectives so ingrained that it becomes difficult to imagine any other perspective (Klein, 1995).

One of the most powerful and influential images of the psyche is found in Plato's philosophy. In *Phaedrus*, the soul is pictured as a charioteer driving two horses, one representing the bodily passions and the other the higher emotions. This metaphor encapsulates the two approaches to consciousness—the biological and the spiritual—that have been pursued, without being reconciled, throughout Western philosophy and science. This conflict generated the "mind-body problem" that is reflected in many schools of social sciences (Capra, 1982). Furthermore, in defining gender identity, placing autonomy and relationship in theoretical opposition to each other is a core problem. Gilligan (1982) calls the ability to balance the needs of self and other the defining mark of moral maturity. It is possible to construct views of self in which one does not experience difference as irreconcilable or the existence of others as an a priori threat to getting what one wants.

The emphasis on rational thought in Western culture is epitomized in Descartes's celebrated statement "*Cogito, ergo sum*"—"I think, therefore I exist"—which equates existence itself with the rational mind rather than with the whole organism. Descartes's *cogito* made mind more certain for him than matter and led him to the conclusion that the two were separate and fundamentally different (Capra, 1982, p. 59). The Cartesian division between mind and matter has had a profound effect on Western thought.

According to Capra (1982), the division between mind and matter led to a view of the universe as a mechanical system consisting of separate objects, which in turn were reduced to fundamental building blocks whose properties and interactions were thought to completely determine all natural phenomena. This Cartesian view of nature was further extended to living organisms, which were regarded as machines constructed from separate parts. This view has served as a rationale for treating nature itself (the natural environment) as if it consisted of separate parts to be exploited by different interest groups.

Exploitation of nature has gone hand in hand with the subjugation of women; through the ages, women have often been identified with nature. From the earliest times, nature was seen not only as a kind and nurturing mother, but also as a wild and uncontrollable female. In prepatriarchal eras, nature's many aspects were identified with the numerous manifestations of the goddess. Under patriarchy, the benign image of nature changed to one of passivity, and the view of nature as wild and dangerous gave rise to the idea that she was to be dominated by man. At the same time, women were portrayed as passive and subservient to men. With the rise of Newtonian science, nature finally became a mechanical system that could be manipulated and exploited, together with the manipulation and exploitation of women (Capra, 1982).

These views (of man as dominating both nature and woman, and the belief in the superior role of the rational mind) have been supported and encouraged by the Judeo-Christian tradition, which adheres to the image of a male god, the personification of supreme reason and the source of ultimate power who rules the world from above by imposing his divine law on it (Capra, 1982). This mechanistic conception of the world is still the basis of most of the social sciences and continues to have a tremendous influence on scientific approaches and the view of self-identity.

❖ BIAS TOWARD YANG COMMUNICATION BEHAVIORS

Capra (1982) shows the framework for our exploration of cultural values and attitudes. He lists the associations of yang (masculine, expansive, demanding, aggressive, competitive, rational, analytic) and yin (feminine, contractive, conservative, responsive, cooperative, intuitive, synthesizing). Looking at this list of opposites, it is easy to see that Western society has consistently favored the yang over the yin—rational knowledge over intuitive wisdom, confrontation over avoidance, science over religion, competition over cooperation, and so on. This emphasis, supported by the patriarchal system, has led to a profound cultural imbalance that lies at the very root of our current state—an imbalance in our thoughts and feelings, our values and attitudes, and our social and political structures (see Capra, 1982). What is good is not yin or yang but the dynamic balance between the two; what is bad or harmful is imbalance.

An inviting parallel exists between our current ideal—the one-sided, centralized, yang-oriented value system—and the classic views of the physical world. Our current ideal of personhood is achieved through self-assertion by displaying yang communication behavior: confronting, demanding, talking, being assertive, being aggressive, being competitive, bragging, and expanding in human (communication) behavior. Integration is furthered by yin behavior: by being responsive, indirect, cooperative, intuitive, yielding, and showing awareness of and consideration for others' feelings. Both yin and yang (i.e., both the integrative and self-assertive tendencies) are necessary for harmonious social and ecological relationships.

The preference for yang-focused human communication is rooted in modern Western philosophical traditions, which have repeatedly made the case for natural self-interest or competitiveness of the individual. In the history of the modern West, ideas such as the natural rights and free will of each individual, or a market consisting of free members who choose to enter it via mutual consent and contract, have played a dominant role in forming many aspects of cultural practices, everyday discourses, and institutions (e.g., Bellah, Madsen, Sullivan, Swidler, & Tipton, 1985). As mentioned previously, the scientific study of human communication in the West has not been value-free; instead, it has tacitly incorporated this individualistic ontology into its theories and models. This is hardly surprising because the model of the person as an autonomous, independent, free entity is the model of most Western social sciences (including psychology, sociology, and economics) and of most of biology as well (Lillard, 1998). Western psychology has given sanction to self-determination, self-interest, and selfishness through its promotion of a particular set of models of human nature.

The mechanistic model of the person is only one (albeit an important and powerful one) of many variants of what researchers have called the independent view of the self. Modern European and North American communication theory is anchored in a philosophical legacy that includes capitalism and the Protestant ethic. These ideas include social contracts, rational profit making, and the actions of a free market made up of individual players (Kitayama & Markus, 1999). It is within the independent view of the self, encompassing all such variants, that the assorted yang-based communication patterns have historically been constructed.

This analysis helps explain why there exists an uncanny resemblance between many theories and focal issues of contemporary human communication and the individualistic model of the person. These theories and issues include a high premium placed on communication approach over avoidance (see Chapters 4 and 5), confrontation over withdrawal in conflict (Chapter 6), talk over silence (Chapter 13), tendency to presuppose fixed attitudes over situation in predicting behavior (Chapter 8), independence over conformity (Chapter 9), internal locus of control over external locus of control (Chapter 10), boastful self-disclosure over negative self-disclosure (Chapter 12), and many more. Although diverse and obviously different in detail, all these processes are consequences of having repeatedly participated in a cultural world framed in terms of the independent view of the self.

The Western culture has consistently promoted and rewarded the yang (the masculine or self-assertive elements of human nature and communication behavior) and has disregarded the yin (the feminine or intuitive aspects). This unnatural split in the human psyche is still with us. Under the patriarchal establishment, this split was projected every-where—into cosmic-spiritual realms, into human culture and customs, and into scientific perceptions of the mental and physical worlds. Our ultimate goal must be nothing less than a thorough redefinition of personhood and human nature. Reaching this objective will have a pro-found effect on the further evolution of our culture and on our under-standing of human communication.

❖   PARTICLE/WAVE PARADOX:
     SOME PRELIMINARY IMPLICATIONS
     OF PERSONHOOD FOR HUMAN COMMUNICATION

The experimental investigation of atoms at the beginning of the 20th century yielded sensational and totally unexpected results. The subatomic particles were nothing like the hard, solid objects of classi-cal physics. These subatomic units of matter turned out to have a dual aspect. Depending on how we look at them, they appear sometime as particles, sometimes as waves. This dual nature is also exhibited by light, which can take the form of either particles or electromagnetic waves. The particles of light, now called *photons*, were first called "quanta" by Einstein—hence the origin of the term "quantum theory" (see Capra, 1982).

This dual nature of matter and of light is very strange. It seems impossible to accept that something can be, at the same time, an entity confined to a very small volume (i.e., a particle) and an entity that is spread out over a large region of space (i.e., a wave). And yet this is exactly what physicists had to accept. For a better understanding of the relationship between this pair of classical concepts, Niels Bohr intro-duced the notion of complementarity. He considered the particle picture and the wave picture to be two complementary descriptions of the same reality, each of them only partly correct and having a limited range of application. Both pictures are needed to give a full account of the atomic reality. A notion quite similar to complementarity has already been used extensively in the Chinese conception of yin/yang; the yin and yang opposites are interrelated in a complementary way.

In contrast to the mechanistic Cartesian view of the world, the worldview emerging from modern physics can be characterized by words such as *organic* and *holistic*. The universe is no longer seen as a machine, made up of a multitude of objects, but has to be pictured as one indivisible, dynamic whole whose parts are essentially interrelated and can be understood only as patterns of a cosmic process (Capra, 1982).

Modern physics provides us with a different view of the physical world and, by analogy, a distinctively different perspective on personhood. Like the physicists, we will have to accept the fact that we must modify or even abandon some of our concepts when we expand the realm of our experience or field of study. Now that physicists have gone far beyond the dualistic model, it is time for the social sciences (including communication) to expand their underlying philosophies.

The nondualistic view of personhood is an appropriate basis not only for the behavioral sciences but also for the social sciences, including human communication. Many communication scholars have embraced conventional, stereotypic images of human nature and personhood. The situation is further aggravated because most communication scholars, in a misguided striving for scientific rigor, avoid explicitly acknowledging the value system on which their models are based and tacitly accept the highly imbalanced set of values that dominates Western culture. These values have led to an overemphasis on yang communication behavior: assertion over avoidance, independence over conformity, talk over silence, and so forth.

Acknowledgment of these values may well make it easier for communication scholars to go beyond the traditional dualistic framework when dealing with the full range of human communication behavior. Throughout this book, I have attempted to show the strikingly consistent preference for yang values, attitudes, and communication patterns. According to Chinese wisdom, none of the values is intrinsically bad, but by deprecating their polar opposites—that is, by focusing on the yang and investing it alone with moral virtue and political power—we have bought into being a biased view of human communication.

Sinha and Tripathi (1994), for instance, argue that the Indian culture and psyche are neither predominantly collectivistic nor individualistic but, rather, incorporate elements of both orientations. Although these elements often conflict with one another and appear to be mutually exclusive, Indians endeavor to combine both orientations in their preferred modes of behavior. They try to incorporate the best of both and frequently display a mixture of collectivistic and individualistic modes at the same time. Although prior work (Hofstede, 1980; Markus & Kitayama, 1991) has discussed independent-interdependent dimensions as unidimensional, recent evidence shows that they are two separate dimensions (see Rhee, Uleman, Lee, & Roman, 1995).

16

Dimensionality of Cultural Identity

One great splitting of the whole universe into two halves is made by each of us . . . We call the two halves by the same names, and . . . those names are "me" and "not me" respectively.

— James (1890, 1918). *The principles of psychology* (I, 289)

❖ UNIDIMENSIONAL MODEL OF SELF-CONSTRUALS

The trend toward viewing the self-concept as including social as well as personal identities is laudable. However, certain erroneous assumptions have been made regarding individuals' personal and social identities. One such assumption is the Aristotelian categorization of the mutually exclusive categories of A and not-A: If you are individualistic (independent), you cannot be collectivistic (interdependent); you are at one end or another of a linear measure (or, occasionally, in between). Every increment of individualism necessarily reduces your collectivism, and vice versa (for further discussion of this issue, see Hampden-Turner & Trompenaars, 1997). For instance, Hofstede (1980) identified these constructs as opposite poles of a value dimension that differentiates world cultures. Most prior work on cultural dimensions presumes, implicitly or explicitly, that cultural categories are linear and exclusive.

Similarly, in dealing with self-construals (as individual-level correlates of individualism and collectivism), there has been a tendency to treat them as bipolar opposites. The main issue concerns the

Figure 16.1   Unidimensional Model of Self-Construals

Independent Self-Construal	Marginal Identity	Interdependent Self-Construal

SOURCE: From Kim and Leung (2000).

dimensionality of these constructs. Are interdependence and independence bipolar opposites (one dimension) or distinct constructs (two
dimensions) (see Rhee, Uleman, & Lee, 1996)? Two distinct models
have guided thinking about this question: a linear, bipolar model and
a two-dimensional model. In the linear model, self-concept is seen as a
continuum from strong independent orientation at one extreme to
strong interdependent orientation at the other. The assumption underlying this model is that a stronger identification with one requires a
weakening of the other (see Figure 16.1).

However, recent work indicates that the separate measures of the
independent and interdependent aspects of the self have an orthogonal
relationship (Kashima et al., 1995; Singelis, 1994). This bidimensional
approach to the self provides additional support for the notion that
some core constructs that vary across cultures may each represent an
independent dimension rather than always occurring as polar opposites of a single dimension.

❖ BIDIMENSIONAL MODEL OF CULTURAL IDENTITY

Theory and research on the related constructs of individualism and
collectivism, independent and interdependent self-construal, and so
forth vacillate between treating them as unidimensional (i.e., opposite
ends of the same continuum) or multidimensional (i.e., independent
constructs). Individualism and collectivism were originally believed to
represent endpoints lying on the same dimension (e.g., Hofstede,
1980). More recent empirical evidence, however, suggests that the
two constructs are orthogonal (Gudykunst et al., 1996; Kim et al.,

1996; Singelis, 1994). Many studies on individualism-collectivism and self-construals fail to consider the possibility that these constructs are multidimensional. Many existing measures of cultural identity are unidimensional. This may lead to misidentification of individuals and faulty conclusions.

Recent empirical work at the individual level supports the multidimensional conception of collectivism and individualism (Cross, 1995; Gudykunst et al., 1996; Kim et al., 1996; Rhee, Uleman, Lee, & Roman, 1995; Singelis, 1994). Some scholars have suggested that individuals can possess both orientations (Kagitcibasi, 1987; Sinha & Tripathi, 1994). It appears that independent and interdependent self-construals are unrelated to one another, not polar opposites as their verbal labels might imply. In 1990, Schwartz noted that viewing collectivism and individualism as polar opposites obscures important differences among types of individualism and types of collectivism.

A bicultural identity is conceptually incompatible with the unidimensional model of self-construals. In the unidimensional model, bicultural individuals are forced to occupy a space between the two cultural poles, suggesting marginal competency and sensitivity in both cultures. Similar to the unidimensional model of acculturation, the unidimensional model of cultural identity is still popular with most researchers. A graphic representation of the two-dimensional model is shown in Figure 16.2. In the unidimensional model, movement away from the independent pole necessarily brings one closer to the interdependent pole. The unidimensional perspective fails to consider alternatives to assimilation, such as the emergence of integrated or bicultural identities. In contrast, this alternative model suggests that there are not merely two extremes, but at least four possible distinct cultural orientations (see Berry & Kim, 1988, for a similar model applied to acculturation). A high score on both dimensions is indicative of bicultural identity; a low score on both dimensions suggests marginal identity. A high score on only one dimension indicates culture-typed identity (either independent or interdependent) (see Figure 16.2).

❖ SUPPORT FOR THE BIDIMENSIONAL MODEL

Improper conceptualization of a culturally embedded sense of self can lead to the dangerous dichotomization of individuals as either

Figure 16.2   Two-Dimensional Model of Self-Construals

Independence

	Independent	Bicultural
High	Independent	Bicultural
Low	Marginal	Interdependent

Low   High

Interdependence

SOURCE: From Kim and Leung (2000).

independent or interdependent. The bulk of intercultural communication research has focused on preferred communication styles of culture-typed individuals. For instance, according to the conventional stereotypes of individualism and collectivism, one might assume that independent selves would always be direct, whereas interdependent selves would always be indirect. This, however, would be an overly simplistic assumption. Theories of the social self focus on cross-cultural differences in whether the self is typically construed as individuated or interpersonal. However, these different self-construals may also coexist within the same individual, available to be activated at different times or in different contexts (Brewer & Gardner, 1996).

In my view, the individual can have an interdependent self-schema, an independent self-schema, both, or neither. According to Niedenthal & Beike (1997), individuals might have separate interrelated and isolated self-concepts in the same domain. This assumption is consistent with Guisinger and Blatte's (1994) contention that "it appears quite likely that natural selection in the intelligent, adaptable, and social Homo Sapiens has resulted in separate developmental lines or sets of tasks, constituting the phenomena and processes of individuality and relatedness" (p. 108). These construals of self, although distinct, have been viewed by Singelis (1994) as not being mutually exclusive but, rather, capable of coexisting.

It was assumed that those with a strong tendency to construe themselves independently (so-called independents) have a weak tendency to construe themselves interdependently, and vice versa (see Brockner & Chen, 1996). But although most prior attempts to measure individualism-collectivism have assumed it to be a single bipolar dimension (Hofstede, 1980), the two aspects of self can coexist. Instead of a person being either independent or interdependent in self-orientation, she or he might exhibit both orientations—that is, simultaneously maintain high independent and high interdependent construals, or simultaneously low independent and low interdependent construals.

Recent findings lend credence to the view that individualism and collectivism are essentially orthogonal dimensions. Cross and Markus (1991) found support for two dimensions of self in their study of stress and coping behavior among North American and East Asian exchange students. East Asian students who viewed the interdependent (collectivistic) aspects of the self as less important than the independent aspects and who had developed the independent aspects reported less stress than those who viewed the independent (individualistic) aspects of the self as less important. When asked to indicate the importance of the independent and interdependent facets of the self, the East Asian exchange students placed much more importance on the interdependent dimension of the self than did the American students, but importance scores for the independent dimension did not differ between the groups. Therefore, the Asian exchange students appeared to have developed an internal, private, autonomous self-system while continuing to retain the interdependent aspects of the self.

Empirical support for the existence of the dual construal of self has also been found by Cross (1995). Certain individuals, whom the author called *biculturals*, had both highly developed independent and interdependent self-construals, the possession of which enabled them to cope better, with less stress, in cultural environments foreign to their own. In other studies, Kim and her associates (Kim & Hunter, 1995; Kim et al., 1996; Kim, Sharkey, & Singelis, 1994) found that self-construals were indeed separate dimensions. Kim et al. (1996) grouped the respondents into four types of culture orientation:

- *Bicultural.* High development of both independent and inter-dependent construals.
- *Independent.* Highly developed independent construal but underdeveloped interdependent construal.
- *Interdependent.* Highly developed interdependent construal but underdeveloped independent construal.
- *Marginal.* Underdevelopment of both construals.

There was a significant main effect of cultural orientation, with bicultural individuals expressing the highest level of overall conversational concern, followed by interdependent, then independent and, finally, marginal individuals expressing the lowest level of concern. Such findings imply a tendency for bicultural and interdependent individuals to be more adaptive than independent or marginal individuals in intercultural conversational settings.

The model of acculturation described by Berry and Kim (1988) posited four modes that are based on an individual's willingness and ability to change, add, and/or retain cultural identity. This model can be understood as a process of adjusting one's self-identity (or not). The four modes are as follows:

- *Assimilation.* Those individuals who assimilate will replace their self-image with the self-view prevalent in the culture in which they wish to belong.
- *Bicultural.* A person who integrates (either from a collectivistic or an individualistic culture) may develop an independent self (or interdependent self) in addition to her original self-concept.
- *Separation.* The result of a choice to retain the original self in lieu of assimilation or integration.
- *Marginalization.* May be the result of a degradation of the original self without its replacement by the new self-image, thus leaving the individual marginal (without any well-defined sense of self).

The point is that some individuals may simultaneously maintain high independent as well as high interdependent self-construals. Berry

Table 16.1   Paradigms in Cultural Identity

Representation of Identity	Interdependent	Independent	Bicultural
Identity	Culture-typed, identity as given		Identity as choice, seeking to understand meaning of cultural identity for oneself
Development	Pre-encounter, unexamined cultural identity, lack of interest or concern with cultural identity		Achieved cultural identity through awareness
Important features	Hierarchical status, roles	Horizontal abilities, thoughts	Multifunctional
Tasks	Fulfilling culturally mandated tasks, preference for values of dominant culture		Self-awareness of culturally mandated tasks and choice making
Basis of self-esteem	Follow cultural heritage and be an ideal member of a culture		Understanding of multiperspective, respect for cultural differences
Communication styles	Culturally patterned behavior, single language as a medium of communication and thought patterns		Dynamic code switching, wider repertoire of communication strategies and styles

SOURCE: From Kim and Leung (2000).

concluded that the integration strategy leads to the best mental health outcomes, whereas marginalization leads to the worst outcomes (Berry, 1999).

The previous discussion is summarized in Table 16.1. Bicultural or multicultural individuals come to a deeper understanding and appreciation of their cultural identity than do culture-typed or marginal individuals. This culmination may require resolution or coming to terms with two or more extremes of cultural identifications. Bicultural or multicultural identity development may continue in cycles that involve further exploration or rethinking of the role or meaning of one's cultural identity.

Adaptability seems to be an important key variable of bicultural communication competence. As has been reviewed previously, adaptability focuses on the ability of the communicator to be flexible in the use of conversational strategies with a variety of people in a variety of situations. A bicultural person who identifies with both independent and interdependent characteristics may develop a repertoire of strategies and use them to adapt to the demands of the different contexts. Having a repertoire of individualistic and collectivistic cultural experiences, rather than either one type or the other, allows one to more adequately adapt in differing situations. On the other hand, the culture-typed person may feel that certain conversational styles are inconsistent with internalized culture-role standards, thus causing psychological discomfort. Bicultural individuals may also demonstrate more adaptive behavior and exhibit higher levels of various types of competence than culture-typed individuals. Therefore, an individual with highly developed interdependent and independent characteristics may acquire a broader range of strategies from which to choose, thus demonstrating greater communication competence.

Because bicultural individuals may identify to a high degree with both independent and interdependent characteristics, they may be free from cultural pressure to restrict their strategy choices to stereotypic roles. Thus, bicultural individuals are more likely than marginal or culture-typed individuals to display conversational adaptability across situations. Similarly, individuals with high independent as well as high interdependent self-construals may be well aware of appropriate communication styles in different cultural contexts, showing a high flexibility for behavioral adaptation. This vision of people as multifaceted also seems to coincide with such concepts as the "universal person" (Walsh, 1973), "multicultural person" (Adler, 1974), and "international person" (Lutzker, 1960). Adler (1974), for example, explains the unique characteristics of the multicultural person as neither totally a part of nor totally apart from her or his culture. For instance, such people may be capable of reconciling the conflicts posed by competing conflict management styles and achieving a high level of communication competence. They may be better able to make deliberate choices in specific situations and to maintain a dynamic balance between avoidance and confrontation, rather than being bound by the culturally imposed emphasis on communicative behaviors.

Multicultural perspectives seek a new way of experiencing the self and the world. The alternative perspectives discussed throughout this chapter can provide creative impetus for the new sensibilities. To choose a particular way of responding is quite different from being automatically drawn or socialized into a certain way of behavior. I predict a general shift away from the unidimensional model toward the bidimensional model of cultural identity.

❖ FORMATION OF BICULTURAL IDENTITY

Both the social identity and the acculturation frameworks acknowledge that cultural identity is dynamic, changing over time and context (Phinney, 1990). In a similar vein, cultural or ethnic identity is considered to be achieved through an active process of decision making and self-evaluation. Cultural identity is not an entity but a complex of processes by which people construct their ethnicity. However, in research based on the social identity or acculturation frameworks, investigators in general have not examined cultural identity at the level of individual change.

In the ego identity model (Marcia, 1980), four ego identity statuses are based on whether people have explored identity options and whether they have made a decision. A person who has neither engaged in exploration nor made a commitment is said to be *diffuse*. A commitment made without exploration, usually on the basis of parental values, represents a *foreclosed* status. A person in the process of exploration without having made a commitment is in *moratorium*; a firm commitment following a period of exploration is indicative of an *achieved identity*.

The formation of a bicultural identity may be thought of as a process similar to ego identity formation that takes place over time, as people explore and make decisions about the role of cultural identity in their lives. Phinney (1990) examined commonalities across various models and proposed a three-stage progression from an unexamined ethnic identity through a period of exploration to an achieved or committed ethnic identity. According to this model, early adolescents and perhaps adults who have not been exposed to cultural identity issues are in the first stage, an unexamined ethnic identity. A second stage is characterized by an exploration of one's own cultural identity search, which is similar to the *moratorium* status described by Marcia (1980) and the *encounter* stage defined by Cross (1995).

These models all have a common thread running through them. Individuals begin with an unexamined racial or ethnic identity.

The individual is then challenged by experiences that make race or ethnicity more problematic. To resolve the conflict, individuals initiate an introspection of their own ethnic or racial identities. This search leads individuals to value their racial, ethnic, or minority group membership and integrate it with other identities. These models suggest that bicultural individuals come to a deeper understanding and appreciation of their cultural identity. This culmination may require resolution or coming to terms with two extremes of cultural identifications. The bicultural identity may not necessarily end with bicultural identity but may continue in cycles that involve further exploration or rethinking of the role or meaning of one's cultural identity.

According to Waterman (1981), by maintaining an outmoded 17th-century conception of individualism, its critics persist in making a dialectical dichotomy between individual and social interests. Because making this dichotomy has been found to be neither conceptually necessary nor predictively useful, a societal ideal entailing the compatible incorporation of both interests appears increasingly plausible. The potential for transcending this dichotomy is offered by a recognition that the ethical pursuit of self-interest can simultaneously provide benefits to others. Based on normative (ethical) individualism in both philosophy and psychology, the value system promotes rather than hinders social well-being and cooperative interdependence. The defining features of normative individualism are (a) eudaimonism (a person's efforts to recognize and live in accordance with the true self), (b) freedom of choice, (c) personal responsibility, and (d) universality involving respect for the integrity of others.

Independent and interdependent orientation may at first sight appear to be conflicting, even mutually exclusive. However, such an interpretation would probably reflect a Western individualistic worldview that pits the individual against the group. Indeed, there is nothing illogical about the coexistence of interdependence and independence orientations; in fact, quite a bit of research and thinking provides evidence for such coexistence (Kagitcibasi, 1996). Conflicting tendencies can cause problems of adjustment. However, this conflict can also be the source of dynamic change and growth rather than static equilibrium. In this process of change, conflicting tendencies confronting one another would lead to new solutions (synthesis) that reflect new adjustments to changing environmental demands.

Several theoretical views carry similar themes; each proposes a formulation combining the two basic needs for interdependence and independence, reminiscent of the model of bicultural identity—for example, "psychology of relatedness" (Kagitcibasi, 1996), "ensembled individualism" (Sampson, 1988), "social individuality" (Lykes, 1985), and "relational individualism" (Chodorow, 1989). A recent analysis, using an evolutionary perspective (Guisinger & Blatt, 1994), proposes two basic developmental lines through natural selection—interpersonal relatedness along with self-definition—which both interact in a dialectical fashion. This is very much in line with the thesis proposed here.

Kagitcibasi (1996) pointed out a similar value bias among Western psychologists towards individualism. She argued that this bias is strongly expressed in the area of developmental psychology, where it is taken for granted that the development of autonomy and independence is a prerequisite for optimal personality and optimal cognitive and moral development (Kagitcibasi, 1987). Consistent with my previous discussion on multicultural identity, Kagitcibasi (1996) notes that a family culture of relatedness and interdependence is not incompatible with socioeconomic development. She proposes a model of family change based on the dual common human needs for agency (autonomy) and communion (relatedness). In this model, Kagitcibasi differentiates three types: X, the collectivistic model based on communion (total interdependence); Z, the individualistic model based on agency (independence); and Y, a dialectical synthesis of the two (Kagitcibasi, 1996). The last model (Y) integrates the two basic needs for autonomy and relatedness through child socialization, which is a recognition of the coexistence of these two basic conflicting needs everywhere.

It is possible for individual loyalties to coexist with communal-familial loyalties and relations in a new synthesis rather than being mutually exclusive. An interdependent interpersonal perspective does not pit the individual against the group and can thus provide scientists with a fruitful base to explore the psychology of relatedness. Similarly, we need to assume a dialectic orientation, given the conflicting nature of the two needs involved. Thus, an independence that does not recognize the need for relatedness and an interdependence that does not recognize the need for autonomy would not do justice to the two basic human needs. A dialectical synthesis of the two would appear to be a more optimizing solution for cultural identity. I predict a general shift toward this model in the field of communication.

Part III of this book dealt with how most current theories of human communication are rooted in Western philosophical presumptions about persons and in layers of practices and institutions that reflect and promote these presumptions. People live by the meanings and practices of multiple sets of cultural contexts (Markus, Mullally, and Kitayama, 1997). The prevailing individualistic values have consequences both for the way in which we do research and in our interpersonal interactions with people who do not build their understanding of communication in the individualistic notions of self. Paralleling the adoption of multicultural perspectives in theory is the emerging notion of bicultural or multicultural communicative competence in practice. As people struggle to come to terms with cultural pluralism, there is a growing recognition of identity challenges in the life of the bicultural or multicultural person and her or his potential communication patterns. In the United States alone, evidence of multicultural people is everywhere. Whether through immigration, sojourning, marriage, adoption, or birth, a wide range of people are actively carrying the frame of reference of two or more cultures (see Bennett, 1993). This chapter elaborates on this point and further emphasizes the applications of bicultural identity in communication competence. It also examines the implications of communication competence that can integrate both autonomy and relatedness.

Modern physics provides us with a different view of the physical world and opens the door to a distinctive perspective on personhood. Recent developments in modern physics suggest a different meaning of order and help us flesh out an alternative personhood ideal. The new concepts in physics have brought about a profound change in our worldview. A dramatic change of concepts and ideas occurred in physics during the first three decades of the 20th century, and that change is still being elaborated in our current theories of matter (Capra, 1982). The modern physics introduced a challenging new way of understanding the physical universe and suggested a different manner of approaching human phenomena as well. Research and theoretical developments, such as those discussed previously in this chapter, look into new combinations (coexistence, synthesis) of individualistic and collectivistic orientations and promise better conceptualizations in this area.

IV

Conclusion

At the fusion of the double spiral there is a vortex, and winds of dissolu-
tion; beyond is a still center and the bliss of union.

— Sjöö and Mor, *The Great Cosmic Mother:*
Rediscovering the Religion of the Earth, 1991, p. 173

Intercultural communication research during the last decade has
perceived the self as either individualistic or collectivistic. In a multicultural society, the development of bicultural or expanded selves
may be viewed as an asset because such perspectives can diminish
rigid culture-typed behaviors. Consciousness of one's own cultural
identity has been called a state of "dynamic betweenness" by
Yoshikawa (1988). The suggestion here is that of (a) continual and com-
fortable movement between cultural identities such that an integrated,
multicultural existence is maintained and (b) conscious, deliberate
choice being made between communication management strategies.
This awareness of living in at least two cultures can eliminate the
dependence upon a single culture for identity (i.e., being culture-
typed). Thus, bicultural individuals can be constructive in dealings

with culturally diverse others and, increasingly, this bicultural identity will be recognized as a resource to be harnessed for professional or social advantage. At present, however, there is a paucity of research on the effectiveness of bicultural individuals in their communication behavior.

Independence and interdependence are cultural organizing principles. Cultures may emphasize one much more than the other, but every culture recognizes both and legitimates some aspects of both. At the individual level, there are elements of both independence and interdependence in every self (Fiske, Kitayama, Markus, & Nisbett, 1998; Greenfield & Cocking, 1994). *Independence* and *interdependence* refer to two different orientations toward society and people. But we should keep in mind that cultures and individuals can balance and develop each of these alternatives in many different ways. Thus, although social practices based on these two cultural orientations may differ dramatically, they are not always diametrical antitheses (Fiske et al., 1998), nor are their psychological consequences always simple opposites.

Research and theory, such as the studies and hypotheses discussed in Part III of this book, look into new combinations (coexistence, synthesis) of individualistic and collectivistic orientations and promise to continue to improve the conceptualizations in this area. A psychology of relatedness would propose a different view of maturity than would a psychology of independence. A better theory would honor the human requirements for agency (autonomy, independence) as well as for communion (relatedness, interdependence). Both of these orientations may be promoted simultaneously in certain cultural settings. This perspective can also contribute to cultural flexibility in Western societies.

Models that acknowledge differences without placing them in hierarchy or opposition are therefore useful. Recognition of normative influences shaping contemporary communication theories may serve as a useful starting point for change. It has been argued that a monocultural image of human functioning has generated ethnocentric theoretical formulations within the field. Thus, the present question is how to engender multiplicity of perspectives. To develop comprehensive and universal theories of human communication, we need to recognize one major stumbling block: a cultural view that the individual is intrinsically separate and self-contained and must resist the collective. In the dominant mentality of contemporary Western culture, self is equated with the autonomous or self-sufficient individual. Therefore, relationality in Western cultures is often constructed as undermining the so-called correct or most powerful kind of selfhood (Klein, 1995). To the extent that personal creativity and individuality are more valued than relationships and to the extent that autonomy is characterized as the pinnacle of psychological and ethical development, there is the implicit suggestion that a caring and relational style of identity makes one less than one might be.

We have to keep in mind the fact that general trends in culture do not affect every person to the same extent. Even within the highly individualistic Western culture, most people are still much less self-reliant, self-contained, or self-sufficient than the prevailing cultural ideology suggests that they should be. Perhaps Western models of the self are considerably at odds with actual individual social behavior and should be reformulated to reflect the substantial interdependence that characterizes even Western individualists (Markus & Kitayama, 1991). Sampson (1977) has argued that the reality of globalization and a shrinking world will force just such a rethinking of the nature of the individual.

These and other innovations are only now beginning to emerge, to be conceptualized, and to be integrated into the human communication literature. The consequence will be an intellectual synergy that will enable us to transcend the limitations imposed by our cultural origins. We may then be able to claim that we have a more truly universal understanding of human communication behavior.

As mentioned previously, the coexistence of opposites may be seen as conflicting and unstable, especially for Westerners with an intellectual heritage of Cartesian dualism. Sinha and Tripathi (1994) note that the use of dichotomies is a heuristic device popular in the West. I want to stress the coexistence of different orientations in the same person or culture, although one or the other orientation may take over at different times and regarding different issues. Construing independence and interdependence as opposite poles of a single dimension assumes that they are mutually exclusive, which is not supported by empirical evidence (see Kagitcibasi, 1996; Kim et al., 1996).

The distinction between the independent and interdependent modes of social participation serves as an initial framework within which many cross-cultural differences and similarities in communication behaviors can be understood, and it also serves as a heuristic device to point out cultural relativity of theories. In this part, I summarize some of the cultural differences and similarities in several domains of human communication that are illuminated by this distinction. Taken as a whole, I believe that this literature will impress upon communication scholars who work only in a monocultural (most often European-American) context that the cultural angle must be taken seriously.

17

Into the Future

Implications for Future Inquiry

An invasion of armies can be resisted, but not an idea whose time has come.

— Victor Hugo, *Histoire d'un Crime*

❖ IDEOLOGY AND BEYOND

At the outset of this book, I noted the close connection between the normative assumptions of a culture and the construction of communication theories. But by suspending a particular set of normative assumptions, scientists may be moved to search anew, to expand the range of potential truths, to reanalyze and resynthesize, and to emerge with conclusions that may challenge the normative system and thus render it more adaptive (Gergen, 1979). By understanding the forces shaping contemporary scientific thought, we become better able to evaluate our present condition and to judge its adequacy. In light of the inherent myopia that constrains any single theoretical perspective, a premium is to be placed on theoretical multiplicity. Any theory that has gained preeminence, any ideology that is pervasive throughout the culture, and any seemingly self-evident normative assumptions about social life pose a threat to the understanding of human communication. In the broadest sense, multiplicity of perspective possesses survival value, and a break in paradigm is thus of greater value than the continued striving for verification.

If a prevailing theoretical structure goes unchallenged, one remains bound to its implications. Many processes once thought to be basic to human social psychology actually vary according to culture. This discovery does not imply that communication researchers cannot formulate valid, highly general explanatory principles. What it shows is simply that, to be valid, such explanatory principles must be formulated with reference to culture (Fiske, Kitayama, Markus, & Nisbett, 1998). It may not always be possible to disentangle the web of culture and to isolate specific assumptions that affect specific communication processes. But we need to explore the interconnections between culture and communication and find out how they operate.

The relative importance accorded to others in the two self-construals has a wide range of communicative implications. In this book, I have outlined some of the communicative consequences of holding a view of the self that includes others and that requires others to define the self. A rapidly expanding body of research suggests that many features of the way people perceive, categorize, or assign causality are to a large extent personal, reflecting the nature of the self that anchors them.

The first step in broadening our current theories of the self and their communicative consequences seems to require becoming self-conscious about what is being taken for granted in the initial formulation of the problem and about the labels that are used. For instance, if a theorist accepts the notion that the self is constantly striving to defend itself from the collective, then influence by others is viewed as a weakness or a failure. But from a perspective that acknowledges interdependence between the self and the collective, social influence, acknowledgment of others, and the inhibition of private thoughts or feelings, even yielding to others, can be framed quite differently; such actions can be construed as essential, positive, and mature (see Azuma, 1986).

With new communication technologies, personal intercultural contact is now a daily fact of life for millions of people. The forecast of the "global village" (Barnlund, 1975) has become contemporary reality. We are rapidly learning that all the villagers are not alike. We must understand the cultural underpinnings of communication theories and ensure that developing new theories are culturally relevant and in tune with pluralistic reality. If cultures remained isolated from each other, differences in communication phenomena might remain inconsequential. But such is not the case. With the increasing commonness of intercultural encounters, the likelihood of negative impact from ethnocentric tendencies in research and theory has also grown tremendously. This review provided a theoretical basis for replacing a single, monocultural view of communication with a multiperspective, multicultural view.

Theories in the social sciences are cultural constructions that reflect a particular orientation to, and interpretation of, reality. I have adopted the notion of interdependent and independent selfways (Markus, Mullally, & Kitayama, 1997) as characteristic patterns of engaging the social world. These selfways provide a guiding orientation to one's subjectivity and thus structure the patterns of communication. Analysis of a particular communication behavior within a cultural context that is different from one's own makes one's own typically transparent selfways become visible.

❖ RECLAIMING CULTURAL RELEVANCE OF COMMUNICATION THEORIES

My discussion of the communicative consequences has by no means exhausted the range of potential consequences of holding an independent or interdependent construal of the self. But it is enough, I believe, to demonstrate that the field of communication must consider the fact that communication processes are culturally contingent. There are two possible ways for the field to proceed from this point: (a) by investigating the cultural limits of our assumptions and (b) by examining psychological variables other than self-construal in attempting to explain cross-cultural differences in belief and communication behavior. I'll now discuss these possible avenues of research in more detail.

We can consider the major phenomena of human communication, such as those reviewed in Part II of this book. One by one, we can analyze our cultural assumptions regarding each of these phenomena. Then we can investigate a sample of the world's cultures to see the cultural limits of our assumptions. This may be an effective and hence appropriate early strategy for establishing that human communication is culturally contingent, because it will reorient the field and facilitate a paradigm shift. However, it is also a backward-looking strategy that may eventually need to be superseded. Clearly, we are only beginning to build the foundation of this field. In spite of so-called scientific theories and sophisticated methodologies, communication theorists are still naive participants of the culture. As such, to reduce misattribution or false interpretations, we need to be totally aware of the social and cultural context in which we create theories and make observations (see Diaz-Loving, 1999).

Self-construal represents a constellation of variables that differentiates people from different cultures. However, it is not the only way to distinguish people from different cultures. Future research needs to also examine psychological variables other than self-construal in attempting to explain cross-cultural differences in belief and communication behavior. Previous work has revealed that there are multiple ways to construe self and that constructions of both construals can be found across cultures. The bulk of research on intercultural variation in the self and communication has centered on U.S.-East Asian comparisons. In developing a perspective on the cultural grounding of the self, it is obviously useful to examine a wide variety of cultures. Although it is much less profuse than the work on East Asian selves, there is a growing body of literature on selves in Indian, Arab, Mexican, and African cultures (Markus et al., 1997; Oyserman, 1993; Sinha & Tripathi, 1994).

These self-construals and their cognitive, emotional, and behavioral consequences are products of particular cultural environments. The psyche can be seen as an internalization of culture, whereas culture can be viewed as an externalization of the psyche. Thus, processes of the self are constructions that bear the mark of past constructions and are also constructors that provide stability to the present and a course of action for the future (Markus et al., 1997). Further analysis of the consequences of different construals of the self may also prove fruitful in understanding some basic human communication issues. As Malpass (1977) pointed out, it is also necessary to examine the relationship of the dimension or dimensions to other variables within each culture. For example, in Brockner and Chen's (1996) study, although the mean level of independent self-construal was not greater in the U.S. sample than in the People's Republic of China (PRC) sample, the patterns of relationships between self-esteem and measures of self-protection reveals that the U.S. sample, on the whole, did have more independent self-construals.

Because individualism is not just a matter of belief or value but also of everyday practice, including scientific practice, it is not easy for theorists to encompass social behavior from a different culture. And it is probably harder still to fathom a different culture in empirical work.

Continued effort to develop culture-universal communication theories may eventually open new and productive possibilities for the analysis of human communication behavior. In general, viewing the self and communication behavior from alternative perspectives may enable theorists to recognize tacit and taken-for-granted values, ideals, and meaning systems.

Given the "Americo-centrism" of most social science (Featherman, 1993), this broadening in the cultural base will help universalize our discipline. As Markus and Kitayama (1991) argue,

> A failure to replicate certain findings in different cultural contexts should not lead to immediate despair over the lack of generality of various psychological principles or to the conclusion of some anthropologists that culturally divergent individuals inhabit incomparably different worlds. Instead, it is necessary to identify the theoretical elements or processes that explain these differences. (p. 248)

I suggest that self-construals may be one such powerful theoretical element in understanding human communication.

Future research must take into consideration the fact that individualism and collectivism exist in all cultures and that individuals hold both individualistic and collectivistic values. This position is consistent with Schwartz's (1990) contention that individualistic and collectivistic values are not necessarily incompatible; they can coexist. If individualism and collectivism coexist at both the cultural and individual levels, then it is critical that future research hypotheses involve very precise predictions regarding the linkages between the various aspects of individualism-collectivism and individuals' behavior (Gudykunst, Guzley, & Ota, 1993). A universally applicable theory should subsume individual-level as well as culture-level issues. Because self-concept provides a link between the norms and values of a culture and the everyday behavior of individuals, it is a promising means of explaining communication styles in different cultures. The notion of self-concept brings the broad cultural variability dimensions to the individual level.

These and other innovations are only now beginning to emerge, to be conceptualized, and to be integrated into the human communication literature. Smith and Bond (1998) claim that a similar evolution in social psychology had to await the diffusion of Western psychology to different cultural milieus and the nurturing of local psychologists who are capable of challenging the biases of the discipline in its own terminology, using its own established procedures. Gordon (1998/1999) argues that the time for multicultural, multidisciplinary, multitheoretic exploration of human communication is at hand. The move within the American communication discipline is in this direction, and the times would also seem propitious for breakthroughs and paradigm shifts in the communication studies discipline at the international level.

As this change occurs, it should let loose an intellectual synergy that will enable us to transcend the limitations imposed by our cultural origins. We may then be able to claim that we have a more truly universal understanding of human communication behavior. I hope that this book will help alert mainstream communication scholars to the need to examine which, if any, supposedly universal phenomena are characteristic of people beyond the boundaries of the United States. Attempting to understand the cultural context of various approaches and traditions within communication will also have a payoff in terms of the intellectual development of individual researchers. In Anastasi's (1972) words, "Exposure to a multiplicity of intellectual traditions, value systems, and perceptual frames of reference frees the individual from narrow ideological constraints and permits the fullest development of individuality" (p. 1098).

If the field of human communication can come to deal more realistically with the multidimensional phenomena of human selfhood, it could make a difference not only to our own profession, but also in our contribution to human welfare. Recent research and thinking show that such a synthesis is becoming a reality.

Postscript

I will add a brief judgmental comment in this postscript. First, it strikes me that the tendency to focus research on nation-based communication—Korean communication, Indian communication, Chinese communication, and the like—often slows the search for theoretical explanations of pancultural communication processes. Seeking generalizations about the impact of this or that kind of philosophy on a certain national group's communication styles, rather than striving to develop and test overarching theoretical propositions and empirical generalizations about the communication styles *in general,* is a failure to pitch research efforts at the proper level of abstraction. Although some culture-specific research dealing with currently hot areas (e.g., Indian theory of communication, Chinese philosophy and human communication) is all but inevitable, it should be buttressed by work focusing on more general theoretical and empirical concerns.

I knew from the beginning of this journey that this book would be controversial in terms of the political and cultural issues it raises. This book will undoubtedly evoke mixed reactions. As pointed out by Kuhn (1970), adherents of conflicting paradigms cannot resolve their differences by resorting to a step-by-step logical refutation. Diametrically opposed paradigms have their bases in differing metaphysical, value, and ideological assumptions. The only path open, then, is to employ old-fashioned "persuasion," to use Kuhn's (1970) term. In his words, "Debates over theory-choice cannot be cast in a form that fully resembles logical or mathematical proof . . . debate is about premises, and its recourse is to persuasion as a prelude to the possibility of proof" (p. 199). To the extent that one accepts Kuhn's insights into the structure of scientific revolutions, debate has even greater immediacy for communication theories.

Everyone who has had an academic education begins with the assumption that scholarship is objective. When what we have been taught as objective science turns out to be culture-bound, it is both disillusioning and illuminating. Athena was born out of Zeus's head. Athena's mind is offspring of traditional authority and bias—until she remembers Metis: Metis who was swallowed and forgotten, but emerges in the present.

References

Achenbach, J. (1993). *Why things are* (Vol. II: The big picture). New York: Ballantine Books.

Adler, P. S. (1974). Beyond cultural identity: Reflections upon cultural and multicultural man. In R. Brislin (Ed.), *Topics in culture learning* (Vol. 2, pp. 23-41). Honolulu, HI: East-West Center.

Ajzen, I., & Fishbein, M. (1980). *Understanding attitudes and predicting social behavior.* Englewood Cliffs, NJ: Prentice Hall.

Alberti, R. E., & Emmons, M. L. (1970). *Your perfect right: A guide to assertive behavior.* San Luis Obispo, CA: Impact.

Alberts, J. K., Miller-Rassulo, M. A., & Hecht, M. L. (1991). A typology of drug resistance strategies. *Journal of Applied Communication Research, 19,* 129-151.

Alexander, R. D. (1987). *The biology of moral systems.* New York: Aldine de Gruyter.

Allen, M., Hunter, J. E., & Dohohue, W. (1989). Meta-analysis of self-report data on the effectiveness of public speaking anxiety treatment techniques. *Communication Education, 38,* 54-76.

Allport, G. (1935). Attitudes. In. C. Murchinson (Ed.), *A handbook of social psychology* (pp. 798-844). Worcester, MA: Clark University Press.

Ames, P. T., Dissanayake, W., & Kasulis, T. P. (Eds.). (1994). *Self as person in Asian theory and practice.* Albany: State University of New York Press.

Anastasi, A. (1972). The cultivation of diversity. *American Psychologist, 27,* 1019-1099.

Asch, S. E. (1952). Effects of group pressure on the modification and distortion of judgments. In G. E. Swanso, T. M. Necomb, & E. L. Hartley (Eds.), *Readings in social psychology* (pp. 2-11). New York: Holt.

Asch, S. E. (1956). Studies of independence and submission to group pressure: I. A minority of one against a unanimous majority. *Psychological Monographs, 70,* (9, Whole No. 417).

Aune, R. K., & Waters, L. L. (1994). Cultural differences in deception: Motivations to deceive in Samoans and North Americans. *International Journal of Intercultural Relations, 18,* 159-172.

Avtgis, T. A., & Brenders, D. A. (1994, November). *The relationship between locus of control, communication apprehension, and esteem protection.* Paper presented at the annual meeting of the Speech Communication Association, New Orleans, LA.

Avtgis, T. A., & Rancer, A. S. (1997). Argumentativeness and verbal aggressiveness as a function of locus of control. *Communication Research Reports, 14,* 441-450.

Ayers, J., & Hopf, T. (1993). *Coping with speech anxiety.* Norwood, NJ: Ablex.

Azuma, H. (1986). Why study child development in Japan? In H. Stevenson, H. Azuma, & K. Hakuta (Eds.), *Child development and education in Japan* (pp. 3-12). New York: Freeman.

Back, K. W. (1951). Influence through social communication. *Journal of Abnormal and Social Psychology, 46,* 9-23.

Barnes, J. A. (1994). *A pack of lies.* Cambridge, UK: Cambridge University Press.

Barnlund, D. (1975). *Private and public self in Japan and the United States.* Tokyo: Simul Press.

Barnlund, D. (1989). *Communication styles of Japanese and Americans.* Belmont, CA: Wadsworth.

Barraclough, R. A., Christophel, D. M., & McCroskey, J. C. (1988). Willingness to communicate: A cross-cultural investigation. *Communication Research Reports, 5,* 187-192.

Barry, H., Child, I., & Bacon, M. (1959). Relation of child training to subsistence economy. *American Anthropology, 61,* 51-63.

Bartlett, J. (2000). *Familiar quotations* (10th ed.; revised and enlarged by N. H. Dole). Retrieved March 20, 2002, from www.Bartleby.com/100/151.65.html (Original work published 1919)

Basso, K. (1990). "To give up on words": Silence in Western Apache culture. In D. Carbaugh (Ed.), *Cultural communication and intercultural contact* (pp. 303-320). Hillsdale, NJ: Lawrence Erlbaum.

Batson, C. D. (1994). Why act for the public good? Four answers. *Personality and Social Psychology Bulletin, 20,* 603-610.

Baumeister, R. F. (1982). A self-presentational view of social phenomena. *Psychological Bulletin, 91,* 3-26.

Baumeister, R. F., & Leary, M. R. (1995). The need to belong: Desire for interpersonal attachments as a fundamental human motivation. *Psychological Bulletin, 117,* 497-529.

Becker, C. (1986). Reasons for the lack of argumentation and goodness-of-fit in the analysis of covariance structures. *Psychological Bulletin, 10,* 93-98.

Belenski, M. F., Clinchy, B. M., Goldberger, N. R., & Tarule, J. M. (1986). *Women's ways of knowing: The development of self, voice, and mind.* New York: Basic Books.

Bellah, R. N., Madsen, R., Sullivan, W. M., Swidler, A., & Tipton, S. M. (1985). *Habits of the heart.* New York: Harper & Row.

Bem, D. J. (1968). Attitudes as self-descriptions: Another look at the attitude-behavior link. In A. G. Greenwald, T. C. Brook, & T. M. Ostrom (Eds.),

Psychological foundations of attitudes (pp. 197-215). New York: Academic Press.

Bennett, J. M. (1993). Cultural marginality: Identity issues in intercultural training. In M. Paige (Ed.), *Education for the intercultural experience* (pp. 109-135). Yarmouth, ME: Intercultural Press.

Berger, C. R., & Metzger, N. J. (1984). The functions of human communication in developing, maintaining, and altering self-image. In C. C. Arnold & J. W. Bowers (Eds.), *Handbook of rhetorical and communication theory* (pp. 273-337). Boston: Allyn & Bacon.

Berry, J. W. (1967). Independence and conformity in subsistence level societies. *Journal of Personality and Social Psychology, 7,* 415-418.

Berry, J. W. (1974). Differentiation across cultures: Cognitive style and affective style. In J. Dawson & W. Lonner (Eds.), *Readings in cross-cultural psychology* (pp. 167-175). Hong Kong, China: University of Hong Kong Press.

Berry, J. W. (1978). Social Psychology: Comparative societal and universal. *Canadian Psychological Review, 19,* 93-104.

Berry, J. W. (1983). The sociogenesis of social sciences: An analysis of the cultural relativity of social psychology. In B. Bain (Ed.), *The sociogenesis of language and human conduct* (pp. 449-458). New York: Plenum Press.

Berry, J. W. (1999). Intercultural relations in plural societies. *Canadian Journal of Psychology, 40,* 12-21.

Berry, J. W., & Kim, U. (1988). Acculturation and mental health. In P. R. Dasen, J. W. Berry, & N. Sartorius (Eds.), *Health and cross-cultural psychology* (pp. 207-236). New York: Academic Press.

Blake, R. R., & Mouton, J. S. (1964). *The managerial grid.* Houston, TX: Gulf.

Bochner, S. (1994). Cross-cultural differences in the self concept: A test of Hofstede's individualism/collectivism distinction. *Journal of Cross-Cultural Psychology, 25,* 273-283.

Bok, S. (1978). *Lying: Moral choice in public and private life.* New York: Pantheon Books.

Bond, M. H. (1998). Managing culture in studies of communication: A futurescape. *Journal of Asian Pacific Communication, 8,* 31-49.

Bond, M. H., & Cheung, T. S. (1983). College students' spontaneous self-concept: The effect of culture among respondents in Hong Kong, Japan, and the United States. *Journal of Cross-Cultural Psychology, 14,* 153-171.

Bond, M. H., Leung, K., & Wan, K. C. (1982). The social impact of self-effacing attributions: The Chinese case. *Journal of Social Psychology, 118,* 157-166.

Bond, R., & Smith, P. B. (1996). Culture and conformity: A meta-analysis of studies using Asch's (1952b, 1956) line judgment task. *Psychological Bulletin, 119,* 111-137.

Bourhis, R. Y., Moise, L. C., Perreault, S., & Senecal, S. (1997). Towards an interactive acculturation model: A social psychological approach. *International Journal of Psychology, 32,* 369-386.

Braithwaite, C. A. (1990). Communicative silence: A cross-cultural study of Basso's Hypothesis. In D. Carbaugh (Ed.), *Cultural communication and intercultural contact* (pp. 321-327). Hillsdale, NJ: Lawrence Erlbaum.

Brenders, D. A. (1987). Perceived control: Foundations and directions for communication research. In M. L. McLaughlin (Ed.), *Communication yearbook 10* (pp. 86-116). Newbury Park, CA: Sage.

Brewer, M. B., & Gardner, W. (1996). Who is this "we"? Levels of collective identity and self representations. *Journal of Personality and Social Psychology, 71,* 83-93.

Brislin, R. W. (1981). *Cross-cultural encounters: Face-to-face interaction.* New York: Pergamon.

Brockner, J., & Chen, Y-R. (1996). The moderating roles of self-esteem and self-construal in reaction to a threat to the self: Evidence from the People's Republic of China and the United States. *Journal of Personality and Social Psychology, 71,* 603-615.

Brown, J. D. (1990). Evaluating one's abilities: Shortcuts and stumbling blocks on the road to self-knowledge. *Journal of Experimental Social Psychology, 26,* 149-167.

Brown, P., & Levinson, S. (1978). Universals in language usage: Politeness phenomena. In E. N. Goody (Ed.), *Questions and politeness* (pp. 56-289). Cambridge, UK: Cambridge University Press.

Brown, C. T., Yelsma, P., & Keller, P. W. (1981). Communication-conflict predisposition: Development of a theory and an instrument. *Human Relations, 34,* 1103-1117.

Bruneau, T. (1995). Empathetic intercultural communication: State of the art and future potential. *Intercultural Communication Studies, 8,* 1-24.

Bryant, B. K. (1992). Conflict resolution strategies in relation to children's peer relations. *Journal of Applied Developmental Psychology, 13,* 35-50.

Bugental, D. P., Henker, B., & Whalen, C. K. (1976). Attributional antecedents of verbal and vocal assertiveness. *Journal of Personality and Social Psychology, 34,* 405-411.

Buhr, T. A., Pryor, B., & Sullivan, M. (1991). A further examination of communication apprehension and information processing. *Cognitive Therapy and Research, 15,* 303-317.

Buller, D. B., & Burgoon, J. K. (1994). Deception. In J. A. Daly & J. M. Wiemann (Eds.), *Communicating strategically: Strategic interpersonal communication* (pp. 191-223). Hillsdale, NJ: Lawrence Erlbaum.

Burgoon, J. K. (1976). The unwillingness-to-communicate scale: Development and validation. *Communication Monographs, 43,* 60-69.

Buriel, R. (1994). Acculturation, respect for cultural differences, and biculturalism among three generations of Mexican American and Euro American school children. *The Journal of Genetic Psychology, 154,* 531-543.

Burroughs, N. F., Kearney, P., & Plax, T. G. (1989). Compliance-resisting in the college classroom. *Communication Education, 38,* 214-229.

Burroughs, N. F., & Marie, V. (1990). Communication orientations of Micronesian and American students. *Communication Research Reports, 7,* 139-146.

Buss, A. R. (1975). The emerging field of the sociology of psychological knowledge. *American Psychologist, 30,* 988-1002.

Buss, A. R. (Ed.). (1979). *Psychology in social context.* New York: Irvington.

Byron, G. (1824). *Don juan.* London.

Cahn, D. D. (1985). Communication competence in the resolution of intercultural conflict. *World Communication, 14,* 85-94.

Campbell, J. D., Trapnell, P. D., Heine, S., Katz, I. M., Lavalle, L. F., & Lehman, D. R. (1996). Self-concept clarity: Measurement, personality correlates, and cultural boundaries. *Journal of Personality and Social Psychology, 70,* 141-156.

Canary, D. J., Cody, M. J., & Marston, P. J. (1986). Goal types, compliance-gaining and locus of control. *Journal of Language and Social Psychology, 5,* 249-269.

Canary, D. J., Cunningham, E. M., & Cody, M. J. (1988). Goal types, gender, and locus of control in managing interpersonal conflict. *Communication Research, 15,* 426-446.

Canary, D., & Spitzberg, B. H. (1987). Appropriateness and effectiveness perceptions of conflict strategies. *Human Communication Research, 14,* 93-118.

Capra, F. (1982). *The Turning Point.* New York: Bantam Books.

Caprara, G. V., & Cervone, D. (2000). *Personality, determinants, dynamics, and potentials.* New York: Cambridge University Press.

Carbaugh, D. (1993). Competence as cultural pragmatics: Reflections on some Soviet and American encounters. In R. L. Wiseman & J. Koester (Eds.), *Intercultural communication competence* (pp. 168-183). Thousand Oaks, CA: Sage.

Carmona, A. E., & Lorr, M. (1992). Dimensions of assertiveness: A cross-cultural comparison of Chilean and U.S. subjects. *Personality and Individual Differences, 13,* 45-48.

Chiu, L. H. (1972). A cross-cultural comparison of cognitive styles in Chinese and American children. *International Journal of Psychology, 8,* 235-242.

Chiu, L .H. (1986). Locus of control in intellectual situations in American and Chinese school children. *International Journal of Psychology, 21,* 167-176.

Chodorow, N. (1989). *Feminism and psychoanalytic theory.* New Haven, CT: Yale University Press.

Choi, I., Nisbett, R. E., & Norenzayan, A. (1999). Causal attribution across cultures: Variation and universality. *Psychological Bulletin, 125,* 47-63.

Chua, E., & Gudykunst, W. B. (1987). Conflict resolution styles in low- and high-context cultures. *Communication Research Reports, 5,* 32-37.

Chusmir, L., & Mills, J. (1989). Gender differences in conflict resolution styles of managers: At work and at home. *Sex Roles, 20,* 149-162.

Cixous, H. (1997). Sorties: Out and out: Attacks/ways out/forays. In C. Belsey & J. Moore (Eds.), *The feminist reader: Essays in gender and the politics of literary criticism* (pp. 91-103). London: Macmillan.

Collier, M., & Thomas, M. (1988). Cultural identity: An interpretive perspective. In Y. Kim & W. Gudykunst (Eds.), *Theories in Intercultural Communication.* Newbury Park, CA: Sage.

Comadena, M. E., & Prusank, D. T. (1988). Communication apprehension and academic achievement among elementary and middle school students. *Communication Education, 37,* 270-277.

Comstock, J., & Buller, D. B. (1991). Conflict strategies adolescents use with their parents: Testing the cognitive communicator characteristics model. *Journal of Language and Social Psychology, 10,* 47-59.

Conrad, C. (1991). Communication in conflict: Style-strategy relationships. *Communication Monographs, 58,* 135-155.

Cook, D. J., & St. Lawrence, J. S. (1990). Variations in presentation format: Effect on interpersonal evaluations of assertive and unassertive behavior. *Behavior Modification, 14,* 21-36.

Cooper, J., & Fazio, R. H. (1984). A new look at dissonance theory. In L. Berkowitz (Ed.), *Advances in experimental social psychology* (Vol. 17, pp. 229-266). San Diego, CA: Academic Press.

Coupland, N., Giles, H., & Wiemann, J. M. (1991). *"Miscommunication" and problematic talk.* Newbury Park, CA: Sage.

Cousins, S. (1989). Culture and selfhood in Japan and the United States. *Journal of Personality and Social Psychology, 56,* 124-131.

Crittenden, K. S. (1991). Asian self-effacement or feminine modesty? Attributional patterns of women university students in Taiwan. *Gender and Society, 5,* 98-117.

Cronen, V., Pearce, B., & Tomm, K. (1985). A dialectical view of personal change. In K. Gergen & K. Davis (Eds.), *The social construction of the person.* New York: Springer-Verlag.

Cross, S. E. (1995). Self-construals, coping, and stress in cross-cultural adaptation. *Journal of Cross-Cultural Psychology, 6,* 673-697.

Cross, S. E., & Markus, H. R. (1991, July). *Cultural adaptation and the self: Self-construal, coping, and stress.* Paper presented at the ninety-ninth annual convention of the American Psychological Association, San Francisco, CA.

Daly, J. A., McCroskey, J. C., & Richmond, V. P. (1977). The relationships between vocal activity and perception of communicators in small group interaction. *Western Speech Communication Journal, 41,* 175-187.

Daly, J. A., & Stafford, L. (1984). Correlates and consequences of social-communicative anxiety. In J. A. Daly & J. C. McCroskey (Eds.), *Avoiding communication: Shyness, reticence, and communication apprehension* (pp. 125-143). Beverly Hills, CA: Sage.

Daly, J. A., Vangelisti, A. L., Neel, H. L., & Cavanaugh, P. D. (1989). Preperformance concerns associated with public speaking anxiety. *Communication Quarterly, 37*, 39-53.

Darley, J. M. (1966). Fear and social comparison as determinants of conformity behavior. *Journal of Personality and Social Psychology, 4*, 73-78.

Delano, A. (1817). *A narrative of voyages and travels in the Northern and Southern Hemispheres; comprising three voyages round the world.* Boston: Printed by E. G. House for the author.

DePaulo, B. M., Kashy, D. A., Kirkendol, S. E., Wyer, M. M., & Epstein, J. A. (1996). Lying in everyday life. *Journal of Personality and Social Psychology, 70*, 979-995.

Deutsch, M., & Gerard, H. B. (1955). A study of normative and informational social influences upon individual judgment. *Journal of Abnormal and Social Psychology, 51*, 629-636.

Deutscher, I. (1966). Words and deeds: Social science and social policy. *Social Problems, 13*, 235-254.

Dickens, C. (1880). The old curiosity shop. Boston: Aldine.

Diaz-Loving, R. (1999). The indigenization of psychology: Birth of a new science or rekindling of an old one? *Applied Psychology: An International Review, 48*, 433-449.

Doherty, W. J., & Ryder, R. G. (1979). Locus of control, interpersonal trust, and assertive behavior among newlyweds. *Journal of Personality and Social Psychology, 37*, 2212-2239.

Doi, L. T. (1973). The Japanese patterns of communication and the concept of *amae. Quarterly Journal of Speech, 59*, 180-185.

Doi, T. (1986). *The anatomy of self: The Individual versus society.* Tokyo: Kodansha.

Dowling, R. E., & Flint, L. J. (1990). The argumentativeness scale: Problems and promise. *Communication Studies, 41*, 183-198.

DuCette, J., Wolk, S., & Friedman, S. (1972). Locus of control and creativity in black and white children. *Journal of Social Psychology, 88*, 297-298.

Dyal, J. A. (1984). Cross-cultural research with the locus of control construct. In H. M. Lefcourt (Ed.), *Research with the locus of control constructs* (Vol. 3). New York: Academic Press.

Dyal, J. A., & Dyal, R.Y. (1981). Acculturation, stress and coping: Some implications for research and education. *International Journal of Intercultural Relations, 5*, 301-328.

Ebesu, A. S., & Miller, M. D. (1994). Verbal and nonverbal behaviors as a function of deception type. *Journal of Language and Social Psychology, 13*, 418-442.

Eisenberg, E. M. (1984). Ambiguity as strategy in organizational communication. *Communication Monographs, 51*, 1713-1722.

Eisenberg, E. M., & Phillips, S. R. (1991). Miscommunication in organizations. In N. Coupland, H. Giles, & J. M. Wiemann (Eds.), *Miscommunication and problematic talk* (pp. 244-258). Newbury Park, CA: Sage.

Eisenberg, E. M., & Witten, M. G. (1987). Reconsidering openness in organizational communication. *Academy of Management Review, 12,* 418-426.

Elliot, S., Scott, M. D., Jensen, A. D., & McDonough, M. (1982). Perceptions of reticence: A cross-cultural investigation. In M. Burgoon (Ed.), *Communication yearbook 5* (pp. 591-602). New Brunswick, CA: Transaction Books.

Ellis, J. B., & Wittenbaum, G. M. (2000). Relationships between self-construal and verbal promotion. *Communication Research, 27,* 704-722.

Emerson, R. W. (1841). "Self-Reliance." In *Essays* (First Series; pp. 35-73). Boston: James Monroe and Company.

Feagin, J. R., & Feagin, C. B. (1996). *Racial and ethnic relations.* Upper Saddle River, NJ: Prentice Hall.

Featherman, D. L. (1993). What does society need from higher education? *Items, 47 (2/3),* 38-43.

Feldstein, S., Alberti, L., & BenDebba, M. (1979). "Self-attributed personality characteristics and the pacing of conversational interaction." In A. W. Seigman & S. Feldstein (Eds.), *Of speech and time* (pp. 73-87). Hillsdale, NJ: Lawrence Erlbaum.

Festinger, L. (1957). *A theory of cognitive dissonance.* Stanford, CA: Stanford University Press.

Festinger, L., & Carlsmith, J. M. (1959). Cognitive consequences of forced compliance. *Journal of Abnormal and Social Psychology, 58,* 203-210.

Filley, A. C., & House, R. J. (1969). *Managerial process and organizational behavior.* Glenview, IL: Scott Publishing.

Fine, M. G. (1991). New voices in the workplace: Research directions in multicultural communication. *Journal of Business Communication, 28,* 259-275.

Fiske, A. P., Kitayama, S., Markus, H. R., & Nisbett, R. E. (1998). The cultural matrix of social psychology. In D. T. Gilbert, S. T. Fiske, & G. Lindzey (Eds.), *The handbook of social psychology* (Vol. 2, pp. 915-981). Boston: McGraw-Hill.

Fox, C. (1997). The authenticity of intercultural communication. *International Journal of Intercultural Relations, 21,* 85-103.

Frager, R. (1970). Conformity and anti-conformity in Japan. *Journal of Personality and Social Psychology, 15,* 203-210.

Friend, R., Rafferty, Y., & Bramel, D. (1990). A puzzling misinterpretation of the Asch "conformity" study. *European Journal of Social Psychology, 20,* 29-44.

Fukuyama, M. A., & Greenfield, T. K. (1983). Dimensions of assertiveness in an Asian-American student population. *Journal of Counseling Psychology, 30,* 429-432.

Fuller, T. (1732). *Gnomologia: Adages and proverbs; wise sentences and witty sayings, ancient and modern, foreign and British.* London: Printed for B. Barker.

Furby, L. (1979). Individualistic bias in studies of locus of control. A. R. Buss (Ed.), *Psychology in social context* (pp. 169-190). New York: Irvington.

Furnham, A. (1984). Studies of cross-cultural conformity: A brief and critical review. *Psychologia, 27,* 65-72.

Galassi, J. P., Delo, J. S., Galassi, M. D., & Bastien, S. (1974). The college self-expression scale: A measure of assertiveness. *Behavior Therapy, 5,* 165-171.

Galvin, K. M., & Brommel, B. J. (1986). *Family communication: Cohesion and change.* Glenview, IL: Scott, Foresman & Co.

Gates, H. L., Jr. (1993, September 20). Let them talk. *New Republic,* 37-49.

Geertz, C. (1973). *The interpretation of culture: Selected essays.* New York: Basic Books.

Gergen, K. J. (1973). Social psychology as history. *Journal of Personality and Social Psychology, 26,* 309-320.

Gergen, K. J. (1979). The positivist image in social psychological theory. A. R. Buss (Ed.), *Psychology in social context* (pp. 193-212). New York: Irvington.

Gervasio, A. H., & Crawford, M. (1989). Social evaluations of assertiveness: A critique and speech act reformation. *Psychology of Women Quarterly, 13,* 1-25.

Gilbert, D. T., Krull, D. S., & Malone, P. S. (1990). Unbelieving the unbelievable: Some problems in the rejection of false information. *Journal of Personality and Social Psychology, 59,* 601-613.

Gilbert, D. T., & Malone, P. S. (1995). The correspondence bias. *Psychological Bulletin, 117,* 21-38.

Gilbert, S. J., & Horenstein, D. (1975). The communication of self-disclosure: Level versus valence. *Human Communication Research, 1,* 316-322.

Giles, H., Coupland, N., & Wiemann, J. (1992). "Talk is cheap . . ." but "My word is my bond": Beliefs about talk. In K. Bolton & H. Kwok (Eds.), *Sociolinguistics today* (pp. 218-243). New York: Routledge.

Gill, C. (1996). *Personality in Greek epic, tragedy, and philosophy.* Oxford, UK: Claredon Press.

Gilligan, C. (1982). *In a different voice: Psychological theory and women's development.* Cambridge, MA: Harvard University Press.

Goffman, E. (1959). *The presentation of self in everyday life.* Garden City, NY: Doubleday.

Goldberg, C. J., & Botvin, G. J. (1993). Assertiveness in Hispanic adolescents: Relationship to alcohol use and abuse. *Psychological Reports, 73,* 227-238.

Goodstadt, B. E., & Hjelle, L. A. (1973). Power to the powerless: Locus of control and the use of power. *Journal of Personality and Social Psychology, 27,* 190-196.

Gordon, M. M. (1964). *Assimilation in American life.* New York: Oxford University Press.

Gordon, R. D. (1998/1999). A spectrum of scholars: Multicultural diversity and human communication theory. *Human Communication, 2,* 1-8.

Greenfield, P. M. (1994). Independence and interdependence as developmental scripts: Implications for theory, research, and practice. In P. M. Greenfield & R. R. Cocking (Eds.), *Cross-cultural roots of minority child development* (pp. 1-37). Hillsdale, NJ: Lawrence Erlbaum.

Greenfield, P., & Cocking, R. (1994). *Cross-cultural roots of minority child development.* Hillsdale, NJ: Lawrence Erlbaum.

Greenwald, A. G. (1980). The totalitarian ego: Fabrication and revision of personal history. *American Psychologist, 35,* 603-618.

Gudykunst, W. B., Guzley, R. M., & Ota, H. (1993). Issue for future research on communication in Japan and the United States. In W. B. Gudykunst (Ed.), *Communication in Japan and the United States* (pp. 291-322). Albany: State University of New York Press.

Gudykunst, W. B., & Kim, Y. Y. (1997). *Communicating with strangers: An approach to intercultural communication.* New York: McGraw-Hill.

Gudykunst, W. B., Matsumoto, Y., Ting-Toomey, S., Nishida, T., Kim, K., & Heyman, S. (1996). The influence of cultural individualism-collectivism, self-construals, and individual values on communication styles across cultures. *Human Communication Research, 22,* 510-543.

Gudykunst, W. B., & Ting-Toomey, S. (1988). *Culture and interpersonal communication.* Newbury Park, CA: Sage.

Guisinger, S., & Blatt, S. J. (1994). Individuality and relatedness: Evolution of a fundamental dialectic. *American Psychologist, 49,* 104-111.

Gurin, P., Gurin, G., Lao, R. C., & Beattie, M. (1969). Internal-external control in the motivational dynamics of Negro youth. *Journal of Social Issues, 25,* 29-53.

Hackman, M. Z., Johnson, C. E., & Barthel-Hackman, T. (1995). Correlates of talkaholism in New Zealand: An intracultural analysis of the compulsive communication construct. *Communication Research Reports, 12,* 53-60.

Hall, E. T. (1976). *Beyond culture.* New York: Anchor.

Hall, J. (1986). *Conflict management survey: A survey of one's characteristic reaction to and handling of conflicts between himself and others.* Conroe, TX: Teleometrics.

Hamaguchi, E. (1985). A contextual model of the Japanese: Toward a methodological innovation in Japan studies. *Journal of Japanese Studies, 11,* 289-321.

Hamilton, J. P. (1991). The development of a communication specific locus of control instrument. *Communication Reports, 4,* 107-112.

Hampden-Turner, C., & Trompenaars, F. (1997). Response to Geert Hofstede. *International Journal of Intercultural Relations, 21,* 149-156.

Hara, K. (2000). The "*kotodama* belief" in Japanese communication style. *Dokkyo Working Papers in Communication, 21,* 125-160.

Harding, S., & Phillips, D. (1986). *Contrasting studies in Western Europe: Unity, diversity, and change.* London: Macmillan.

Hart, R. P., & Burks, D. M. (1972). Rhetorical sensitivity and social interaction. *Speech Monographs, 39,* 75-91.

Heaton, R., & Duerfeldt, P. (1973). The relationship between self-esteem, self-reinforcement, and the internal-external personality dimension. *Journal of Genetic Psychology, 123,* 3-13.

Heine, S. J., & Lehman, D. R. (1997a). The cultural constructions of self-enhancement: An examination of group-serving biases. *Journal of Personality and Social Psychology, 72,* 1268-1283.

Heine, S. J., & Lehman, D. R. (1997b). Culture, dissonance, and self-affirmation. *Personality and Social Psychology Bulletin, 23,* 389-400.

Heine, S. J., Lehman, D. R., Markus, H. R., & Kitayama, S. (1999). Is there a universal need for positive self-regard. *Psychological Review, 106,* 766-794.

Henderson, M., & Furnham, A. (1982). Self-reported and self-attributed scores on personality, social skills, and attitudinal measures as compared between high nominated friends and acquaintances. *Psychological Reports, 50,* 88-90.

Henley, W. E. (1920). "Invictus." In *Poems* (pp. 83-84). London: Macmillan.

Hewes, D., & Planalp, S. (1987). The individual's place in communication science. In C. R. Berger & S. H. Chaffee (Eds.), *Handbook of communication science* (pp. 146-183). Newbury Park, CA: Sage.

Ho, D. Y. F. (1976). On the concept of face. *American Journal of Psychology, 81,* 867-884.

Hofstede, G. (1980). *Culture's consequences: International differences in work-related values.* Beverly Hills, CA: Sage.

Hofstede, G. (1983). Dimensions of national cultures in fifty countries and three regions. In J. Deregowski, S. Dzirawiec, & R. Annis (Eds.), *Explications in cross-cultural psychology* (pp. 389-407). Lisse, The Netherlands: Swets & Zeitlinger.

Hogan, R. (1975). Theoretical egocentrism and the problem of compliance. *American Psychologist, 39,* 972-973.

Hogan, R. T., & Emler, M. P. (1975). The biases in contemporary social psychology. *Social Research, 45,* 478-534.

Hsieh, T. T., Shybut, J., & Lotsof, E. J. (1969). Internal versus external control and ethnic group membership. *Journal of Consulting and Clinical Psychology, 33,* 122-124.

Huang, L C., & Harris, M. B. (1973). Conformity in Chinese and Americans: A field experiment. *Journal of Cross-Cultural Psychology, 4,* 427-434.

Ifert, D. E. (2000). Resistance to interpersonal requests: A summary and critique of recent research. In M. Roloff (Ed.), *Communication yearbook 23* (pp. 125-161). Thousand Oaks, CA: Sage.

Imai, M. (1981). *16 ways to avoid saying no.* Tokyo: The Nihon Keizai Shimbun.

Inagaki, Y. (1985). *Skills in self-expression* [in Japanese]. Tokyo: PHP.

Infante, D. A. (1981). Trait argumentativeness as a predictor of communicative behavior in situations requiring argument. *Central States Speech Journal, 32,* 265-272.

Infante, D. A. (1982). The argumentative student in the speech communication classroom: An investigation and implications. *Communication Education, 31,* 141-148.

Infante, D. A., Chandler, T. A., & Rudd, J. E. (1989). Test of an argumentative skill deficiency model of interspousal violence. *Communication Monographs, 56,* 163-177.

Infante, D. A., & Gordon, W. I. (1985). Superiors' argumentativeness and verbal aggressiveness as predictors of subordinates' satisfaction. *Human Communication Research, 12,* 117-125.

Infante, D. A., & Rancer, A. S. (1982). A conceptualization and measure of argumentativeness. *Journal of Personality Assessment, 46,* 72-80.

Infante, D. A., & Rancer, A. S. (1996). Argumentativeness and verbal aggressiveness: A review of recent theory and research. In B. Burleson (Ed.), *Communication yearbook 19* (pp. 318-351). Thousand Oaks, CA: Sage.

Infante, D. A., Trebing, J. D., Shepherd, P. E., & Seeds, D. E. (1984). The relationship of argumentativeness to verbal aggression. *Southern Speech Communication Journal, 50,* 67-77.

Infante, D. A., & Wigley, C. J. (1986). Verbal aggressiveness: An interpersonal model and measure. *Communication Monographs, 53,* 61-69.

Inkeles, A., & Smith, D. H. (1974). *Becoming modern: Individual change in six developing countries.* Cambridge, MA: Harvard University Press.

Ishii, S. (1984). *Enryo-sasshi* communication: A key to understanding Japanese interpersonal relations. *Cross Currents, 11,* 49-58.

Ishii (1998). Developing a Buddhist en-based systems paradigm for the study of Japanese human relationships. *Japan Review, 10,* 109-122.

Ishii, S., & Bruneau, T. (1988). Silence and silences in cross-cultural prospective: Japan and the United States. In L. Samovar & P. Porter (Eds.), *Intercultural communication* (pp. 246-251). Belmont, CA: Wadsworth.

Iwao, S. (1988, August). *Social psychology's models of man: Isn't it time for East to meet West?* Invited address to the International Congress of Scientific Psychology, Sydney, Australia.

James (1890, 1918). *The principles of psychology* (Vols. I and II). New York: Dover.

Joe, V. C. (1971). Review of the internal-external control construct as a personality variable. *Psychological Reports, 28,* 619-640.

Johnson, F. (1985). The Western concept of self. In A. Marsella, G. De Vos, & F. L. K. Hsu (Eds.), *Culture and self* (pp. 91-138). London: Tavistock.

Johnson, F. A., & Marsella, A. J. (1978). Differential attitudes toward verbal behavior in students of Japanese and European ancestry. *Genetic Psychology Monographs, 97,* 43-76.

Jones, E. E., & Gordon, E. M. (1972). Timing of self-disclosure and its effect on personal attraction. *Journal of Personality and Social Psychology, 2,* 348-358.

Jordan, J. V. (1991). Empathy and self boundaries. In J. V. Jordan, A. G. Kaplan, J. B. Miller, I. P. Stivey, & J. L. Surrey (Eds.), *Women's growth in connection* (pp. 67-80). New York: Guilford Press.

Kacmar, K. M., & Carlson, D. S. (1994). Using impression management in women's job search processes. *American Behavioral Scientist, 37,* 682-696.

Kagitcibasi, C. (1987). Individual and group loyalties: Are they possible? In C. Kagitcibasi (Ed.), *Growth and progress in cross-cultural psychology* (pp. 94-103). Lisse, The Netherlands: Swets & Zeitlinger.

Kagitcibasi, C. (1996). *Family and human development across cultures: A view from the other side.* Hillsdale, NJ: Lawrence Erlbaum.

Kane, T. R., & Tedeshi, J. T. (1973). Impressions created by conforming and independent persons. *Journal of Social Psychology, 91,* 109-116.

Kashima, Y., Siegel, M., Tanaka, K., & Kashima, E. S. (1992). Do people believe behaviors are consistent with attitudes? Toward a cultural psychology of attribution processes. *British Journal of Social Psychology, 31,* 111-124.

Kashima, Y., Yamaguchi, S., Kim, U., Choi, S.-C., Gelfand, M. J., & Yuki, M. (1995). Culture, gender, and self: A perspective from individualism-collectivism research. *Journal of Personality and Social Psychology, 69,* 925-937.

Kiesler, C. A., & Kiesler, S. B. (1969). *Conformity.* Reading, MA: Addison-Wesley.

Kilmann, R. H., & Thomas, K. W. (1975). Interpersonal conflict-handling behavior as reflections of Jungian personality dimensions. *Psychological Reports, 37,* 971-980.

Kim, H.-J., & Markus, H. R. (1999). Deviance or uniqueness, harmony or conformity? A cultural analysis. *Journal of Personality and Social Psychology, 77,* 785-800.

Kim, M. S. (1993). Culture-based conversational constraints in explaining cross-cultural strategic competence. In R. L. Wiseman & J. Koester (Eds.), *Intercultural communication competence* (pp. 132-150). Newbury Park, CA: Sage.

Kim, M. S. (1994). Cross-cultural comparisons of the perceived importance of conversational constraints. *Human Communication Research, 21,* 128-151.

Kim, M. S. (1995). Toward a theory of conversational constraints. In R. L. Wiseman (Ed.), *Intercultural communication theory* (pp. 148-169). Thousand Oaks, CA: Sage.

Kim, M. S. (1999). Cross-cultural perspectives on motivations of verbal communication: Review, critique, and a theoretical framework. In M. Roloff (Ed.), *Communication yearbook 22* (pp. 51-89). Thousand Oaks, CA: Sage.

Kim, M. S. (2001). Perspectives on human communication: Implications for transcultural theory. In V. H. Milhouse, M. K. Asante, & P. O. Nwoso (Eds.), *Transcultural realities* (pp. 3-31). Thousand Oaks, CA: Sage.

Kim, M. S., Aune, K., Hunter, J. E., Kim, H.-J., & Kim, J. S. (2001). The effect of culture and self-construals on predispositions toward verbal communication. *Human Communication Research, 27*, 382-408.

Kim, M. S., & Hunter, J. E. (1993a). Attitude-behavior relations: A meta-analysis of past research—focusing on attitudinal relevance and topic. *Journal of Communication, 43*, 101-142.

Kim, M. S., & Hunter, J. E. (1993b). Relationships among attitudes, behavioral intentions, and behavior: A meta-analysis of past research, part 2. *Communication Research, 20*, 331-364.

Kim, M. S., & Hunter, J. E. (1995, November). *A test of an ethno-cultural model of conflict styles.* Paper presented at the annual meeting of the Speech Communication Association, San Antonio, TX.

Kim, M. S., Hunter, J. E., Miyahara, A., Horvath, A., Bresnahan, M., & Yoon, H. J. (1996). Individual- vs. culture-level dimensions of individualism and collectivism: Effects on preferred conversational styles. *Communication Monographs, 63*, 29-49.

Kim, M. S., Kam, K., Singelis, T. M., Wilson, G., & Sharkey, W. (1998, March). *A test of a cultural model of deceptive communication.* Paper presented at the conference on Interdisciplinary Theory and Research on Intercultural Relations, Fullerton, CA.

Kim, M. S., Klingle, R. S., Sharkey, W. F., Park, H. S., Smith, D. H., & Yuego, G., et al. (2000). A test of a cultural model of patient's motivation for verbal communication in patient-doctor interactions. *Communication Monographs, 67*, 262-283.

Kim, M. S., & Leung, T. (2000). A Multicultural View of Conflict Management Styles: Review of Past Research and Critical Synthesis. In M. Roloff (Ed.), *Communication yearbook 23* (pp. 227-269). Thousand Oaks, CA: Sage.

Kim, M. S., & Sharkey, W. F. (1995). Independent and interdependent construals of the self: Explaining cultural patterns of interpersonal communication in multi-cultural settings. *Communication Quarterly, 43*, 20-38.

Kim, M. S., Sharkey, W. F., & Singelis, T. M. (1994). The relationship between individual's self-construals and perceived importance of interactive constraints. *International Journal of Intercultural Relations, 18*, 117-140.

Kim, M. S., Shin, H. C., & Cai, D. (1998). The influence of cultural orientations on the preferred forms of requesting and rerequesting. *Communication Monographs, 65*, 47-66.

Kim, M. S., & Wilson, S. R. (1994). A cross-cultural comparison of implicit theories of requesting. *Communication Monographs, 61*, 210-235.

Kim, Y. Y. (1988). *Communication and cross-cultural adaptation: An integrative theory.* Clevedon, UK: Multilingual Matters.

Kincaid, D. L. (1987). *Communication theory: Eastern and Western perspectives.* San Diego, CA: Academic Press.

Kirkbride, P. S., Tang, S. F., & Westwood, R. I. (1991). Chinese conflict preferences and negotiating behavior: Cultural and psychological influences. *Organization Studies, 12,* 365-386.

Kitayama, S., & Markus, H. R. (1999). *Yin* and *Yang* of the Japanese self: The cultural psychology of personality coherence. In Cervone, D. & Shoda, Y. (Eds.), *The coherence of personality: Social-cognitive bases of consistency, variability, and organization* (pp. 242-302). New York: Guilford Press.

Kitayama, S., Markus, H. R., Matsumoto, H., & Norasakkunkit, V. (1997). Individual and collective processes in the construction of the self: Self-Enhancement in the United States and self-criticism in Japan. *Journal of Personality and Social Psychology, 72,* 1245-1267.

Klein, A. C. (1995). *Meeting the great bliss queen: Buddhists, feminists, and the art of the self.* Boston: Beacon.

Kleinke, C. L., & Kahn, M. L. (1980). Perceptions of self-disclosures: Effects of sex and physical attractiveness. *Journal of Personality, 48,* 191-205.

Klopf, D. W. (1984). Cross-cultural apprehension research: A summary of Pacific Basin studies. In J. A. Daly & J. C. McCroskey (Eds.), *Avoiding communication: Shyness, reticence, and communication apprehension* (pp. 157-169). Beverly Hills, CA: Sage.

Klopf, D. W. (1995). *Intercultural encounters: The fundamentals of intercultural communication.* Englewood, CO: Morton.

Klopf, D. W., & Ishii, S. (1976). A comparison of the communication activities of Japanese and American adults. *ELEC Bulletin, 53,* 22-26.

Klopf, D. W., Thompson, C. A., & Sallinen-Kuparinen, S. (1991). Argumentativeness among selected Finnish and American college students. *Psychological Reports, 68,* 161-162.

Koester, J., & Olebe, M. (1988). The behavioral assessment scale for intercultural communication effectiveness. *International Journal of Intercultural Relations, 12,* 233-246.

Koper (1994, July). *Cultural differences in the perception of deceptive behavior.* Paper presented at the annual conference of the International Communication Association, Sydney, Australia.

Kuhn, T. S. (1970). *The structure of scientific revolutions.* Chicago: University of Chicago Press.

Kurman, J., & Sriram, N. (1997). Self-enhancement, generality of self-evaluation, and affectivity in Israel and Singapore. *Journal of Cross-Cultural Psychology, 28,* 421-441.

LaFromboise, T., Coleman, H. K., & Gerton, J. (1993). Psychological impact of biculturalism: Evidence and theory. *Psychological Bulletin, 114,* 395-412.

LaPiere, R. (1934). Attitudes versus actions. *Social Forces, 13,* 230-237.

Lapinski, M. K. (1996). *Deception and the self: A cultural examination of information manipulation theory.* Unpublished master's thesis, University of Hawaii, Honolulu.

Lavine, S. D., & Karp, I. (1991). Introduction: Museums and multiculturalism. In I. Karp and S. D. Lavine (Eds.), *Exhibiting cultures: The poetics and politics of museum display* (pp. 1-9). Washington, DC: Smithsonian Institution Press.

Layman's parallel Bible: King James version, modern language Bible, living Bible, revised standard version. (1991). Grand Rapids, MI: Zondervan Bible Publishers.

Lebra, S. L. (1984). Nonconfrontational strategies for management of interpersonal conflict. In E. S. Krauss, T. P. Rohlem & P. G. Steinhoff. (Eds.), *Conflict in Japan* (pp. 41-60). Honolulu: University of Hawaii Press.

Lebra, T. S. (1991, March). *Cultural factors that influence communication in Japan and the United States.* Paper presented as a plenary address at a conference on Communication in Japan and the United States, California State University, Fullerton.

Lebra, T. S. (1992, June). *Culture, self, and communication.* Paper presented at the University of Michigan, Ann Arbor.

Lee, A. Y., Aaker, J. L., & Gardner, W. L. (2000). The pleasure and pains of distinct self-construals: The role of interdependence in regulatory focus. *Journal of Personality and Social Psychology, 78,* 1122-1134.

Lee, H., & Rogan, R. (1991). A cross-cultural comparison of organizational conflict management behaviors. *International Journal of Conflict Management, 2,* 181-199.

Lefcourt, H. (1966). Internal versus external control of reinforcement: A review. *Psychological Bulletin, 65,* 206-220.

Lefcourt, H. M. (1992). Durability and impact of the locus of control construct. *Psychological Bulletin, 112,* 411-414.

Leung, T. & Kim, M. S. (1997). *A revised self-construal scale.* Unpublished manuscript, University of Hawaii at Manoa, Honolulu.

LeVine, R. (1973). *Ego functions and sociocultural evolution.* Paper presented to the American Psychoanalytic Association and the American Psychiatric Association, Honolulu, HI.

Lillard, A. (1998). Ethnopsychologies: Cultural variations in theories of mind. *Psychological Bulletin, 112,* 3-32.

Littlejohn, S. W. (1996). Communication theory. In T. Enos (Ed.), *Encyclopedia of rhetoric and composition: Communication from ancient times to the information age* (pp. 117-121). New York: Garland.

Littlejohn, S. W. (2002). *Theories of human communication* (7th ed.). Belmont, CA: Wadsworth/Thomson Learning.

Locke, J. (1894). *An essay concerning human understanding.* Oxford: Claredon Press.

Lustig, M. W., & Andersen, P.A. (1991). Generalizing about communication apprehension and "avoidance": Multiple replications and meta-analyses. In J. W. Neulip (Ed.), *Replication research in the social sciences* (pp. 297-328). Newbury Park, CA: Sage.

Lutzker, D. (1960). Internationalism as a predictor of cooperative behavior. *Journal of Conflict Resolution, 4,* 426-430.

Lykes, M. B. (1985). Gender and individualistic vs. collectivistic bases for notions about the self. *Journal of Personality, 53,* 356-383.

Ma, R. (1990). An exploratory study of discontented responses in American and Chinese relationships. *Southern Communication Journal, 55,* 305-318.

Malpass, R. S. (1977). Theory and method in cross-cultural psychology. *American Psychologist, 32,* 1069-1079.

Mann, L. (1988). Culture and conformity. In M. H. Bond (Ed.), *The cross-cultural challenge to social psychology* (pp. 182-195). Newbury Park, CA: Sage.

Mann, T. (1927). *The magic mountain* (2 vols.). London: Secker.

Marcia, J. (1980). Identity in adolescence. In J. Adelson (Ed.), *Handbook of adolescent psychology* (pp. 159-187). New York: Wiley.

Markus, H., & Kitayama, S. (1991). Culture and the self: Implications for cognition, emotion, and motivation. *Psychological Review, 98,* 224-252.

Markus, H. R., & Kitayama, S. (1994). A collective fear of the collective: Implications for selves and theories of selves. *Personality and Social Psychology Bulletin, 20,* 568-579.

Markus, H. R., & Kitayama, S. (1998). The cultural psychology of personality. *Journal of Cross-Cultural Psychology, 29,* 63-87.

Markus, H. R., Mullally, P. R., & Kitayama, S. (1997). Selfways: Diversity in modes of cultural participation. In U. Neisser & D. A. Jopling (Eds.), *The conceptual self in context* (pp. 13-59). Cambridge, UK: Cambridge University Press.

Markus, H. R., & Wurf, E. (1987). The dynamic self-concept: A social psychological perspective. *Annual Review of Psychology, 38,* 299-337.

Marsella, A., DeVoss, G., & Hsu, F. L. K. (1985). *Culture and the self.* London: Tavistock.

Masters, J. C., Burish, T. G., Hollon, S. D., & Rimm, D. C. (1987). *Behavior therapy: Techniques and empirical findings.* New York: Harcourt Brace Jovanovitch.

Matsumoto, D., Weissman, M. D., Preston, K., Brown, B. R., & Kupperbusch, C. (1997). Context-specific measurement of individualism-collectivism on the individual level: The individualism-collectivism interpersonal assessment inventory. *Journal of Cross-Cultural Psychology, 28,* 743-767.

McClintock, C. G. (1972). Social motives: A set of propositions. *Behavioral Science, 17,* 438-454.

McCroskey, J. C. (1972). The implementation of a large-scale program of systematic desensitization for communication apprehension. *Speech Teacher, 21,* 255-264.

McCroskey, J. C. (1977). Oral communication: A summary of recent theory and research. *Human Communication Research, 4,* 78-96.

McCroskey, J. C. (1982). Oral communication apprehension: A reconceptualization. In M. Burgoon (Ed.), *Communication yearbook 6* (pp. 136-170). Beverly Hills, CA: Sage.

McCroskey, J. C., Andersen, J. F., Richmond, V. P., & Wheeless, L. R. (1981). Communication apprehension of elementary and secondary students and teachers. *Communication Education, 30,* 122-132.

McCroskey, J. C., & Daly, J. (1976). Teachers' expectations of the communication apprehensive child in the elementary school. *Human Communication Research, 3,* 269-277.

McCroskey, J. C., Daly, J., Richmond, V., & Cox, B. (1975). The effects of communication apprehension on interpersonal attraction. *Human Communication Research, 2,* 51-65.

McCroskey, J. C., & Richmond, V. P. (1987). Willingness to communicate. In J. C. McCroskey & J. A. Daly (Eds.), *Personality and interpersonal communication* (pp. 129-156). Newbury Park, CA: Sage.

McCroskey, J. C., & Richmond, V. P. (1993). Identifying compulsive communications: The Talkaholic Scale. *Communication Research Reports, 10,* 107-114.

McCroskey, J. C., & Richmond, V. P. (1995). Correlates of compulsive communication: Quantitative and qualitative characteristics. *Communication Quarterly, 43,* 39-52.

McCroskey, J. C., Richmond, V., Daly, J. A., & Falcione, R. L. (1977). Studies of the relationship between communication apprehension and self-esteem. *Human Communication Research, 3,* 269-277.

McCroskey, J. C., Richmond, V., & Stewart, R. A. (1986). *One on one: The foundations of interpersonal communication.* Englewood Cliffs, NJ: Prentice Hall.

McIntyre, T. M., Mauger, P. A., Margalit, B., & Figueiredo, E. (1989). The generalizabililty of aggressiveness and assertiveness factors: A cross-cultural analysis. *Personality and Individual Differences, 10,* 385-389.

Meichenbaum, D. (1977). *Cognitive behavior modification.* New York: Plenum.

Meyer, J. W. (1988). The social construction of the psychology of childhood: Some contemporary processes. In R. M. Lerner & E. M. Hetherington (Eds.), *Child development in life span perspective* (pp. 47-65). Hillsdale, NJ: Lawrence Erlbaum.

Miike, Y. (2000, August). *Toward an Asian standpoint of communication theory: Some initial assumptions.* Paper presented at the Pacific and Asian Communication Association Convention, Honolulu, HI.

Miller, G. R. (1983). Telling it like it isn't and not telling it like it is: Some thoughts on deceptive communication. In J. I. Sisco (Ed.), *The Jensen lectures: Contemporary communication studies* (pp. 91-116). Tampa: University of South Florida.

Miller, G. R., & Steinberg, M. (1975). *Between people: A new analysis of interpersonal communication*. Chicago, IL: Science Research Associates.

Miller, G., & Stiff, J. B. (1993). *Deceptive communication*. Newbury Park, CA: Sage.

Miller, L. C., Cooke, L. L., Tsang, J., & Morgan, F. (1992). Should I brag? Nature and impact of positive and boastful disclosures for women and men. *Human Communication Research, 18*, 364-399.

Miller, J. G. (1984). Culture and the development of everyday social explanation. *Journal of Personality and Social Psychology, 46*, 961-978.

Monge, P. R. (1998). Communication theory for a globalizing world. In J. S. Trent (Ed.), *Communication: Views from the helm for the 21st century* (pp. 3-7). Boston: Allyn & Bacon.

Moscovici, S. (1980). Toward a theory of conversion behavior. In L. Berkowitz (Ed.), *Advances in experimental social psychology* (Vol. 2, 3rd ed., pp. 209-239). New York: Academic Press.

Mullen, B., & Riordan, C. A. (1988). Self-serving attributions in naturalistic settings: A meta-analytic review. *Journal of Applied Social Psychology, 18*, 3-22.

Myers, D. (1987). *Social psychology*. New York: McGraw-Hill.

Nagao, M. (1991). *Assertive behaviors and perceptions of assertiveness as communication competence: A comparative study of American and Japanese students*. Unpublished master's thesis, Ohio University, Athens.

Nicotera, A. M. (1989, April). *Argumentativeness and social desirability: Investigation of an instrument*. Paper presented at the meeting of the Central States Communication Association, Kansas City, MO.

Nicotera, A. M. (1993). Beyond two dimensions: A grounded theory model of conflict-handling behavior. *Management Communication Quarterly, 6*, 282-306.

Niedenthal, P. M., & Beike, D. R. (1997). Interrelated and isolated self-concepts. *Personality and Social Psychology Review, 1*, 106-128.

Nishiyama, K. (1993, June). *Japanese negotiators: Are they deceptive or misunderstood?* Paper presented at the meeting of the Communication Association of Japan, Tokyo.

Ochs, E. (1988). *Culture and language development*. Cambridge, UK: Cambridge University Press.

Olaniran, B. A., & Roach, K. D. (1994). Communication apprehension and classroom apprehension in Nigerian classrooms. *Communication Quarterly, 42*, 379-389.

Oyserman, D. (1993). The lens of personhood: Viewing the self and others in a multicultural society. *Journal of Personality and Social Psychology, 65*, 993-1009.

Parish, S. (1994). *Moral knowing in a sacred Hindu city* (Vol. 19). New York: Columbia University Press.

Park, R. E. (1928). Human migration and the marginal man. *American Journal of Sociology, 5*, 881-893.

Pascale, R. T., & Athos, A. G. (1981). *The art of Japanese management*. New York: Simon & Schuster.

Patterson, M. L. (1983). *Nonverbal behavior: A functional perspective*. New York: Springer-Verlag.

Paul, R. A. (1995). Act and intention in Sherpa culture and society. In L. Rosen (Ed.), *Other intentions: Cultural contexts and the attribution of inner states* (pp. 15-45). Santa Fe, NM: School of American Research Press.

Peabody, D. (1985). *National characteristics*. Cambridge, UK: Cambridge University Press.

Pedersen, P. (1991). Counseling international students. *Counseling Psychologist, 19*, 10-58.

Phinney, J. S. (1990). Ethnic identity in adolescents and adults: Review of research. *Psychological Bulletin, 108*, 499-514.

Ponterotto, J. G., Casas, J. M., Suzuki, L. A., & Alexander, C. M. (Eds.). (1995). *Handbook of multicultural counseling*. Thousand Oaks, CA: Sage.

Pruitt, D. G., & Rubin, J. Z. (1986). *Social conflict: Escalation, stalemate, and settlement*. New York: Random House.

Prunty, A., Klopf, D., & Ishii, S. (1990). Argumentativeness: Japanese and American tendencies to approach and avoid conflict. *Communication Research Reports, 7*, 75-79.

Putnam, L. L., & Wilson, C. E. (1982). Communication strategies in organizational conflicts: Reliability and validity of a measurement. In M. Burgoon (Ed.), *Communication yearbook 6* (pp. 629-652). Beverly Hills, CA: Sage.

Rahim, M. A. (1983). A measure of styles of handling interpersonal conflict. *Academy of Management Journal, 26*, 368-376.

Rahim, M. A., & Bonoma, T. V. (1979). Managing organizational conflict: A model for diagnosis and intervention. *Psychological Reports, 44*, 1323-1344.

Rajecki, D. W., Ickes, W., & Tanford, S. (1981). Locus of control and reaction to strangers. *Journal of Personality and Social Psychology, 7*, 282-289.

Ramanaiah, N., & Deniston, W. (1993). NEO personality inventory profiles of assertive and unassertive person. *Psychological Reports, 73*, 336-338.

Ramirez, M. (1983). *Psychology of the Americas*. New York: Pergamon Press.

Rancer, A. S., & Baukus, R. A. (1987). Discriminating males and females on belief structures about arguing. In L. B. Nadler, M. K. Nadler, & W. R. Todd-Mancillas (Eds.), *Advances in gender and communication research* (pp. 155-173). Lanham, MD: University Press of America.

Rancer, A. S., Baukus, R. A., & Infante, D. A. (1985). Relations between argumentativeness and belief structures about arguing. *Communication Education, 34*, 37-47.

Rancer, A. S., & Dierks-Stewart, K. J. (1985). The influence of sex and sex-role orientation on trait argumentativeness. *Journal of Personality Assessment, 49*, 69-70.

Ray, J. (1670). *A collection of English proverbs*. Cambridge, UK: Printed by J. Hayes.

Rhee, E., Uleman, J. S, & Lee, H. K. (1996). Variations in collectivism and individualism by ingroup and culture: Confirmatory factor analyses. *Journal of Personality and Social Psychology, 71,* 1037-1054.

Rhee, E., Uleman, J. S., Lee, H. K., & Roman, R. J. (1995). Spontaneous self-descriptions and ethnic identities in individualistic and collectivistic cultures. *Journal of Personality and Social Psychology, 69,* 142-152.

Richmond, V. P., & McCroskey, J. C. (1985). *Communication: Apprehension, Avoidance, and Effectiveness.* Scottsdale, AZ: Gorsuch Scarisbrick.

Richmond, V. P., & McCroskey, J. C. (1992). *Communication: Apprehension, Avoidance, and Effectiveness* (3rd ed.). Scottsdale, AZ: Gorsuch Scarisbrick.

Richmond, V., & Roach, K. D. (1992). Willingness to communicate and employee success in U.S. organizations. *Journal of Applied Communication Research, 20,* 95-115.

Riegel, K. F. (1972). Influence of economic and political ideologies on the development of developmental psychology. *Psychological Bulletin, 78,* 129-141.

Roberts, T. (1991). Gender and influence of evaluations on self-assessments in achievement settings. *Psychological Bulletin, 109,* 297-308.

Rothbaum, F., Pott, M., Azuma, H., Miyake, K., & Weisz, J. (2000). The development of close relationships in Japan and the United States: Paths of symbiotic harmony and generative tension. *Child Development, 71,* 1121-1142.

Rotter, J. B. (1954). *Social learning and clinical psychology.* Englewood Cliffs, NJ: Prentice Hall.

Rotter, J. B. (1966). Generalized expectancies for internal versus external control of reinforcement. *Psychological Monographs: General and Applied, 80* (1, Whole No. 609, pp. 1-28).

Rotter, J. B. (1975). Some problems and misconceptions related to the construct of internal versus external control of reinforcement. *Journal of Consulting and Clinical Psychology, 43,* 56-67.

Rubin, A. M. (1993). The effect of locus of control on communication motivation, anxiety, and satisfaction. *Communication Quarterly, 41,* 161-171.

Rubin, R. B., & Rubin, A. M. (1992). Antecedents of interpersonal communication motivation. *Communication Quarterly, 40,* 305-317.

Rudman, L. (1998). Self-promotion as a risk factor for women: The costs and benefits of counterstereotypical impression management. *Journal of Personality and Social Psychology, 74,* 629-645.

Ruiz, R. (1981). Cultural and historical perspectives in counseling Hispanics. In D. Sue (Ed.), *Counseling the culturally different* (pp. 186-215). New York: Wiley.

Ryder, A. G., Alden, L E., & Paulhus, D. L. (2000). Is acculturation unidimensional or bidimensional? A head-to-head comparison in the prediction of personality, self-identity, and adjustment. *Journal of Personality and Social Psychology, 79,* 49-65.

Sadana, T., & Norbeck, E. (1975). Prophecy continues to fail: A Japanese sect. *Journal of Cross-Cultural Psychology, 6,* 331-345.

Sallinen-Kuparinen, A. (1986). Finnish Communication Reticence: Perceptions and Self-Reported Behavior. University of Jyväskylä. *Studia Philologica Jyväskyläensia, 19.*

Saltzman, C. E. (1986). One hundred and fifty percent persons: Models for orienting international students. In R. M. Paige (Ed.), *Cross-cultural orientation: New conceptualizations and applications* (pp. 247-268). Lanham, MD: University Press of America.

Samarin, W. (1965). The language of silence. *Practical Anthropology, 12,* 115-119.

Sampson, E. E. (1977). Psychology and the American ideal. *Journal of Personality and Social Psychology, 35,* 767-782.

Sampson, E. E. (1988). The debate on individualism: Indigenous psychologies of the individual and their role in personal and societal functioning. *American Psychologist, 43,* 15-22.

Saville-Troike, M. (1985). The place of silence in an integrated theory of communication. In D. Tannen & M. Saville-Troike (Eds.), *Perspectives on silence* (pp. xi-xvii). Norwood, NJ: Ablex.

Schooler, C. (1990). Individualism and the historical and social-structural determinants of people's concerns over self-directedness and efficacy. In J. Rodin, C. Schooler, & K. W. Schaie (Eds.), *Self-directedness: Cause and effects through the life course* (pp. 19-49). Hillsdale, NJ: Lawrence Erlbaum.

Schwartz, S. H. (1990). Individualism-collectivism: Critique and proposed refinements. *Journal of Cross-Cultural Psychology, 21,* 139-157.

Schweder, R. A., & Bourne, E. J. (1984). Does the concept of the person vary cross-culturally? In A. Marsella & G. White (Eds.), *Cultural conceptions of mental health and therapy* (pp.97-137). New York: Reidel.

Scollon, R. (1985). The machine stops: Silence in the metaphor of malfunction. In D. Tannen & M. Saville-Troike (Eds.), *Perspectives on silence* (pp. 21-30). Norwood, NJ: Ablex.

Seeman, M. (1997). The elusive situation in social psychology. *Social Psychology Quarterly, 60,* 4-13.

Segall, M. H. (1986). Culture and behavior: Psychology in global perspective. *Annual Review of Psychology, 37,* 523-564.

Shakespeare, W. (1818). *Hamlet, a tragedy.* London: W. Simpkin and R. Marshall.

Sharkey, W. F., & Singelis, T. M. (1995). Embarrassability and self-construal: A theoretical integration. *Personality and Individual Differences, 19,* 919-926.

Sherif, M. (1935). A study of some social factors in perception. *Archives of Psychology, 27* (No. 187).

Sillars, A. L. (1980). Attribution and communication in roommate conflict. *Communication Monographs, 47,* 180-200.

Simpson, J. A., & Weiner, E. S. C. (Eds.). (1989). *Oxford English Dictionary* (2nd edition; Vol. 15). Oxford, England: Oxford University Press.

Singelis, T. M. (1994). The measurement of independent and interdependent self-construals. *Personality and Social Psychology Bulletin, 20,* 580-591.

Singelis, T. M., & Brown, W. J. (1995). Culture, self, and collectivist communication: Linking culture to individual behavior. *Human Communication Research, 21,* 354-389.

Sinha, D., & Tripathi, R. C. (1994). Individualism in a collectivist culture: A case of coexistence of opposites. In U. Kim, H. C. Triandis, C. Kagitcibasi, S. C. Choi, & G. Yoon (Eds.), *Individualism and collectivism: Theory, method, and applications* (pp. 123-136). Thousands Oaks, CA: Sage.

Sistrunk, F., & Clement, D. E. (1970). Cross-cultural comparisons of the conforming behavior of college students. *Journal of Social Psychology, 82,* 273-274.

Sjöö, M., and Mor, B. (1991). *The great cosmic mother: Rediscovering the religion of the earth* (2nd ed.). San Francisco, CA: HarperSanFrancisco.

Smith, C. E., Steinke, J., & Distefano, M. K. (1973). Perceived locus of control and future outlook among psychiatric patients. *Journal of Community Psychology, 1,* 40-41.

Smith, M. B. (1991). *Values, self, and society: Toward a humanist social psychology.* New Brunswick, NJ: Transaction.

Smith, P. B., & Bond, M. H. (1998). *Social psychology across cultures.* London: Prentice Hall Europe.

Steele, C. M. (1988). The psychology of self-affirmation: Sustaining the integrity of self. In L. Berkowitz (Ed.), *Advances in experimental social psychology* (Vol. 21, pp. 261-302). San Diego, CA: Academic Press.

Stevenson, B. (Ed.). (1967). *The home book of quotations: Classical and modern* (p. 979). New York: Dodd, Mead & Co.

Stevenson, B. (Ed.). (1979). *The Macmillan book of proverbs, maxims, and famous phrases.* New York: Macmillan.

Stonequist, E. V. (1935). The problem of marginal man. *American Journal of Sociology, 7,* 1-12.

Straus, A. (1977). Northern Cheyenne ethnopsychology. *Ethos, 5,* 326-352.

Sue, D. W., Arredondo, P., & McDavis, R. J. (1992). Multicultural counseling competencies and standards: A call to the professional. *Journal of Counseling and Development, 70,* 477-486.

Sue, D., Ino, S., & Sue, D. M. (1983). Nonassertiveness of Asian Americans: An inaccurate assumption? *Journal of Counseling Psychology, 30,* 581-588.

Sue, D. W., & Sue, D. (1981). *Counseling the culturally different: Theory and practice.* New York: Wiley.

Suzuki, S., & Rancer, A. S. (1994). Argumentativeness and verbal aggressiveness: Testing for conceptual and measurement equivalence across cultures. *Communication Monographs, 61,* 256-279.

Tanaka, T. (1987). Self-deprecative tendencies in self-evaluation through social comparison. *Japanese Journal of Experimental Social Psychology, 27,* 27-36.

Tannen, D. (1985). Silence: Anything but. In D. Tannen & M. Saville-Troike (Eds.), *Perspectives on silence* (pp. 93-111). Norwood, NJ: Ablex.

Taylor, S. E., & Brown, J. D. (1988). Illusion and well-being: A social psychological perspective on mental health. *Psychological Bulletin, 103,* 193-210.

Tesser, A. (1986). Some effects of self-evaluation maintenance on cognition and action. In R. M. Sorrentino & E. T. Higgins (Eds.), *Handbook of motivation and cognition: Foundations of social behavior* (pp. 435-464). New York: Guilford Press.

Thibodeau, R., & Aronson, E. (1992). Taking a closer look: Reasserting the role of the self-concept in dissonance theory. *Personality and Social Psychology Bulletin, 18,* 591-602.

Thomas, J. (1983). Cross-cultural pragmatic failure. *Applied Linguistics, 4,* 91-112.

Thomas, K. W. (1976). Conflict and conflict management. In M. Dunnette (Ed.), *Handbook of industrial and organizational psychology* (pp. 889-935). Chicago, IL: Rand McNally.

Thomas, K. W., & Kilmann, R. H. (1978). Comparison of four instruments measuring conflict behavior. *Psychological Reports, 42,* 1139-1145.

Thompson, C. A., & Ishii, S. (1990). Japanese and American compared on assertiveness/responsiveness. *Psychological Reports, 66,* 829-830.

Tice, D. M., Butler, J. L., Muraven, M. B., & Stillwell, A. M. (1995). When modesty prevails: Differential favorability of self-presentation to friends and strangers. *Journal of Personality and Social Psychology, 69,* 1120-1138.

Ting-Toomey, S. (1988). Intercultural conflict styles: A face-negotiation theory. In Y. Y. Kim & W. B. Gudykunst (Eds.), *Theories in intercultural communication* (pp. 213-235). Newbury Park, CA: Sage.

Ting-Toomey, S. (1989). Identity and interpersonal bonding. In M. K. Asante & W. B. Gudykunst (Eds.), *Handbook of international and intercultural communication* (pp. 163-185). Newbury Park, CA: Sage.

Ting-Toomey, S. (1991). Intimacy expressions in three cultures: France, Japan, and the United States. *International Journal of Intercultural Relations, 15,* 29-46.

Ting-Toomey, S. (1994). Managing intercultural conflicts effectively. In L. A. Samovar & R. E. Porter (Eds.), *Intercultural communication: A reader* (pp. 360-372). Belmont, CA: Wadsworth.

Ting-Toomey, S., Gao, G., Trubisky, P., Yang, Z., Kim, H. S., & Lin, S. L., et al. (1991). Culture, face maintenance, and styles of handling interpersonal conflict: A study in five cultures. *The International Journal of Conflict Management, 2,* 275-296.

Tobin, J. (2000). Using "The Japanese Problem" as a corrective to the ethnocentricity of Western theory. *Child Development, 71,* 1155-1158.

Triandis, H. C. (1988). Collectivism vs. Individualism: A reconceptualization of a basic concept in cross-cultural psychology. In G. Verma & C. Bagley

(Eds.), *Cross-cultural studies of personality, attitudes and cognition.* London: Macmillan.

Triandis, H. C. (1989). The self and social behavior in differing cultural contexts. *Psychological Review, 96,* 506-520.Triandis, H. C. (1995). *Individualism and collectivism.* Boulder, CO: Westview.

Trilling, L. (1972). *Sincerity and authenticity.* Cambridge, MA: Harvard University Press.

Tripathi, R. C. (1988). Aligning development to values in India. In D. Sinha & H. S. R. Kao (Eds.), *Social values and development: Asian perspectives.* New Delhi: Sage India.

Trompenaars, F. (1993). *Riding the waves of culture.* London: Economist Books.

Trubisky, P., Ting-Toomey, S., & Lin, S. L. (1991). The influence of individualism-collectivism and self-monitoring on conflict styles. *International Journal of Intercultural Relations, 15,* 65-84.

Tsujimura, A. (1987). "Some characteristics of the Japanese way of communication." In D. L. Kincaid (Ed.), *Communication theory from eastern and western perspectives.* New York: Academic Press.

Walsh, J. E. (1973). *Intercultural education in the community of man.* Honolulu: University of Hawaii Press.

Ward, C., & Kennedy, A. (1992). Locus of control, mood disturbance, and social difficulty during cross-cultural transitions. *International Journal of Intercultural Relations, 16,* 175-194.

Waterman, A. S. (1981). Individualism and interdependence. *American Psychologist, 36,* 762-773.

Watson, K. W., Monroe, E. E., & Atterstrom, A. (1989). Comparison of communication apprehension across cultures: American and Swedish children. *Communication Quarterly, 37,* 67-76.

Weiss, H., & Sherman, J. (1973). Internal-external control as a predictor of task effort and satisfaction subsequent to failure. *Journal of Applied Psychology, 57,* 132-136.

Weisz, J. R., Rothbaum, F. M., & Blackburn, T. C. (1984). Standing out and standing in: The psychology of control in America and Japan. *American Psychologist, 39,* 955-969.

Wheeless, L. R. (1975). An investigation of receiver apprehension and social context dimensions of communication apprehension. *Speech Teacher, 24,* 261-268.

Williams, T. P., & Sogon, S. (1984). Group composition and conforming behavior in Japanese students. *Japanese Psychological Research, 26,* 231-234.

Wood, P. S., & Mallinckrodt, B. (1990). Culturally sensitive assertiveness training for ethnic minority clients. *Professional Psychology: Research and Practice, 21,* 5-11.

Wortman, C. B., & Brehm, J. W. (1975). Responses to uncontrollable outcomes: An integration of reactance theory and the learned helplessness model. In

L. Berkowitz (Ed.), *Advances in experimental social psychology* (Vol. 9, pp. 277-336). New York: Academic Press.

Yoshida, T., Kojo, K., & Kaku, H. (1982). A study on the development of self-presentation in children. *Japanese Journal of Educational Psychology, 30,* 30-37.

Yoshikawa, M. J. (1988). Cross-cultural adaptation and perceptual development. In Y. Y. Kim & W. B. Gudykunst (Eds.), *Cross-cultural adaptation: Current approaches.* Newbury Park, CA: Sage.

Yum, J. O. (1988). The impact of Confucianism on interpersonal relationships and communication patterns in East Asia. *Communication Monographs, 55,* 374-388.

Zakahi, W. R. (1985). The relationship of assertiveness to communication competence and communication satisfaction: A dyadic assessment. *Communication Research Reports, 2,* 36-40.

Zangwill, E. (1925). *The melting pot.* New York: Macmillan.

Index

About the Author

Min-Sun Kim (Ph.D., Michigan State University, 1992) is Professor in the Department of Speech at the University of Hawaii at Manoa. Her research focuses on the role of cognition in conversational styles among people of different cultural orientations. She has applied her models (based on conversational constraints) in many areas, including requesting, re-requesting, conflict styles, and communication motivation. She has conducted extensive research and has published more than 40 research papers in major communication journals. Her two newest theoretical developments, focusing on relativity of communication constructs, appeared in two consecutive volumes (22 and 23) of *Communication Yearbook*.

Dr. Kim is the recipient of numerous top paper awards in major international communication conferences and was recently invited to give a keynote speech, *Paradigms of Cultural Identity*, at the third annual conference of the David C. Lam Institute for East-West Studies in Hong Kong. She has served as a Division Secretary for the International and Intercultural Communication Division of the International Communication Association. Since 1994, Dr. Kim has also served as a workshop leader for the annual Summer Workshop for the Development of Intercultural Coursework at Colleges and Universities (which is run by the Center for International Business Education and Research at the University of Hawaii at Manoa). She is currently serving as an Associate Editor for *Communication Reports* and also as a reviewer for various communication journals.

66567146R00137

Made in the USA
Lexington, KY
17 August 2017